CREATING A

MARKET-SENSITIVE

CULTURE

The Institute of Management (IM) is at the forefront of management development and best management practice. The Institute embraces all levels of management from students to chief executives. It provides a unique portfolio of services for all managers, enabling them to develop skills and achieve management excellence.

If you would like to hear more about the benefits of membership, please write to Department P, Institute of Management, Cottingham Road, Corby NN17 1TT.

This series is commissioned by the Institute of Management Foundation.

CREATING A

MARKET-SENSITIVE

CULTURE

Anticipate change,
act fast,
do it today

ANDREW BRUCE and
KEN LANGDON

the Institute
of Management
FOUNDATION
PITMAN
PUBLISHING

London · Hong Kong · Johannesburg
Melbourne · Singapore · Washington DC

To the long-suffering Nicki and Penny, and
the long-suffered Alfi, Jonathan, Kate and Steve.

PITMAN PUBLISHING
128 Long Acre, London WC2E 9AN
Tel: +44 (0)171 447 2000
Fax: +44 (0)171 240 5771

A Division of Pearson Professional Limited

First published in Great Britain in 1997

ISBN 0 273 62631 0

British Library Cataloguing in Publication Data
A CIP catalogue record for this book can be obtained from the British Library

10 9 8 7 6 5 4 3 2 1

Typeset by Pantek Arts, Maidstone, Kent.
Printed and bound in Great Britain by Bell and Bain Ltd, Glasgow.

The Publishers' policy is to use paper manufactured from sustainable forests.

ABOUT THE AUTHORS

Andrew Bruce works as a management consultant, facilitator and trainer. His first consulting years were spent with an international firm of consultants. Major clients included Nissan, Hewlett-Packard and Northern Telecom.

An engineer by training, he served a short service commission with the Army and worked in a variety of engineering and commercial roles for a manufacturer of processing machinery including special projects in Australia. This gave him the hands-on experience necessary for his later role as a consultant.

Since forming the Organisational Competency Company, he has continued to work with clients in a variety of roles to effect organisational change and performance improvement.

He is currently working on the implementation of the organisational sensitivity model with a number of international organisations, both profit-making and public service. These projects frequently involve using a 'war room' (or knowledge centre) concept to redesign the organisation's strategy and processes.

Andrew also works as a tutor for the Open Business School.

Ken Langdon has a background in the technology industry where he was in sales and account management with a computer major, prior to being a director of a start-up company for its first five years.

He has been a consultant and trainer for some 11 years during which time he has assisted a number of large and small companies to improve their strategic planning processes. He is the author of *Key Accounts are Different – Solution Selling for Account Managers* (Pitman Publishing, 1995). He is also a contributor to the *FT Handbook of Management* (Pitman Publishing, 1995).

Both Andrew and Ken now spend most of their time training and facilitating management teams in the discipline of creating 'organisational sensitivity'.

Andrew Bruce
OCC
17 Bisham Village
Maidenhead, SL7 1RR
01628 488466

Ken Langdon
KPL Associates
24 St Mark's Road
Maidenhead, SL6 6DE
01628 782193

ACKNOWLEDGEMENTS

Andrew Bruce gratefully acknowledges the following people who have all, in some way or another, contributed to the ideas contained in this book.

John Roberts (Professor of Marketing, Australian Graduate School of Management) – the vitality of positive attitude
John showed me that the 'attitude' that people adopt when dealing with each other can either stimulate innovation and energy levels or it can suppress and resist. It is therefore the 'oil' in human relationships.

Ben Tregoe (Founder and Chairman of Kepner-Tregoe) – the importance of understanding values, and the power of 'process thinking'
Ben's pioneering work in the use of creative and rational processes for resolving strategic and operational issues continues to inspire millions of people worldwide every year. He showed me that, even when confronted with ambiguity and uncertainty, a sound 'thinking process' will always provide a way forward. Furthermore, use of such techniques must always be within a clear understanding of organisational and individual beliefs and values.

William Hextall (Managing Director, Kepner-Tregoe UK Ltd) – the necessity to keep looking forward and to be prepared to take risks
A single phrase coined by William over the years has had a significant impact on my ability to cope with adversity – 'it is what it is'. In too many organisations the first question asked by managers when faced with a crisis is, 'Whose fault is it?' This is the blame culture. Stating 'it is what it is' encourages people to accept the reality of the current situation and, rather than waste time dwelling on the past, to focus on the solution. This then enables people to take the risks necessary in their work if the boundaries of current thinking are ever to be pushed forward.

Michael Jones (Director, Quality and Customer Satisfaction, Nortel Ltd) – the value of creating a vision and the need to have the courage of your convictions
Change in organisations will not happen unless there is sufficient motivation, often created by a crisis. Michael envisioned a completely new way in which organisations could and should operate. Vision was essential. He also demonstrated enormous courage in persuading people to spend time on quality thinking and analysis rather than jumping into action.

CONTENTS

PART 4 • CHANGES

What tools do managers need to create?

FOREWORD

The Institute of Management's study *Management Development to the Millennium* confirmed that the demands on managers today are very different from those of ten, or even five, years ago. The demands of the new century will be even more different.

However managers should welcome the pressures that today's dynamic marketplace puts upon them – managing change to achieve something better is a principal, probably on-going task of management.

As the management world has become very much more complicated, a key skill is to be prepared for, and wherever possible predict, the changes that will occur in future. New technology, changing markets and changing organisational cultures are all crucially important influences on managers' behaviour and activities.

Technology is the key to combining the advantages of a very large organisation with the advantages of a very small one, while the competitive nature of the national and global marketplace means that total quality is becoming the minimum standard required to compete. Cultural changes however can never be forced. In a learning organisation there has to be a shift from dominant attention to short-term success towards creating a context that stimulates managers to experiment with opportunities in favour of long-term growth. Organisations must be dynamic – they have to change, both out of necessity and by choice. The manager's job of today therefore focuses more on action and less on analysis, with more emphasis on intervention than on planning. These changes are happening in almost all organisations, both large and small, in both the private and public sectors. So whether you work for a giant multinational or a small local company, it is likely that you will have to change your way of working to keep up with the shifts in your market and benefit from the new opportunities of the new century.

I therefore unreservedly commend *The Millennium Manager* series both for its forward-looking approach and for continuing the debate around the direction of management and management development for UK plc.

Roger Young
Director General, Institute of Management

THE
MILLENNIUM
MANAGER

PRIORITY SKILLS FOR THE MANAGER OF 2001

In July 1995, the Institute of Management published a report, *Management Development to the Millennium*, based on interviews with opinion formers at the most senior managerial level of industry and commerce – all who had high expectations of their managers in their ability to lead and grow their organisations.

Managers are expected to have the ability to operate across a broad range of skills and competencies. The *Management Development to the Millennium* report identified those skills and competencies that senior managers felt were essential for management and organisational success into the new millennium.

The following table from the report shows a list of the priority skills selected by respondents. Three-quarters of the managers surveyed indicated a clear focus on the 'harder' skills of strategic thinking and change management. Nevertheless, over four in ten endorsed the importance of facilitating others to contribute, in other words a classic 'softer' skill.

Skills for the manager in the next millennium

Base: 1,241 respondents

Strategic thinking, eg longer term, broader perspective, anticipating
Responding to and managing change
An orientation towards total quality/customer satisfaction
Financial management, eg role and impact of key financial indicators
Facilitating others to contribute
Understanding the role of information and IT
Verbal communication, eg coherent, persuasive
Organisational sensitivity, eg cross-functional understanding
Risk assessment in decision making

This book addresses the indicated skill – *organisational sensitivity*. Other books in the **Pitman/IM Millennium Manager** series concentrate on some of the other skills listed above.

WHAT'S IN IT FOR YOU? – A QUICK OVERVIEW

Organisational sensitivity is a term used to define the situation of an organisation whose right hand is well aware of what its left hand is doing. Such an organisation is remarkably sensitive to its customers' needs and wants, and to other external influences such as its competitors and suppliers. In this way it is able to maintain and expand its position as a supplier of products and services which achieve high levels of customer satisfaction.

There are two capabilities which enable the creation of such an organisation:

➡ the awareness of the need for change

➡ the ability to change successfully.

'Management Development to the Millennium', a report published by the Institute of Management in 1994, recorded the results of a survey of many managers from many industry sectors. The managers identified organisational sensitivity, including cross-functional understanding, as a key skill for managers in the new millennium. This should not come as a great surprise. Whatever it is called, organisational sensitivity has always been one of the determinants of the success of organisations.

This book provides tools and techniques for achieving all aspects of organisational sensitivity. The ideas are not simply based on academic or conceptual thinking but on a combination of sound 'applied common sense', and the guiding principle of 'what works in practice'.

The principles are not complex but reasonably straightforward to understand and easy to apply. They do, however, require some commitment and discipline as the application of the principles makes us think differently about how our organisations work. The book provides a practical tool for any manager who believes that the performance of his or her organisation or team can be improved, and who is willing to challenge the current way of thinking.

Please read and challenge the ideas presented, and complete the self-analysis exercises at the end of each of the later chapters. If you agree that managing organisations is not as complex as it often appears, then you will be able to apply these techniques in your own organisation and teach them to other members of your team.

'The first and wisest of them all professed
To know only, that he nothing knew'

Milton

PREPARING FOR SUCCESS

The scope of the book and
a plan for using it.

Continuing radical change will result in a need for managers in the new millennium to be even more action-oriented than now. They will need to understand and react to trends in their environment, initiated both inside and outside traditional organisational boundaries. In short, managers will strive to improve their own and their companies' *organisational sensitivity*. They will also need a clear model of their organisation to enable them to understand what drives performance and how to improve it. This introduction outlines how such a route map can be created using this book.

What will drive the organisation of the 2000s?

The shock of recessions which appear to occur after shorter intervals of real growth have eventually stopped being a shock. Indeed, managers are now so recession-weary that they make decisions with survival, their own and their organisations', primarily in mind. They look at risk with an eagle eye and evaluate options carefully but quickly. Thus recession becomes a key driver of management decision making. 'Will this still be a good expansion when times are hard?' 'If consumer spending slows down, will this marketing strategy still make sense?'

This primary focus on cycles and their organisations' sensitivity to them tends to combine managers' main emphasis of working. Suddenly there is a dual function to perform: maintaining the cost consciousness demanded by recession and thinking through and implementing a strategy for growth.

The other cliché of the nineties from which the new millennium manager will have learned is best summed up as the 'chaotic environment'. Managers are learning how to cope with, and indeed encourage, continuous change.

To ensure this change is for the better and related to the strategic route of the whole enterprise, managers will require a crystal clear understanding of what drives performance.

Being sensitive to what you need to know

These factors of recession and the chaotic environment are further indicators of management's dependence on information, or rather 'knowledge', and its communication. They make the requirement sharper.

The necessary knowledge used to be at a functional level. That is, 'I know about my part of the business, and it's senior management's job to make sure that we all work together, isn't it?'

The problems of such a functional or vertically isolated approach became clear in the profit centre environment of the seventies and eighties. A simple example and then a more complex one illustrate why managers nowadays are required to understand how their whole organisation operates.

CASE STUDY

Each separate part is right but the business gets it wrong

A simple example of divisionalisation going haywire is found in Autodiv a car distributor and garage. The new car sales function is a separate profit centre from both the repair shop and second-hand sales. This divisionalisation was deemed very sensible when introduced, as it forced managers, who up until then, had considered only sales volume, revenue and customer satisfaction, to pay more attention to profitability.

A typical problem resulting from the 'divisionalised' approach is best illustrated by an example. If customers wish to purchase a car from new car sales, trading in their existing car which has been maintained by Autodiv, the transaction will affect all three divisional profit and loss accounts.

New car sales will make a sale and gain, as profit, the margin between sales price minus cost of sales. They will sell the trade-in car on to second-hand sales. Second-hand sales division will then sell it and make the profit of sales price minus trade-in price minus cost of any repairs necessary before resale. The repair shop will make a profit on the price charged to second-hand sales for work carried out. Whilst the deal for Autodiv as a whole may be worth while, if each division operates in isolation from the others the desirability of doing the deal may not emerge. For example, if sales drops below the equivalent of a 15 per cent discount, they will not achieve the profit per unit target set in their objectives. When new car sales offer the trade-in car to second-hand division, they may receive less than they wish to give the customer as a fair trade-in price.

> The fair trade-in price may only work if the repair shop reduces the cost to second-hand sales department of the work necessary to prepare the trade-in vehicle for resale. Unfortunately the repair shop cannot do this as it drops the profitability of the deal to below their objective.
>
> The matter is thrown further into confusion by the system of charging for overheads. This is done as a percentage of sales turnover for each division. Thus each inter-company transaction incurs a charge.
>
> No matter that the company as a whole was going to make a satisfactory return on the transaction, the individual profit centres lack the necessary knowledge to detect this. The sale is lost and a competitor wins.

This need for excellent transfer of knowledge and an ability to respond to it is known as *organisational sensitivity*. Everybody has to look inside and outside the organisation, first of all listening to the environment around them and then, most importantly, taking appropriate action.

Even in the small environment of a local garage, organisational sensitivity is an issue. Now let us expand the size of the problem by considering a large multi-national.

CASE STUDY

It looked good from where I was standing

A large multi-national had four major product groups. The chief executives of the groups were active traders of businesses, buying and selling to enhance shareholder value. In product group A a deal was hatched to sell an overseas subsidiary to a local conglomerate. It had financial and strategic benefits to that product group.

Unfortunately, the Chief Executive acted in ignorance of the fact that the company being sold was also a major customer, buying components from subsidiary B in product group C.

When the deal went through, the new owners promptly switched component suppliers to take advantage of their increased volumes and by so doing nearly drove subsidiary B out of business.

So, the topic of this book, organisational sensitivity, is driven by two key management requirements:

➡ ensuring that managers have the information they require to make sound strategic and operational decisions in a fast-moving competitive environment

➡ ensuring that managers have a broad cross-functional knowledge, so that actions taken benefit the organisation as a whole.

The rewards for succeeding in these two areas will be sustained performance improvement, both in the short and long term. The penalty for failure is easy to illustrate. Consider the time it took two of the major players in the computer industry of the eighties, IBM and Digital, to react to new technologies which very quickly revolutionised the whole technology scene. Time enough for them to record years of massive losses.

Using knowledge to make decisions

It is now many years since chief executives the world over made a statement to IT directors to the effect 'Get my managers the information they require, make it available to them at the right time and stop making excuses'. But still in many organisations middle managers make decisions with much less than the required information. This is true to such an extent that chief executives are reviewing whether or not that is the right instruction. Middle managers remain like a pilot flying a plane without instruments. And at the holding Board level it can be worse.

To continue the aircraft analogy, the holding Board of a company is to their operating divisions what the airline is to individual planes. The loop of information transfer and feedback needs to recognise that the operators of an individual aircraft are to some extent the eyes and ears of the airline. They will be the first to spot changes to airports and other signs of competitive threat. They need to feed this back.

The pilots hope meanwhile that back at base, senior managers are walking the corridors of power to understand the altering environment, and keeping up with developments in all types of legislation, technology and business practice. Again, having understood the situation, everyone has to hope that the Board makes the necessary changes to policy and strategy which keeps the enterprise on its toes and sharp against the competition.

The quality of management decision making is influenced both by the quality of the 'thinking processes' and the quality of the information used as inputs. Of course, most managers recognise the inadequacy of the inputs on which they are operating, but still are under pressures, of time and feasibility, to make decisions in a knowledge vacuum.

We will use the formula:

$$\text{Inputs + Processes = Output}$$

to remind ourselves that the quality of output, customer deliverables for example, depends on the quality of the inputs and processes.

Similarly in terms of critical thinking we will use the formula:

$$\text{Knowledge + Thinking = Management decision}$$

where the quality of the knowledge and thinking determines the quality of the decision.

Within this book, the word 'knowledge' is used to distinguish **required** information from **available** information. Managers need to evaluate critically the role of information transfer. How do you make sure that information is transferred from external and internal sources to reach the places it needs to be?

The downside is fatal. Most corporate failures can be directly linked to two factors:

➡ not having the right information at the right time

➡ not understanding the implications of available information.

These factors inevitably lead to the taking of inappropriate action. There are many detailed symptoms of this transfer and availability going wrong:

➡ picking up the wrong data

➡ picking up the data at the wrong time

➡ spreading information through the organisation without having the connecting bridges to make it make sense

➡ hoarding information as a source of power

➡ re-inventing the wheel in many different parts of the organisation

➡ failing to learn from mistakes (or successes!)

Even once these points are fixed the stage is not yet set for continuous success. In the case of a long-term project, an organisation has to ensure that all the projects in place remain relevant right through to completion. It has not been unusual for a major project to be finely monitored and completed on time and within budget, only to be found at the end to fail to deliver the advantages sought. While they were busy playing the game, life or the environment or the competition moved the goalposts.

Managers need to overcome these problems and move their organisations, or their parts of their organisations, from organisational confusion to organisational competency.

About this book

In Chapters 1 and 2 we will examine why a manager needs to understand whole organisational thinking. Starting from finding out what actually drives organisational performance, we will introduce a model which will be effective at corporate or departmental level for managers wishing to create organisational sensitivity.

Chapters 3 and 4 look at the reality of organisational confusion with some or all of the elements of the sensitivity model not working as planned. In particular we will demonstrate that the restrictive impact of functional thinking adversely impacts performance by focusing on internal issues rather than the customer and other key drivers of the organisation.

Chapters 5 to 10 suggest the new management skills which will be required to implement the new model, from customer-focused analysis to the need for critical thinking.

The final four chapters are about the tools which managers need to create. We will show how cross-functional reports and performance indicators drive the creation of an organisation-wide knowledge centre. The organisation then deploys technology to complete the transformation to organisational sensitivity.

Case studies and examples

Throughout the book we will illustrate the theory with practical examples. Every one of the incidents in the cases we refer to is real. While we will use knowledge of many organisations to try and make things clear, we will keep coming back to one major case study, Europower.

Having said the cases are real, we do not refer to any real companies. This enables us to get the point of the study over without getting into too much detail.

Europower: organisational sensitivity and a major utility

From work which we have done in a number of utility companies throughout Europe, we will create an eclectic corporation. Or perhaps it should be the opposite of an eclectic corporation, in that it will start with many of the negative aspects of organisational confusion. The products will be electricity and gas and the illustrations will be both in the generating, or manufacturing, side and in the customer-facing side where the product is distributed and delivered to millions of customers.

This organisation will illustrate in macro terms what it means to create organisational sensitivity from the top of a large company down and throughout the divisions and structures.

We will learn about strategic planning, cross-functional process management, knowledge transfer and the essential element of managing the people who are managing change. We will try to understand overall how performance improvement starts from the customer and the competition.

In detail we will look at establishing the correct performance indicators. To take two examples from Europower: can performance measures be set which are comparable in generating plants with very different technologies and efficiencies? How do you maintain safety standards, said to be paramount in the boardroom and widely ignored and shortcut in the real world of storms and dissatisfied customers?

But many managers are considering their own divisions, departments or teams, rather than the whole organisation. Can organisational sensitivity be created at a local level without the active co-operation of Head Office? Or even with a potential lack of direction or knowledge vacuum originating from Head Office?

We think it can, and we will use many short case studies to illustrate this. Here is an example of a manager trying to assist his organisation by pointing out mutual dependencies amongst departments operating in a competitive field. The intention is good, the implementation leaves much to be desired.

Organisational sensitivity in a sales office

A computer salesperson in the late sixties and early seventies sold a high-value, high-price and high-margin product to an immature market. Eventually, by the eighties, computer salespeople found themselves selling low-price, low-margin products to a sophisticated and price-sensitive market.

Reacting to that change is well chronicled in terms of the corporations. These cases will look at the people implications of those changes and the necessary development of cross-functional understanding.

Starting with a simple tale of production, we discover a salesman, Ken, who is struggling to meet targets and to sell this year's new product, the L3407.

In an initiative from top management designed to impress the salespeople with the need for maximum effort and successful selling, letters are sent from the production line to individual salespeople who are below target for the year.

'Dear ....Ken...........,

The supervisors and staff on the L3407 product line are sorry to see that you have not been able to meet your product mix target and have to date sold....O.......of this new and innovative product.

This note is just to let you know that we hope things get better and that you achieve more success. After all,.......Ken........., we are dependent on you.'

This first faltering try to enable positive action by providing inputs from one department to another clearly missed the mark.

Those parts of Ken's reply we can print went something like:

'If the L3407 were about three times as fast, had a mean time between failure of longer than five minutes and actually worked to specification, I might have a chance of selling it. Perhaps, since you are dependent on me, we should change jobs. You could not sell fewer machines than me, and I certainly could not make a more dead-in-the-water, uncompetitive dud of a product'.

Top management cancelled that initiative and thought again.

Action points

At the end of each part of the book, starting from Chapter 5 which is the start of the look at new management skills, you will be offered models and checklists to enable you to improve performance by critically examining your own environment. You can look at your whole organisation, or a division of it, or your team or even just yourself. Briefed with illustrations from the real cases, you will have the opportunity to apply a number of processes and methods of thinking as you go through the book. These processes will enable the knowledge transfer, skills and cultural change which underlies organisational sensitivity.

As we all go into the 21st century with our organisations driven by fear of recession and the requirement for continuous change, we need to transfer the right knowledge to the right people at the right time, with an organisational sensitivity which stops one part of the organisation cutting another part's throat.

SELF-ASSESSMENT

Rate your organisation or unit on a scale of 1 to 5.

1   Do you really understand what drives performance in your organisation? ☐

2   Do you understand what determines whether you will outperform competition in the future or fail to exist? ☐

3   Is it clear how your strategy is linked to day-to-day operational processes, the availability and requirements for knowledge and the capability and motivation of people in all functions? ☐

4   How much does it feel as though your organisation is in control as opposed to being buffeted from one change to the next – a state of constant confusion? ☐

5   How well are the changes in the external environment understood – is the impact and urgency of changes in technology, society or legislation anticipated and managed effectively? ☐

6   How well are the changes in the competitive environment understood – is the impact of customer and competitor changes anticipated and managed effectively? ☐

7   How prepared is the organisation for long-term survival as opposed to short-term operational performance – is it really understood how the organisation will survive and grow? ☐

8   How effectively do functions and management levels work together as a team? ☐

9   How restrictive is the level of functional thinking; how strong is the 'political' influence? ☐

10 Do clear performance indicators and targets exist? ☐

11 Do they focus on key outputs? ☐

12 Do they provide the right information to the right people in the right format at the right time? ☐

13 Are the right people allocated to the right jobs? ☐

14 Do they understand the requirements for success? ☐

15 Do they have the necessary capabilities, resources and rewards to succeed? ☐

16 Does the culture support what the organisation is trying to achieve? ☐

17 Does it encourage thinking and learning? ☐

18 Are decisions made with the necessary knowledge? ☐

Action plan

Throughout this book, we will use chapter checklists to ask you to assess areas of concern (the low scores) and develop an action plan for their resolution before moving on to the next chapter. For the moment, we simply ask you to reflect on each of the above questions to assess whether the ideas in this book are likely to be of value to you.

Clearly, if you score highly throughout, we suggest that you replace the book on the shelf or pass it to a colleague. Where you feel you and your organisation have room for improvement, we ask you to do one more thing.

We are going to be presenting many ideas – some will be confirmation of something familiar, but many will challenge fundamentally the way you view organisational design. Many managers from a variety of industries and levels have found that this new way of looking at organisations has given them great insights and clarity. The only prerequisite is an open mind! Please challenge the ideas and take what you find useful.

Mindmaps

For each chapter there is a 'mindmap' which describes the contents of the chapter and the thread of linking logic which connects the concepts and processes. Here is the mindmap for the whole book. You should start to read it from the rectangle at 12 o'clock.

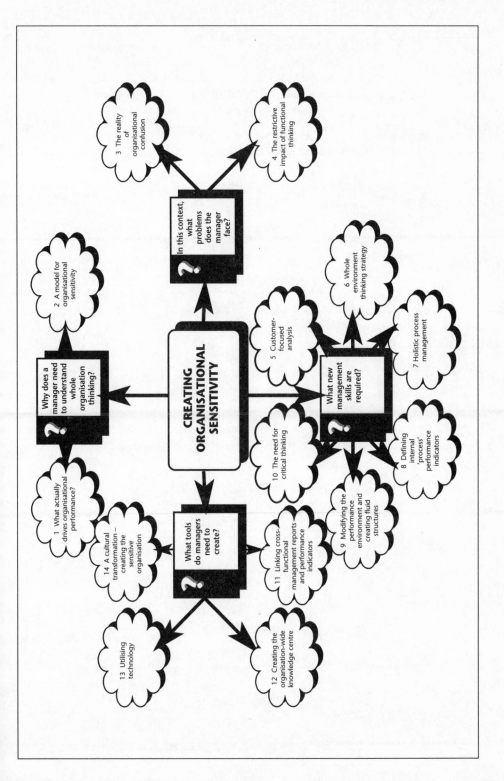

CONTEXT

Why does a manager need to understand whole organisation thinking?

'If it were done when 'tis done,
then 'twere well that it were done quickly.'

Macbeth

WHAT ACTUALLY DRIVES ORGANISATIONAL PERFORMANCE

A focus on performance reveals the four organisational fundamentals or drivers.

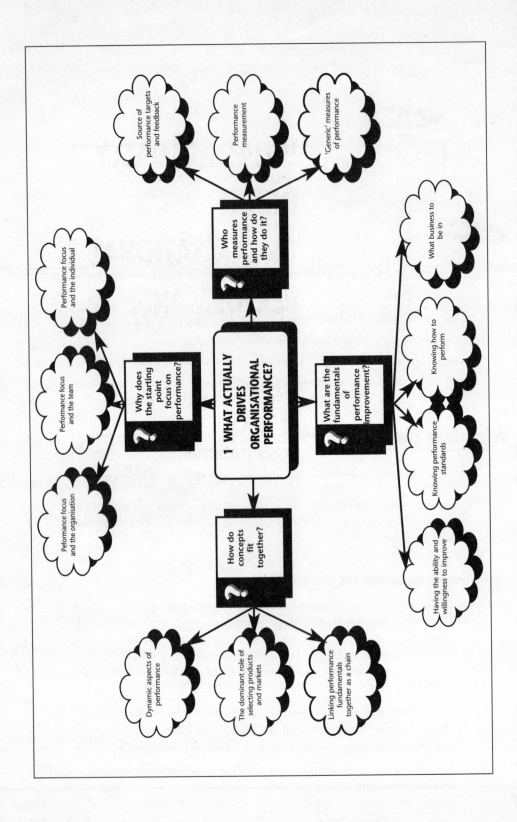

There is an ever-increasing pressure on managers to improve performance. Unfortunately it is still rare for managers to be told what really drives performance. Without this, improvement has a random focus.

Objectives

By the end of this chapter readers will be able to explain these four fundamental elements necessary for an organisation to be truly sensitive:

- ➡ know what business the organisation is in
- ➡ know how to perform in chosen markets
- ➡ transfer knowledge to people who can solve problems
- ➡ have people who are willing and able to improve the organisation.

Why does the starting point focus on performance?

The best way for managers to consider the reasons for concentrating on performance is to consider the alternative. If a management team allows the organisation to ignore the continuous checking of real performance, it may not survive. If a team does not transfer this focus to individuals, they may not survive.

Performance focus and the organisation

The survival of an organisation requires that action is taken in time. To act in time requires that managers detect changes from any direction, external or internal, which are going to make the current way of doing things irrelevant. Many such changes are detected by hard performance indicators such as sales figures, production costs and profit slippages – as long as you are measuring the right indicators.

Even more fundamental changes emerge from the marketplace, which, in order to understand the breadth of organisational sensitivity, we ought to describe as the **global** marketplace.

Here is a terrifying example of the failure of industry to react to competition from a long way off.

Sometimes when managers react to a change in the sales figures, they are already too late

The manufacturing base in most Western countries has shrunk over the last 20 years, nowhere more dramatically than in the UK. Becoming uncompetitive can take a long time to realise, and the causes of the problem even longer.

So it was with many UK companies whose first indicators of a drop in competitiveness came in the sales figures. Investigation of this drop led to pressure on the salesforce to sell at list price, at a time when they were finding it harder and harder to resist discounting.

Once managers were sure that the salesforce had a real price problem, they looked again at direct and indirect costs. Production departments found various ways of making cuts, but were comparing their own past performance and UK competitor's as their benchmark.

By the time the scope of the cost base problem was realised, there was no alternative to, for those that could, closing production capability in the UK and shifting it to the Far East. Those that could not do this either became distributors of Far Eastern-sourced products or simply went out of business.

They paid for their lack of sensitivity to the worldwide manufacturing scene.

Performance focus and the team or department

Now consider the knowledge requirements from a team's point of view. Estates management teams, IT departments, car fleet runners and many other teams no longer exist within the infrastructure of the organisation for whom they provide services. The reason for this is normally cost reduction as well as improved focus on core activities. Many teams did not make an intact transition to the outsourcing era.

In the struggle to prove their value to the organisation, outsourced units have to agree and hit performance targets measured by quality and quantitative measures. This then becomes a driver of the teams left inside the company as managers take responsibility for providing satisfactory service both to meet current needs and to adapt to new requirements as they emerge.

Performance focus and the individual

The same need occurs at individual level. Unless we as individuals are aware of the need for change, and are willing to react to it, we are likely to find ourselves part of the group's downsizing plan.

A salesperson who has made target year after year by demonstrating products and selling to purchasing departments finds it hard to appreciate that a new environment has crept up. In this environment salespeople are required to know what their products will actually do to the bottom line of their customer. This solution selling comes hard to individuals who have spent a lifetime in product-based pitching and selling.

Unless they or their managers have the sensitivity to see their development areas such individuals may pay the cost by losing their jobs. There are a lot of middle-aged *early retirers* who failed to welcome the new challenge, and instead scoffed at new-fangled sales methods being introduced by managers, often their juniors in years.

The final reason for this focus on performance lies in the changed attitude that employers, to begin with, and employees eventually understood. Jobs are no longer for life. In this new culture the real benefits of new

Jobs are no longer for life.

technologies cannot be held back by issues of paternalistic feelings towards staff, no matter how long their service has been. Many people see this removal of a person's 'right' to a job as a cruel manifestation of the selfishness or greed of the eighties. But in reality, it has always been the same, only now we are having to acknowledge it.

For example it was easy enough for a company like IBM in the past to declare a policy of 'no redundancies' at a time when they were growing at 20 to 25 per cent per year. But if new technologies and competition overwhelm the organisation to a point when it is losing billions of dollars a year then such a policy is simply irrelevant.

This will be an unsatisfactory state of affairs for the individual whose 'feel good' factor is secondary to.the 'feel insecure' reality. And yet organisations must be able to do better. The progress towards organisational sensitivity is essential if organisations are to avoid the crises which lead to massive and sudden downsizing.

The correct performance measures of the factors which are critical for an organisation's, a team's or an individual's survival are at the heart of developing a competent and sensitive enterprise.

Who measures performance and how do they do it?

The glib answer to 'Who judges performance' has to be 'The global marketplace'. Measures are ultimately determined by the users or purchasers of products and services. They will use two forms of comparison – absolute, 'Do I really need this thing, or is there a way round it?' and comparative, 'Can I get a better one, or better value from anywhere else?'

What is the best source of performance targets and feedback?

Too many organisations think, through arrogance or ignorance, that they know best. They may be setting top class quality measures and controls in place, but if they do not reflect how their customers see the world they will be irrelevant.

CASE STUDY

Measuring customer satisfaction by the supplier's criteria

A major supplier of large and midi-sized computer systems used a complex, computerised system for measuring customer satisfaction. It covered hardware performance, software performance, the speed of reaction of engineers and support people and many other detailed issues of supplier performance.

Most of the company's account managers used the questionnaire slavishly. Indeed, their appraisal scheme included the requirement for a positive result from the annual customer survey. Managers looked at the reports which the system produced, and these were many, compared them with others and last year's and were generally well satisfied with the high scores coming from the grand majority of the customer base.

The trouble was that it was a self-fulfilled history. Since it concentrated on what the supplier thought was important, and incidentally knew it did well, the scores were bound to be high and getting higher.

Some account managers were more customer focused, and tried to agree another type of customer satisfaction questionnaire which reflected the customer's whole attitude to and plans for the use of computer technology. They got some frightening results as customers, still very loyal and friendly, started to talk of concerns and then backed off saying 'Of course that is not really in your company's area of operation'.

> Too true. Underneath the facade of near total satisfaction loomed a revolution in the way customers wanted to do their computing. A sea change towards personal computing was about to wash over the supplier, and the customer satisfaction survey foresaw it not.

We will return to this topic in further chapters which cover defining and transferring knowledge of customer issues and setting up the knowledge centre to ensure the organisation reacts in time to changes in customer requirements and competitive pressures.

How do we measure performance?

The simplest measures are brought down to a financial figure or set of figures. Indeed, at the holding Board level of a conglomerate, key financial indicators may be the only measures necessary. This leaves the operating companies to be concerned about other issues to do with softer data such as quality or competitiveness. This can be successful enough if the operating companies have the required sensitivity to their customers and the rest of the outside world.

As we will see, a company can rely to an extent on financial indicators, but will have to look at others based on something less easy to define and indeed less finite. And yet, if the warning signs are to work, managers have to define their targets and tasks in a way which they can measure, at least to an extent where a lamp glows in three states – green because there is no problem, amber because the ideal range is being threatened and finally red when the problem has reached the stage of hampering the company's short-term goals or long-term strategy.

What we can set and report on are all those factors that influence performance as defined by customers in terms of deliverables, service, reliability and so on. These measures relate directly to the provision of 'benefits' to the customer, both short- and long-term.

We can also report on measures relating to the cost and timeliness of the product or service provided. (See Figure 1.1.)

Put briefly and from the customer's point of view:

➡ what does it do for me? (benefits)

➡ when can I have it? (timeliness)

➡ how much does it cost? (cost)

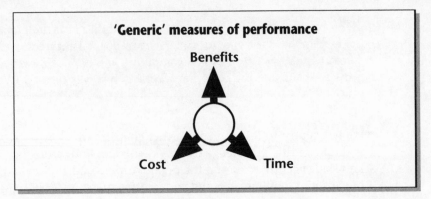

'Generic' measures of performance

FIGURE 1.1

Can we define the fundamentals of organisational sensitivity?

In order to exploit the model for organisational sensitivity, an organisation must first recognise and group the fundamentals which drive good enterprise.

 In order to be successful in a competitive world, an organisation must:

→ know *what* business it is in, and equally important what business it is not in

→ know *how* to perform effectively and efficiently in its chosen markets

→ gather and transfer performance data to people who can take action to resolve problems

→ have people who have both the ability and the willingness to resolve problems and continuously improve the organisation.

The organisation must know what business it is in, and equally important what business it is not in

The knowledge of what business a company is in, and what it is not in, provides an opportunity to outline the process of building organisational sensitivity and creating a knowledge centre.

In subsequent chapters we will argue that a successful company has fully worked out four key elements: strategic planning, knowledge transfer, process management and people management. No matter whether we consider a corporation striving towards organisational competence, or a manager trying to improve divisional performance, these are the key elements.

In terms of the active choice of what business to be in, an organisation must first understand its strategy. Choosing products, services, markets and customers is a complicated decision, in part because there are an awful lot of possibilities with a lot of parameters. Do we choose the segments of high volume and low risk, or high margin and greater room for error? Do we go by short-term profitability, or long-term opportunity? When do we decide that a cash cow is running out of steam and make the difficult decision of major change?

Managers must beware of the fashionable, particularly when they can afford to follow the latest craze.

Managers must beware of the fashionable, particularly when they can afford to follow the latest craze.

CASE STUDY

He diversified them up to the top of the hill and demerged them down again

History repeatedly shows that when a company becomes successful and then cash-rich, Boards have a habit of pushing money into other companies, or plant or people which represent large jumps into new products and markets. Oil companies in the late seventies and early eighties were arguably at this stage. They spent on acquisitions as well as research and development and on production facilities to compete in markets which were the specialities of other players.

This removed the large cash balances from the balance sheet and made everyone look very busy trying to make the most of the capital available. Hindsight makes us question how well the diversification strategy was thought out. When the competitors struck back, the oil price went soft and recession reappeared, many oil companies found themselves the owners of assets which they could not exploit. The selection of the *what* in the 'Know what business it is in' had gone wrong. In particular they had failed to define what businesses they were *not* in.

It was of course new management teams which implemented the divestment programme and pushed the companies back to core business.

In Chapter 6 we will invite you to evaluate critically your own organisation from the *what* perspective. You will be asked to make sure you understand what your core business is and on what basis you compete. Vague terms are not sufficient. To sell 'fast-moving consumer goods into the home market', offers too many opportunities for divisions and managers to move away from core business. Make sure that the strategy gate you provide for operations to pass through has two posts, otherwise everything will get through.

Over time, of course, the basis on which organisations compete changes, mainly due to changes in the marketplace or through technical opportunity. The organisation needs to recognise that fact and avoid the pitfalls of improving efficiency in a dead or dying operation. It does not matter how efficiently you produce black and white televisions if the product has been superseded by colour. Sticking to the knitting is a good mantra as long as the market still wants jumpers.

In short, some products and some markets are significantly more attractive and profitable than others, and activity needs to be prioritised and focused on those areas. It requires managers to foresee change and react in time, changing the strategy even when very difficult changes are required.

It is advisable, although sometimes very hard to do, to get out of a dying industry before you are forced to close all your operations and fire your staff. The meltdown of the British coal industry, apart from its political implications, might have been less traumatic if management and staff had seen the changes coming and planned a way through.

An organisation must know how to perform effectively and efficiently in its chosen markets

Knowing what business to be in implies making choices about products and markets. Unfortunately it is not as simple as just deciding what to do. Organisations must also understand what it takes to carry out the decision successfully. What have you got to get right to succeed in your chosen products, services and markets? (This is what the cash-rich oil companies in the previous example took for granted and what caused the problems.)

Knowing what it has to get right allows the organisation to determine the inputs it requires to process through a series of activities to deliver the outputs which are measured by benefits, cost and timeliness to customers. It can also calculate the urgency of activities in relative terms to meet customer specifications.

Here is an example of a company reacting to changes in its customers' environment which meant that the supplier had to change *how* it went about delivering benefits, even though it had not changed its products, services or markets.

CASE STUDY

'Knowing the engineering need' changed to 'knowing the customers' revenue and profit needs'

In the telecommunications industry, huge revenues were earned by the suppliers of the public switches and all the transmission equipment required to carry voice and data traffic. When there was little competition to the telephone operators, frequently nationalised or quasi-nationalised businesses, these facilities were supplied on an engineer to engineer basis.

One big organisation, the supplier, sold to another the products and services agreed at technical level to develop the network along agreed lines, taking advantage of new technologies as they emerged.

Competition changed all of that. Successful suppliers had to start to understand their customers' marketplace and competitive threats. They started to calculate the impact of their proposals on their customers' profit and loss account as well as their own. They were in a solution-selling environment and needed to have a whole new network of contacts within each customer. Suddenly the marketing department of the telephone operator came heavily into the picture.

Slowly a new decision-making process came into being. The operator's marketing department with the agreement of its sales organisation started to push for a new facility or application which it recognised that the market was demanding. The chain then moved to the product line managers who passed a more detailed description of the requirement to the design and build team. Design and build itself had to take much more close note of how the product would be presented to and used by the telephone companies' end users.

From design and build the proposal went to operations who had to determine what the technical requirement from suppliers was. This then went into the tendering processes carried through by the very powerful purchasing department.

Traditionally the major suppliers of switching and transmission products had formed relationships with operations and purchasing. **In the new competitive environment they had to develop high and wide relationships in all the other areas as well.**

The final step in this exercise in developing sensitivity to customer requirements was to have the suppliers' marketing people coming up with initiatives for the network operator. The chain of added value from the suppliers had lengthened from the technical wizards and purchasing to the opportunity to add value in almost every aspect of the customers' decision-making process.

In the end it became as important to come up with the big idea which benefited the customers' business as to maintain cost and quality measures of the products and services supplied.

Knowing how to compete today does not guarantee success tomorrow. Once the supplier has put in place contacts and processes which ensure it remains a major player it then has to remain sensitive to changes. Consider the impact of a far-reaching change in the computer market on a company such as Compaq and then on Compaq's suppliers.

Compaq used to compete in the PC industry on the basis of quality but had to respond to the radical change towards cost being the main market driver. Eventually the market became a 'commodity' market. The speed of change was awesome.

In this environment Compaq had first to redefine *what* business it was in, and if that still included the PC market. That decision having been made, managers then had to redefine *how* they were going to compete in the future. Without this redefinition they would have become uncompetitive and lost market share.

We are therefore starting to see the fundamentals as a chain where the organisation will only be as strong as its weakest link. The sensitivity issue is broader than normal performance measures. Here is a performance measure concerned with 'green' issues.

CASE STUDY

'How can you help us to improve the environment?'

Hewlett-Packard is a company which promotes itself heavily as making huge efforts to become more environmentally friendly. Indeed in a recent annual report the President, Lew Platt, stated:

'In this message I would like to focus on two main topics: what we did to improve our cost and expense structures and thus profitability, and how we fulfilled our commitment to corporate citizenship'.

Inside the part on corporate citizenship, the environment loomed large. Talking to a major purchasing manager in the company, one could easily see that any supplier to Hewlett-Packard had better be sensitive to this requirement if it wished to remain a supplier. Simply put, HP demands continuous improvement from its suppliers in terms of the environment as a prerequisite for a supplier/customer relationship. It was almost already too late for a supplier to recognise this when it was summoned to a meeting to have this fact explained and spelt out.

A supplier could not simply decide it wanted to do business with Hewlett-Packard, it also had to understand how it needed to behave to be successful.

Even if organisations do not compete on costs, there is now a maximum acceptable price for competing. Once again a good illustration of this is the Western companies withdrawing from manufacturing because their costs of manufacture were too high. This is often incorrectly blamed on labour costs, but often relates directly to the degree of complexity in the manufacturing processes and the manufactured goods. IBM had at one time processes which were simply too cost intensive for their chosen market.

We have seen how an organisation's sensitivity to its customers and its customers' customers is a key determinant of how to perform effectively and efficiently in its chosen markets.

Knowing, theoretically, how to do things is a big step forward, but we need to monitor constantly how effectively we are and will be performing.

An organisation must gather and transfer performance data to people who can take action to resolve problems

This principle does not relate to technology, but to all the ways in which information is shared between the different stakeholders of the organisation. This includes formal and informal communications, meetings, documentation, analysis, management reports and so on.

The first requirement in this area is to gather the right information in the right format at the right time. Simply stated, it has been singularly difficult to achieve. Documentation and information recording are rarely the most enjoyable part of a job which requires great skill such as design or project management.

In this next example we see a link between the previous fundamental of knowing how we can be successful and the requirement to put in place performance data to reflect this. Sometimes the importance will only emerge in the future, but it is possible to recognise the data requirement if managers concentrate on the *how* to remain successful.

CASE STUDY

Europower: staff memory saves the day

Europower had inherited a hydro-electric generator which had been a very important plant in the early fifties. It remained part of base load (ie generating electricity 24 hours a day) though of course with constant modification.

One such major overhaul involved the removal and repair of a gate in the dam which was, of course, under water. The repair was of such a nature that the plant had to close down, and the managers made their best efforts at assessing the timescale and cost of the work. They agreed to be back 'on the bars' within seven days.

The project had a disastrous start, in that the removal of the gate was unexpectedly difficult and had not been accomplished by day four. The overall timescale was plainly at risk.

It happened that one of the existing work people had a father who had retired from working at the same site. When told of the problems he remembered the installation of the gate many years previously and that they had had to design and make a special tool. He was brought in to help with the search for the tool, but, as luck would have it, even the building where he remembered it being kept had been knocked down.

Engineers sat down with the man and slowly but surely redesigned the tool from the man's memory and what drawings they had of the gate. His recollection saved the company a fortune.

The value of information gathering can sometimes be realised years later and the possible requirement can be very hard to anticipate. Having gathered the information, how does an organisation turn this intellectual capital into a reliable asset?

Organisations which have not made real progress towards organisational sensitivity generally approach the topic of information gathering using the wrong questions. This leads to the information gathered being relatively easy to collect and in the main historical. By historical we mean 'This is how we have always got our management reports, so they and their format must be right'. The correct question is more far-reaching. Are we measuring the indicators that will tell us how effectively we are meeting customer expectations in our chosen products, services and markets?

CASE STUDY

If you ask the wrong question, you'll get the wrong answer

A manufacturer of mobile telephones had decided to put time money and talent into designing an ultra-efficient telephone, and put aside a year to do it.

By careful setting of objectives and creating well-documented and agreed action plans it managed a very efficient project. It met all the customer benefit, time and cost parameters set.

On completion of the project the manufacturer discovered that several competitors had moved on to new technology with significant improvement, thus denying them a competitive edge and damaging their competitiveness. The question asked within the project was 'Are we meeting our objectives?' To this question the answer was 'Yes'. The question should have been 'Are we addressing our underlying need to remain competitive in this field'. The answer to this one was 'No'.

Looked at from a management perspective, the information provided tends to lead to two different comments from middle management. Either 'They tell us nothing' which is the keep them in the dark or mushroom approach, or 'They give us so much data we cannot find what we really need'. This second phenomenon warns us of the truth which is that if information is poorly presented to managers they will ignore it. It also highlights a lack of focus on what really drives performance. An organisation which is developing sensitivity spends a lot of time trying to organise information in a way which enhances understanding.

Finally we have to get the information to a 'forum for resolution' which allows the correct action to be taken. This passing of information to the right people at the right time in the right format has to be functionally independent. Performance of one function is rarely isolated from that of others. It is even rarer that the solution to performance problems is found in one function. Most important data needs cross-functional dissemination.

> *If we do not have the people with the ability and willingness to keep us on track, organisational performance will suffer.*

Following these first three fundamentals of organisational sensitivity we get to the people issue. We can know where we are going, understand how to get there and be in a position to know how well we are performing, but if we do not have the people with the ability and willingness to keep us on track, organisational performance will suffer.

Organisations must have people who have both the ability and the willingness to resolve problems and continuously improve the organisation

Having got the first three fundamentals right, the people issue becomes the determinant of success. Senior management needs to look at the plan and maturely decide whether the people involved have the skills and understanding to make the plan happen. Then it needs to check that everybody involved wants to make the plan work and will benefit from a successful implementation.

This happens proactively and reactively. In the proactive sense we can determine the skills and capability implications of a new way of working. In the reactive sense we analyse what skills and capabilities we require to get back on track. Managers need to check that a new way of doing things is implementable by the people involved.

CASE STUDY

Nice plan, pity about the team

A systems integrator was developing an account plan for a key account. He put in the necessary time and effort to ensure a good plan. The 'natural planning team' was gathered and included elements of marketing as well as production to ensure that the resultant plan was within the company's strategy and ability to deliver.

The members of the team started from the right point and looked first at the customer's vision for the future and then the customer's strengths and weaknesses in achieving that vision. They then considered their own vision within the account and their own strengths and weaknesses in achieving their aspirations.

A major weakness for the selling team was lack of knowledge outside the division of the target company where it already did a lot of business. In the action planning section of the team event, the team members were set milestones and actions to plug this knowledge gap. The team had to go high and wide into the customer, seeing senior and middle managers to paint a picture of the other divisions thereby determining new opportunities. A key part of this was a calling matrix for senior managers of all disciplines within the supplier organisation to help the account managers to gain access to customer executives. Their weight, it was thought, would add credibility to the requests for meetings and the meetings themselves.

At a plan review some months later little progress had been made.

An examination of the strategy and actions served to confirm that the plan was solid and correct. The planning facilitator who helped to confirm this then put his finger on the problem. Some members of the team did not have the skill to carry out conversations with senior managers at the right level. This was leading to poor meetings which in turn led to the collapse of motivation of the team to get this part of the plan implemented. The facilitator noted that, of course, everybody had a full schedule selling and implementing projects into their traditional market in the account. This meant that they had a cast iron excuse for failing to make progress in the new areas.

The problem was compounded by the attitude of the supplier senior managers involved. This was also new ground for them and they were less than motivated to help in such selling activity. They declared a lack of skill and therefore unwillingness to help, or worse they felt threatened by the exposure they were being asked to accept.

Either the plan had to be modified or the people trained in new skills. However, some of the team and managers would never have the necessary skills, and this in the end had to lead to changes in the team if the plan was still preferred.

Understanding what it takes to be successful does not mean we have it!

This simple example pales when you consider the radical change required when a company has determined to move into new markets with new products. If the move also involves competing on a different basis from normal then the people issue and other problems are compounded.

Many 'performance improving' initiatives fail because they have not involved and engaged the energy and commitment of those necessary to make the changes happen. Many initiatives never actually carry through into an internalised change to the culture and modus operandi of the organisation.

This is a vicious circle. If staff start to see a number of initiatives being launched amid senior management hype and glossy presentation, they become more and more cynical as management fail to see them through.

CASE STUDY

More new initiatives and processes than man can handle

In Europower, management was facing major changes to its field of operation caused by the imminent arrival of competition. It had to change from being a state-owned monopoly to a privately owned corporation in a competitive market. It needed to compete with generating companies as well as regional distributors.

Management could see the cliff ahead and had some years to prepare. After a long time it was reluctantly conceded that the cliff was that much closer, but the march of the entire company was still directly towards it.

A review showed no lack of initiatives. Going round the company you could find many projects in various states of implementation. There were Total Quality Management initiatives, competitive analysis initiatives, there were downsizing and rightsizing initiatives together with their attendant voluntary severance initiatives. Here were new processes for strategic planning, there teams working on globalism and internationalism. 'A new focus for information technology' report had recommended a series of IT initiatives.

Overall this was a massive exercise in negotiating with staff unions the new environment for industrial relations, backed up, of course, with an initiative for communication called 'Relationships, a new way forward.'

> All of this was well-meaning and aimed at the heart of the new strategy, but all was doomed to fail because the company was trying to make progress on all fronts and making little on any.
>
> In the end management forfeited the trust and respect of the majority of the people who were involved in changing radically how they went about their everyday tasks.

You may have heard of this as the 'BOHICA' effect or 'bend-over-here-it-comes again'.

The four organisational fundamentals required for success – a summary

 In order to be successful in a competitive world, an organisation, team or individual must:

➡ know what business it is in, and equally important what business it is not in

➡ know how to perform effectively and efficiently in its chosen markets

➡ gather and transfer performance data to people who can take action to resolve problems

➡ have people who have both the ability and the willingness to resolve problems and continuously improve the organisation.

Linking performance fundamentals as a chain

These four fundamentals can be viewed as a chain where the organisation will only be as strong as its weakest link. The focus of management should be on that weakest link. Much time and money is wasted by an organisation trying to correct weaknesses in areas which are not on the critical path towards the weakest area of the four.

It does not matter how clear the vision of the future is, how efficiently operations are being run, or how effective is an organisation's understanding of its chosen market if the people within the organisation are not committed to activities which are consistent with and sensitive to other functions both external and internal.

For an example of this, one only has to turn to the tragedy of Timex in Dundee where a clear vision for the future was backed up by a plan for efficient servicing of a growth market. Unfortunately the plan was neither understood nor accepted by the workforce. This complete failure of trust and communication resulted in the death of the factory and the loss of all the jobs.

You may be close to a successful negotiation with staff in one area of the business, but if the agreement you are about to make has a divisive and otherwise negative impact on another division, then your organisational sensitivity must warn you of this. In this example, managers do not have control over an important ingredient in change activities.

CASE STUDY

Europower: the staff organisation was out of sync with the business organisation

In Europower there are a number of craft unions which remain strong in almost all parts of the organisation. Following the restructuring of the business into divisions and profit centres, a huge problem arose when dealing with unions who still worked across the whole organisation.

Their sensitivity between divisions was better than management's and the business paid the penalty. An agreement made with the craftsmen in generation when applied to distribution was so costly that distribution managers had to risk industrial unrest in order to get it changed. The eventual compromise still made the distribution business considerably less efficient than was the original plan.

The dominant role of selecting products, services and customers

Whilst it is true that the fundamentals link together as a chain, the selection of products, markets and customers will be seen as having a dominant role. Most organisations have to survive with a certain number of constant or changing inefficiencies. Most organisations recognise difficulties which cannot in the short term be corrected. But if the organisation is making the wrong products or trying to serve the wrong customers then it is on the slippery slope.

This external aspect of organisational sensitivity will be the subject of the early recommendations of this book.

Hierarchy of performance fundamentals

Whilst many of the examples given so far have focused on the organisation as a whole, these same fundamentals apply at all levels of the organisation down to the individual.

Any team, whether servicing internal or external customers, needs to understand what products and services it is providing and to whom. It needs to understand how to do the necessary tasks, and it needs to know how it is performing. Finally in the chain it needs to make sure it has the necessary skills and motivation to perform the tasks in a way that meets customer-defined performance objectives.

In the case of individuals, career planning and success in their chosen jobs is linked to the same fundamentals.

Dynamic aspects of performance

Finally it must be recognised that performance requirements change constantly. This means that sustained performance requires that the shape and nature of an organisation's objectives and activities change more or less continuously.

This dynamic aspect can only be met by an organisation which moulds fluid structures and ensures that the sensitivity of each individual and team is high both cross-functionally and outwardly.

All the links in the chain react in this dynamic way. Managers therefore need a model to assess the situation and the need for change. This model for creating organisational sensitivity is the core of this book.

'Get your retaliation in first.'

Anonymous football manager

A MODEL FOR ORGANISATIONAL SENSITIVITY

Managing the whole is
only possible if we
understand how all the
pieces fit together.

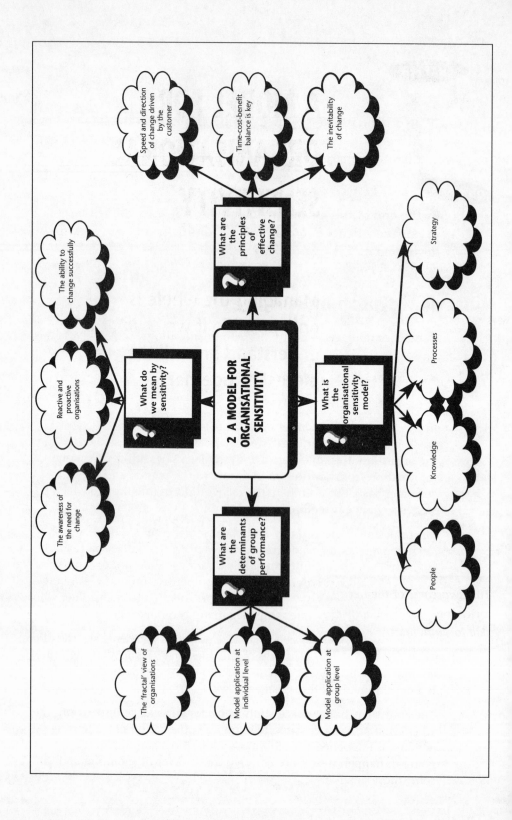

The organisational sensitivity model is based on the four elements that determine organisational performance identified in Chapter 1. It also reflects the 'principles of effective change'.

By the end of this chapter readers will be able to define the essential elements of organisational sensitivity and a model for describing it.

What do we mean by sensitivity?

In practice managers need to develop organisational sensitivity in two steps:

➡ awareness of the need for change

➡ the ability to change successfully.

In the first the organisation makes sure that its listening mechanisms are in place and recognised. This awareness is easier in some parts of the organisation than others. For example, a sales office will get its information from continuous exposure to the market and the customer base. But even here the recognition of intelligence which suggests change is required can cause difficulties.

Most salesforces are strongly motivated to get results. This leads to salespeople reacting, sometimes over-reacting, to changes particularly in competitive offerings. Their understanding of new features in competitive products is at best sketchy and at worst planted by a customer who after all is negotiating to purchase something.

The awareness of the need for change is a development skill for managers.

When, therefore does management take the dire warnings of the salesforce seriously enough to commit to radical change? Thus the awareness of the need for change is a development skill for managers.

The ability to change successfully converts knowledge into action where that knowledge is founded on an appreciation of something which has happened – reaction, or on an understanding of what is going to happen next – pre-emptive action. We will examine both in some more detail.

Awareness of the need for change

As time passes, little or large misfits or inconsistencies arise between organisations and the external and competitive environment in which they operate. The people in an organisation are continuously sensing these misfits as customer complaints, for example, or competitive announcements. They are feeling for them or having them dramatically thrust upon them

At high level this is known as 'strategic drift' which is a good phrase to describe the slow but sure movement of the world away from the position for which the current organisation was prepared.

In the 1970s a politician commenting on the inexorable rise of inflation likened it to a bath in which the water was getting hotter a quarter of a degree at a time. 'At what point do we, who are sitting in the bath, agree that we are being scalded?' he enquired.

But strategic drift as a phrase can hide the potential for what might be better described as 'tactical avalanche'. From technology to commodity prices, from government regulation to mad cow disease, these avalanches are evidence of management's need to be aware of strategic drift early. Increasing competitiveness in today's marketplace forces organisations to detect drift more and more quickly, with antennae which are growing increasingly sensitive.

There is no disagreement that the external and competitive environments are continuously changing. What can be argued is the question of how often, and how radically, to change the organisation to adapt and maintain fit. In most circumstances organisations make incremental steps as they react to or pre-empt change. Figure 2.1 opposite shows this relationship.

The 'reactive organisation'

In different industries this pressure to recognise strategic drift has a different timescale. Consider the timescale of the car industry.

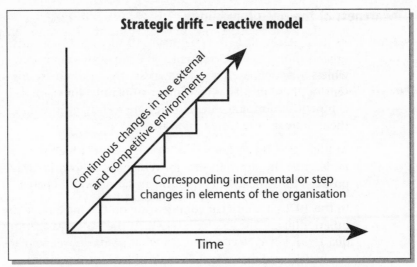

FIGURE 2.1

How quickly can you change your product if it happens to be a mass-produced car?

In a mature industry such as car manufacturing, the established players will continue to monitor gradual changes in customer expectations and competitor activity. This results in a series of model changes and interim 'facelifts' to cope with external events.

Sometimes these external events have long-felt repercussions. For example, environmental issues, combined with the price of oil, have forced a drive to produce cleaner more efficient cars.

Despite the enormous improvements in getting new features incorporated, and the slashing of time to market for new models, there is still a development cycle for a new model of some three years.

This means that there will always be a certain amount of misfit between the latest model and the expectations of a customer or the deliverables of a competitor. Particularly in styling, managers are asking how long it will take for a design to appear out of date.

As in all things the exception proves the rule. Consider the slow rate of change in the look of a Mercedes. That company's brand image and reputation allow it to plough a different furrow, emphasising the timelessness of the design, and therefore the holding of the car's resale value. It will be interesting to see what the strategy will be when Mercedes completes its move into compact, cheaper cars.

This example illustrates the need to forecast customer expectations proactively. Figure 2.2 shows how the proactive organisation stays ahead of strategic drift.

The flexible and proactive organisation ('thought leaders')

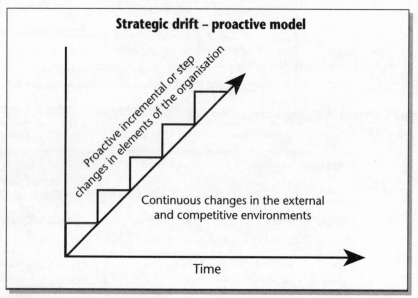

Strategic drift – proactive model

Proactive incremental or step changes in elements of the organisation

Continuous changes in the external and competitive environments

Time

FIGURE 2.2

In every aspect of the organisation we are continuously asking some questions.

➡ Do we have our antennae in place to detect change in the external and competitive environment?

➡ When we detect misfit do we know how to decide when and how much to change?

➡ Do we have the skills and capabilities to produce measured reaction to the antennae?

The ability to change successfully

To start the process of improving an organisation's ability to handle change successfully, we will return to the four key elements of an organisation introduced in Chapter 1:

➡ strategic planning

➡ process management

➡ knowledge transfer

➡ people management.

As the organisation reacts to stimuli, its reactions can be traced to one of these elements. It can change its strategy as the result of drift or avalanche. It can change its processes, reorganise part of its knowledge transfer and encourage its people to deal with and indeed welcome the new way of doing things.

Figure 2.3 puts the organisation into a redoubt, assailed by the forces of change in the external and competitive environment. Except, the redoubt has implications of hard edges, while the sensitive organisation softens these to allow for rapid alteration in its activities. This allows flexibility and responsiveness, characteristics of a 'sensitive' organisation ensuring that the degree of misfit is kept as small as possible.

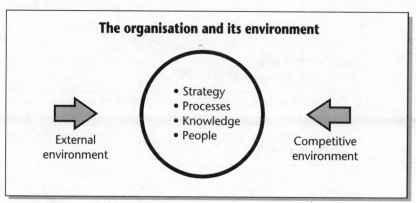

The organisation and its environment

External environment

- Strategy
- Processes
- Knowledge
- People

Competitive environment

FIGURE 2.3

Any change from an external source can trigger change, and each change potentially ripples into another element of the model. A change in the environment, like an instruction from a regulator, may, to start with, have the biggest impact on the strategic plan. But eventually that change will impact processes and knowledge requirements. And, of course, every change depends on the people implementing it for its success.

Similarly a change in technological infrastructure which makes it possible for all the PCs in an organisation to communicate with each other will certainly alter the knowledge transfer and people elements, but it may well have the significance of changing strategy.

A client once likened its organisation 'bubble' as shown in Figure 2.3 to a jelly. It suggested that a change in any one external factor will have an impact, greater or smaller, on *all* elements of the organisation. The ability of the organisation to flex and respond to changes was vital to its success – this ability was affectionately known as the 'wobble factor'! Here is how the health service had to cope with a change in strategy.

CASE STUDY

Changing the concepts of health care

For a dramatic example of the organisational sensitivity model at work we need only consider the creation and change in function of trust hospitals. The dramatic changes to them over the last few years have been caused not only by government legislation, but also by changes in customer requirements and expectations.

One policy statement from the Department of Health was to effect an alteration on the emphasis for caring for the mentally ill. The transfer of care was from the traditional hospitals to the community. For the trust hospitals themselves, this forced a transformation in traditional areas of operation. The old performance measures such as occupancy levels or discharge rates became meaningless overnight.

Professional judgement as well as many other processes had to change. The provision of services in a dispersed setting necessitated fundamental changes to the way activities were conducted. Knowledge which, up to that point, had stayed within the hospital had to be transferred into other people's hands. The roles and responsibilities of all the staff involved were equally transformed and the resultant sense of concern and foreboding enormous. Those hospitals which made and motivated managers to think through and plan for the changes in the context of the sensitivity model were much more likely to change in time and avoid mistakes which in the world of health can be both catastrophic and fatal.

Thus the whole organisation was compelled to change to keep up with a strategic issue. The problem of how and when to respond to external trends is further complicated by planning timescales.

Managers at all levels must divide their attention between the long term and the short term. Unfortunately busy managers are often heard to say that they regret it, but they do not have time for strategy.

Unfortunately busy managers are often heard to say that they regret it, but they do not have time for strategy.

Lack of resources, elements of activity outside their control and the general fire-fighting of today's problems make strategic thinking look like a luxury.

Unfortunately, if a business is too busy taking and producing orders to consider the long term, it runs the danger of not providing what will be required in the future. In this case the long term is left to look after itself, and it becomes clearer and clearer that the organisation has no future. The jelly remains intact and as before, except nobody wants to eat it! Sometimes this kills an industry.

CASE STUDY

Oblivion for the lack of a push button

It is widely believed that the demise of the British motor-cycle industry was brought about by nothing so dramatic as the huge changes in government policy as we have seen in hospitals. Rather it was brought about by management's inability to believe that customers really did prefer a starter button to a kick-start.

In Chapter 1 we talked about the strategy, the 'what', and processes, the 'how'. An organisation's performance and ability to change successfully depends on the appropriateness of the strategy – the what, and the efficiency of the processes – the how. Figure 2.4 shows the relationship of these two elements to the future success of the organisation.

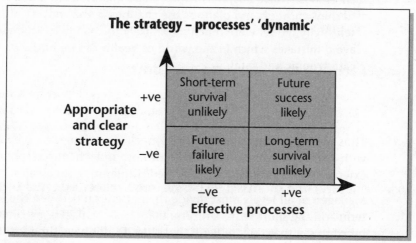

FIGURE 2.4

Any model reflecting the whole organisation must show the critical relationship between these two separate but inter-related elements.

CASE STUDY

Can we wait for the processes to catch up?

In Europower, management's priority was to set a strategy and communicate this to all the people in the organisation. In the distribution part of the business this meant taking tough decisions on what was core business and what could go through a process of evaluation for outsourcing.

Decisions were made of an aspirational type, because the financial processes in place made it impossible to make an accurate comparison between the potential profit and loss accounts of internal departments and the costs of outsourcing.

Add to this that the workforce had yet to agree to any change in the way they worked or were remunerated and Europower is at this stage in the bottom left box of the strategy matrix. It had an appropriate strategy, but its processes remained obstinately ineffective.

Principles of effective change

Before we establish the organisational sensitivity model we must understand what principles lie behind effective change. Management's awareness of the need for change and its ability to change successfully will channel change through these rules.

Changes are customer- and competitor-driven

No matter how much we enjoy producing products or providing services, if sooner or later our customer either does not want to buy or consume them, or prefers to use a competitor, then survival must mean change.

Speed and direction of internal change must reflect external trends

Change for the sake of change is not enough – it must be in the right direction and at the right speed. For every internal change in activity we should ask 'How will this improve our organisation's short- or long-term performance in the marketplace?'

Time-cost-benefits question is key

There are three 'generic' measures of meeting customer expectations and for any particular product/market combination, the balance will be different.

➡ **What will it do for me?**
➡ **When can I have it?**
➡ **How much will it cost?**

This is sometimes termed the 'basis of competition' as it relates to the bases on which a firm must compete for the customer of its chosen marketplace. The balance between the three generic criteria will change over time – the key is that an organisation must understand what the criteria are and reflect these indicators internally throughout all processes

Inputs + process = outputs model applies

The 'quality' of product and service 'outputs' (as measured by the three generic criteria) will always be dependent on the quality of the inputs (materials, information, facilities etc), and the activities completed within the organisation's processes

Holistic view of organisation is required

Changing just one part of an organisation in isolation is not enough. Changing what we want the salesforce to sell will achieve nothing unless our sourcing or operations groups can meet the demand. In the same way, altering the mission of an organisation will change nothing unless its processes, people and ultimately its information systems also change.

Changes will happen whether they are managed or not

The inevitable and continuous nature of change must be recognised. (It is rather like snow in winter in the UK – it always comes and it always catches people by surprise.) A more positive and proactive approach to managing change is required, which ultimately reduces the disruptive impact in fulfilling current orders

The inevitable and continuous nature of change must be recognised.

Effective management and individual performance will not overcome poor organisational design

Inspirational leadership and workforce commitment are vital ingredients of effective teams but they are not enough in isolation! In the field of armed conflict, the majority of battles fought throughout the ages have been won and lost on the management of the logistic chain – not the motivation and commitment of the fighting troops!

The organisational sensitivity model

Whatever managers have imagined as the model for a functionally oriented company, the needs of the millennium require a model which allows for and encourages organisational sensitivity. Making sure that the right hand knows what the left hand is doing, making departmental decisions in the context of understanding the rest of the organisation and reacting in time to changes in the external and competitive environment requires a new way of looking at the organisation.

Criteria for model design

To find a usable model we must ensure that it has the following characteristics. The model must:

➡ demonstrate the dynamic aspect of organisations – encompassing today and tomorrow

➡ include the vital four elements of an organisation

➡ reflect the fundamentals of performance improvement

➡ allow critique of the current organisational state – the plan, the actual and the gap

➡ show clearly and visibly the proactive and reactive nature of knowledge transfer.

The organisational sensitivity model

Each of the four elements of the model (see Figure 2.5) will be examined in detail over the following sections. At first glance, however, key features required for organisational sensitivity become apparent:

➡ the total organisation is represented by the shaded area, showing that suppliers and customers, strategy and processes are all integral

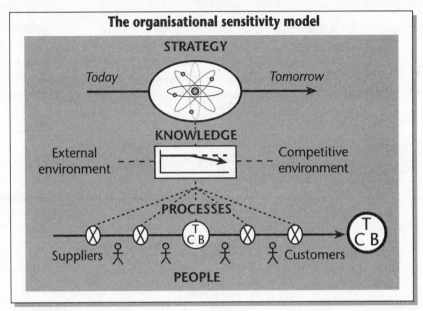

FIGURE 2.5

parts, so all will require detailed understanding and proactive management

➡ strategy is dynamic with the dual role of linking the visions of today and tomorrow, and providing a framework for the whole organisation

➡ the transfer of knowledge lies at the heart of the organisation (externally, knowledge transfer allows managers to implement proactive change, internally, it encourages the evolution of processes to allow timely reactive change to problems and in both cases the focus is not on data but only on those key areas where actual performance is different to the plan)

➡ processes start with the supplier and end with the customer's customer (the end user) (this organisational picture reflects the need to understand the effectiveness of all processes and mirror the performance measures of benefits, time and cost throughout all internal activities)

➡ people are shown as the foundation of the organisation where their deployment and capabilities should be spread throughout the processes as required.

Strategy

Strategy provides the framework within which the organisation operates (covered in more detail in Chapter 6). It clearly articulates what products and services will be provided, and to which markets and customers. Perhaps more importantly, it also articulates what it will not do and who it will not work with. For each of these chosen markets it will specify on what basis it will compete in order to be successful and what its stated purpose or source of advantage will be. It should also reflect the guiding principles of stakeholders and create the culture which will define the nature of the relationships with all stakeholders, internal and external. It will have achieved nothing if it does not also identify the direction and the speed of change in terms of products, markets and capabilities, and also the extent to which the strategy will be planned or opportunistic (how tight or loose) – it must therefore guide day-to-day decision making.

Finally, strategy will also be ineffective if it is not communicated to, understood by and committed to by all those involved in implementation.

Using Directline as an example, we can see how a market-driven strategy can drive a product design, the *what*, which enables a process, the *how*, of selling which is distinct and competitive.

Its strategy of selling only standard, and therefore high-volume, insurance products and avoiding non-standard or high-risk customers ensured that they were highly focused. It also kept clear of the costs of complexity and allowed the organisation to compete in the marketplace on the basis of price.

It is essential then that everyone understands how their role can be carried out to reflect the strategy, and they need to understand it in a way which is relevant to them.

CASE STUDY

Communicate the strategy in the listener's terms

It is worth stating early on the importance of translating a strategy statement into terms which are meaningful for the people you are trying to get to. This is often forgotten, particularly when management is promulgating a lofty mission statement. The following may be a very good message to get to your shareholders and customers:

'Europower's purpose is to provide world-class energy products and services, whilst at the same time maintaining and developing the integrity of our distribution and generating capabilities. We will meet the requirements of our customers, sustain growth in earnings and make an appropriate contribution to the communities in which we conduct our business'.

However, such a mission statement will achieve little unless translated into local practical terms when communicating with other stakeholders. It will do little, for example, for a storeman in a small sub-store of engineering parts in the far-flung corners of the country where you operate.

It is almost certainly not enough to hang the Board's mission statement in every canteen in the organisation.

It is worth noting that terms such as stakeholder are used broadly. For example, stakeholder in the environment of a trust hospital would include the patients and their relatives and friends.

Processes

Processes provide the means by which strategy is achieved (inputs + **processes** = outputs) – the way in which operational and support activities are conducted in order to provide products and services to markets and customers, (covered in more detail in Chapter 6). Capability 'gaps' identified in the strategy (those capabilities that will be required for future success but that are not currently available), will influence future process development.

These gaps in capability are not always the obvious ones.

CASE STUDY

It was not the selling process which was going wrong

A boatyard's selling team was struggling with a large sales campaign. At stake was a size of order very much bigger than the norm for this particular company. The members of the team were getting on well with some of the key people in the buying organisation, but had deep feelings of foreboding. Their selling instincts told them that all was not well and they felt that whatever was being said, the competition was being preferred.

The leader asked a facilitator to help them replan and refocus the sales campaign. With the team together, the facilitator was quickly able to see the team spirit and enthusiasm so often connected with a winning bid. The team had most of the bases covered with a good understanding of the customer requirement, real knowledge of the benefits the customer would gain from buying the team's products and services and a well thought through argument as to an appropriate basis of decision which suited the customer and put this team in its best possible light.

Why then did the team feel so wary about the result? On further probing the only loud noises of dissent concerned other functions within the selling organisation. Put bluntly, they were not used to the size of the deal and were putting obstacles in the way of the team to absolutely ensure that they were covered when the project came to implementation. It was hard for the selling team to get commitment of the resources required to assemble the technical and financial side of the bid. Nobody from marketing felt dedicated to helping the team win. The divisions were passing the requests for information amongst all the involved people but without any real co-ordination. In short the problem was not the selling process but the 'bid process'.

Once this was understood, the selling team set a new set of objectives concerned with bringing the key internal people together, getting their commitment to winning the bid and making sure that the bid was properly organised.

When the sale was made, the successful team asked the customer for a debrief on the campaign. All the key people in the customer commented on the moment when the supplier performance changed and for the first time the buyers felt the supplier could actually handle a project of this size. The moment, of course, occurred when the bid process was sorted out.

Detailed process design will be driven by external customer needs and expectations, where the balance in terms of time, cost and benefits criteria are clearly understood and are reflected throughout all internal processes. All activities will be understood to the extent required to achieve a balance between **alignment** to the specified process objectives, and **empowerment** of the people completing each activity. The contribution of each process to the organisation's short- and long-term success will be clearly identified and the key decision points, where critical choices are made, will be proactively monitored and managed. Finally, roles and responsibilities will be clarified to an appropriate level.

Examples of efficient and effective processes are often found in 'commodity' marketplaces where competition is typically focused on price. The Royal Mail now has a worldwide reputation for the way it distributes letter post throughout the UK. The efficiency of its processes provides an effective deterrent to prospective competitors.

Knowledge

Knowledge provides the organisation with the information required to make the best proactive decisions about the future and reactive decisions concerning crises (**inputs** + processes = outputs). This information combines external information about an organisation's external and competitive environments and its internal operations. The right information will be gathered from the right sources and provided to the right people at the right time in the right way (covered in more detail in Chapters 10 and 11).

Effective knowledge transfer also ensures that managers do not suffer from knowledge overload as is becoming the case at Europower.

CASE STUDY

Europower threatens to drown under the weight of plans

Once the distribution business unit of Europower had completed its plans at senior management level, it got into the habit of sending out minutes of the review meetings to the next level down. In this way managers were getting the entire plan by electronic mail on a monthly basis.

All the managers were interested in that part of the plan which was functionally relevant and in little else. They tended to skim through until they found their initials or the initials of their boss.

The next step was for these managers, who reported to the top team, to produce their own plans. This was done on a regional basis. The regional teams went through the strategic thinking and produced a plan. Much of it derived from the senior management plan and a good connection was made between the two. However, the second-level managers were worried that this second plan would add to the bureaucratic administration and cause overload.

> The IT department solved the problem by making sure that only changes to the plans were reported and activities were listed in the order of those responsible.

All informal and formal communications channels form part of the transfer of knowledge. Knowledge transfer therefore encompasses the effectiveness of meetings as well as the way the organisation learns both from the past and from its successes and failures.

People

People are the first and last link in the chain to organisation success. Organisations must have people who have the capability and the willingness to perform the tasks expected of them (covered in more detail in Chapter 8).

People are the first and last link in the chain to organisation success.

Performance will be directly related to the clarity of the expectations required of them, people's skills and knowledge, the availability of the necessary resources, and the rewards and feedback provided. Whilst these systemic elements are required for success, the culture and management style must also be supportive of the desired way of working.

Whilst the management of people is presented as a discrete element within the model, it is of course people who plan strategy, implement processes and gather and transfer organisational knowledge. Getting people involved can be a complicated process. It is at Europower.

CASE STUDY

Conflicting structures at Europower undermine the credibility of the whole strategy

Following a consultant's report, Europower decides to move away from its traditional civil service-oriented method of operation with its emphasis on budgets, towards a more commercially oriented approach which made everyone much more conscious of the need to make profits. It needed to make profits not only to satisfy its shareholders but also to provide the investment money for the future.

An early move was to restructure the organisation into business units. This was a radical change from the monolithic approach of the past. Initially suspicious, the staff in the organisation warmed to the new situation when the logic was described and management's vision for the future communicated.

Unfortunately as we have seen, the structure of trade unions did not change. They remained completely centralised, trying to negotiate agreements which cut across the business units. This led to great frustration as the needs of one business unit, different from the others, could not be written into agreements because the unions still sought company-wide salaries, terms and conditions.

The result of this was protracted negotiations between personnel departments and unions at the same time as management was trying to roll out a huge raft of changes. Eventually middle managers as well as the shop floor became utterly cynical about management's ability to make new strategies and processes work. They knew that they would be stopped in their tracks by the impossibility of following through changes to working practices and conditions.

There is a strong link between processes and people, with the design of the processes taking into account the abilities of the people who will be balanced with the needs of the processes.

One of the reasons for the success of Hewlett-Packard is said to be the way it manages its people. The 'HP way' focuses on getting all the parts of the human resources system correct and mutually supportive. This is backed up by the culture created by their management teams where the phrase MBWA (managing by walking around) was coined. The management of their people was perhaps the key differentiator which allowed them to respond to quickening changes in their industry and continue to grow profits. Slower to change, IBM and Digital suffered the consequences.

Determinants of group performance

The model which we will use to show the progress of a whole organisation towards sensitivity also fits any group which wants to achieve the same thing. You can apply it at any level, function, division or team, right down to an individual who is attempting to carry out his or her role within an understanding of the whole environment.

At the group level, the external environment will include all of the other groups within the organisation and the distinct relationships with them. The competitive environment includes internal groups competing for budgets and resources, but perhaps more importantly in this age of 'outsourcing', it includes external groups! Strategic planning, process management, knowledge transfer and people management for a team or group will use exactly the same principles and concepts used at the organisational level. Each part of the organisation can be viewed as a 'fractal' – just as with a cauliflower, if you break it into its component parts, each component looks like the whole.

PART 2

CONCERNS

In this context, what problems does the manager face?

'With ruin upon ruin, rout on rout,
Confusion worse confounded.'

Milton

THE REALITY OF ORGANISATIONAL CONFUSION

Recognising the starting point and the pitfalls in creating organisational sensitivity.

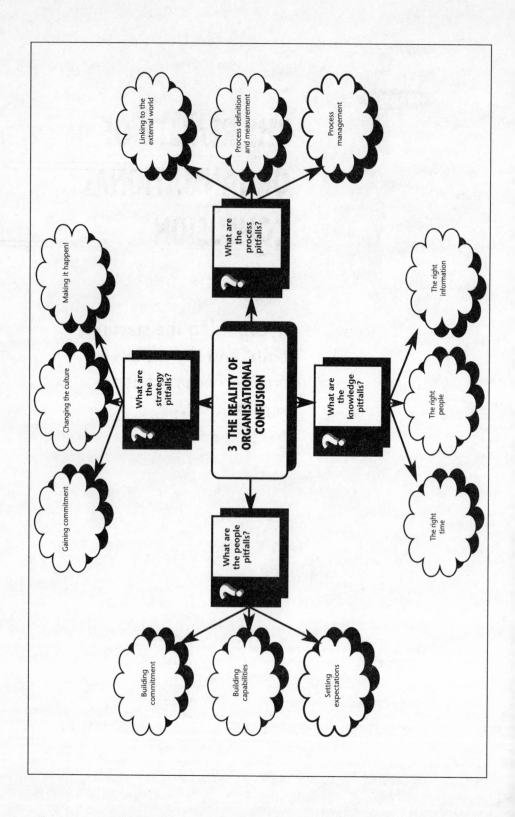

3 THE REALITY OF ORGANISATIONAL CONFUSION

What are the strategy pitfalls?
- Making it happen!
- Changing the culture
- Gaining commitment

What are the process pitfalls?
- Linking to the external world
- Process definition and measurement
- Process management

What are the knowledge pitfalls?
- The right information
- The right people
- The right time

What are the people pitfalls?
- Building commitment
- Building capabilities
- Setting expectations

The picture painted in the previous chapter is the ideal. Unfortunately all pieces of the organisational jigsaw are rarely in place in any organisation at any one time. The reality is often a confused state where one or more of the elements are not working according to the plan.

By the end of this chapter readers will have identified a list of obstacles which are currently hindering their progress towards organisational sensitivity, whether for an entire organisation, a division, a team or an individual. They will complete an exercise which identifies the weakest links in the organisational sensitivity model.

Introduction

The picture of the organisation with suppliers, customers, strategy and processes as integral parts takes a lot to build and to maintain once it is created. Most organisations have some dysfunction in one or more of the areas, which we can represent as the model of organisational confusion (Figure 3.1).

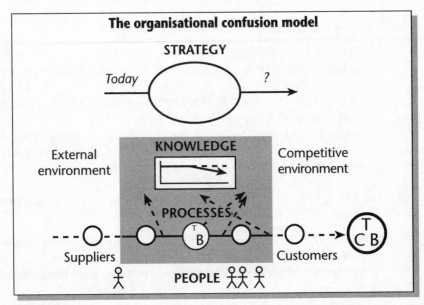

FIGURE 3.1

Perhaps the first significant thing to notice about this model is the lack of integration of strategic thinking or the strategic plan with the rest of the organisation. There is a simple test for this. As we shall see, the last element of the strategic plan is the preparation of activity plans. The simple test is 'Do managers on a daily or at least weekly basis update the action plans driven by the strategic plan?'

In many cases the answer is 'No'. Whether we are talking about the corporate business plan or a divisional plan, they tend not to be dynamic documents. Too often the strategic planning department sits outside the real world of the operating divisions. The result is this lack of integration.

In many organisations planning activity is carried out on an annual basis, with one manager from the division responsible for updating the text of the plan and the numbers. There is no commitment from the rest of the team and no chance that the plan is the focal point of the team's performance measures.

The responsiveness of such a dysfunctional business is inevitably very slow. The operating divisions will probably not take cognisance of what the planners are saying and real change will only occur when the outside world demonstrates dramatically the need for it.

Notice also in organisational confusion how suppliers and customers are seen to be external to the organisation and not part of the driving factors of benefits, time and cost. Once again there are some simple tests to find out whether or not this is true of your organisation. Are purchasers making suppliers aware of the long-term trends and strategies in the organisation? Are customers part of the strategic planning of the organisation directly as well as indirectly?

The people are also set outside the processes of the organisation in the model of organisational confusion. This means that the plan and the processes take little, if any, account of the skills and abilities of the people. The simple test here is probably morale. People who are not treated as part of the whole will react by feeling low and working towards results which they probably know are not really what the organisation as a whole requires. In some large organisations it is astonishing how many managers you can find whose objectives and goals are quite out with the strategy of the organisation. Yet these managers are rewarded by incentive schemes or promotion prospects for attaining these objectives.

Finally it is no surprise to find that the sensitivity of the confused organisation to the external world is very low. It almost has a life of its own where movements in the marketplace whether from the market or the competition are scarcely noticed.

In order to analyse the problems of confusion in an organisation there are more detailed questions to answer.

Identifying the pitfalls in strategic thinking and planning

Take the organisation or part of the organisation you wish to analyse and use this section to consider where the key weak areas are as a starting point for producing action plans.

Are people committed to the strategy and does it anticipate problems and opportunities?

Issue	Supplementary questions
No vision or strategy exists	Can managers articulate to their people, customers and suppliers where the organisation will be in, say, five years' time if all goes well?
	Could a salesperson describe the product and marketing strategy of the organisation?
The strategy is not communicated throughout the organisation	Is there a mechanism for doing this?
	Are significant changes automatically communicated?
The strategy is not understood and committed to by those necessary for its implementation	Has the strategy been translated into terms which are meaningful at each level?
	Do managers ensure that their people can articulate their part in the strategy?
Strategic changes are too reactive	When did your organisation last cause a reaction from its competition?
	Are managers complaining of always being in 'fire-fighting' mode?
	Does your strategic plan include possible threats and activities to counter them?

It is extraordinary how long organisations can survive without a well thought out strategy. Until, that is, something occurs which points to the deficiency dramatically.

You know how important the existence of a plan is when something goes wrong

A contractor had built up a very large and profitable business with a property developer. There was a good fit with the quality and values of the two companies and both were on similar growth paths. There was no strategy in the contractor to guard against over-reliance on one customer, and slowly but surely it became very much a follower in the partnership. The developer called the shots and the contractor organised itself to respond magnificently.

The developer was taken over and the contractor informed that apart from existing projects there would be no others from this source. Despite the fact that there was some time to get other customers, the contractor was unable to find an answer to the new environment. Potential customers could not make themselves understood, so imbued was the contractor in the ways of its erstwhile customer.

It was interesting to note that if something in the organisation could go wrong, it did. Communication became poor, some key people left and confusion reigned. An employee said that it was like being on a ship where everywhere you looked had broken down at the same time. Eventually the company was split into smaller pieces and sold, at low price, to other players.

It is not possible to maintain a long-term future without an identifiable and specific strategic plan.

Can everyone take part in strategic planning and is it in the working culture?

Issue	Supplementary questions
No formal strategy education and training has been given to or exists within the teams, at the top and lower down	Can members of the teams think strategically? Do members of the teams have the patience to form plans where

Issue	Supplementary questions
	the results are achieved some time ahead?
There is no clear process for strategy formulation	Are your plans annual and no more than a matrix of figures?
	Can you understand from reading the plans what the team is going to do and who is responsible for which activities?
	Do planning teams have access to some form of facilitation from outside the team?
There are no clearly defined roles and responsibilities for strategic management	Are all your performance measures within the timescale of a year?
	Are disciplines in place which ensure that teams spend some of their time together looking at longer term issues?
There are no clear links with operations	Are there cross-references in operational plans to the strategic plan and vice versa?
	Do the non-numeric objectives in operational plans reflect the objectives in the strategic plan?
	Do the plans of the staff departments of the organisation overlap considerably with the strategic plan?

Of course a strategy will itself have to adjust to events, in which case other changes may well be necessary.

CASE STUDY

If you change the strategy make sure you change the culture too

A technology company prided itself on the quality and feature-richness of its products. The engineers were used to spending what they determined was necessary in terms of their time and money to keep the product at the quality they sought. The time came, however, when cost pressures were being felt at Board level. The Board realised that some of these pressures arose from the design and build part of the organisation.

It decided to put in processes for budget supervision and passed these down to middle management. Unfortunately the Board did not understand that at the project manager level there was absolutely no understanding of costs or cost control. In this case the strategy change towards maintaining quality inside new restraints on spending had not been properly communicated to the project managers who remained unable to describe what management was trying to do, and therefore unable to take their part in the strategic shift.

Are people in a position to implement the strategy in the way envisaged by management?

Issue	Supplementary questions
The underlying values and beliefs are not understood	Can people at all levels explain what the underlying values are in terms which are meaningful to their roles?
	Can people explain by examples how these values change how they go about their jobs?
The characteristics and boundaries of products, services and markets are not clearly specified	Can everyone concerned articulate these?
	Are they regularly updated?
The purpose of the organisation and its source of competitive advantage are unclear	If you gave everyone a questionnaire would they come up with the same unique and competitive advantages?
	Would these be the same if you gave the questionnaire to a customer?

At Europower they seemed to believe for a while that if you proclaimed values and beliefs often enough, you would end up living by them.

CASE STUDY

Europower: if it's not true it's better not to say it

In Europower, the values and beliefs were set down in great detail following a long process of discussion attended by the shareholders, in this case the government, management and staff represented by a number of unions. The resultant document contained commitments on both sides to communicate with each other regularly, to consult on all major issues and to put in place a series of bodies to make this happen.

The implementation started, but was quickly overtaken by events. The management decided that the time for radical change had come. It put together a complicated set of issues, from a price increase to downsizing and faced owners and staff with the challenge of negotiating on all these fronts for a once and for all improvement in how the company operated.

The negotiations lasted some two years. The consultative processes were of little help since the reality was that there were two sides, management and unions locked in heavy negotiations which became rancorous and harder as time progressed.

In the end the negotiation was more or less successful; but how futile was the earlier work where both parties were pretending to a relationship which did not exist.

Identifying the pitfalls in organisational processes

Do the processes link all the external factors to the organisation?

Issue	Supplementary questions
Organisational processes are not defined or understood. They have evolved over time and are not documented other then through common practice	Does a master list of process maps exist at all levels of the organisation?
Processes are not linked together to provide a seamless transition of inputs from suppliers through to outputs to customers	Do your purchasing people understand your customers' expectations?

Issue	Supplementary questions
	Are the systems involved in all aspects of customer satisfaction consistent and do they communicate with each other?
	Are service people involved in the process of product design?
Processes are not focused on satisfying the end-user	Does the product plan anticipate changes in the end-user requirement, or is it confined to your particular customer?
	Do your marketing processes reach out to the end-user?
	Do your selling processes take into account the end-user?
Customer use and purchasing criteria are not understood in terms of time, cost and benefits	Are you certain which attributes of the products and services are most important to your customers?
	Does your whole organisation understand the way customers trade off attributes to get to their preferred solution?
Internal process performance measures do not reflect the customer's purchasing criteria	Are the reasons why customers purchase from us understood? Are these reasons reflected in internal monitoring mechanisms?
Customer and supplier processes are not understood and the interactions between them are not defined	Do we understand what we can do to help customers become more profitable, or to help suppliers to be more effective?
	Are costs (fixed and variable) monitored and actively managed by those actually doing the work?

Another look at green issues illustrates the importance of linking external factors into an organisation's processes.

The supplier side of environmental friendliness

A major buyer of components started a considerable push towards 'green' policies in its manufacturing processes. Any supplier who failed to recognise this was in great danger of losing the customer. If the customer had to bring weight to bear to make the supplier change, then that was already taken against them when new contracts were in the offing. The customer preferred suppliers who understood the green strategy and made efforts to conform.

Are the processes well defined with relevant performance measures?

Issue	Supplementary questions
There is no effective quality and cost management of activities within the processes	Is quality and the cost of quality constantly monitored in relation to how it affects the customer?
	Are costs (fixed and variable) monitored and managed by those actually doing the work?
Key value and decision points within the process are not defined	Since all activities in a process are not equally important, have you identified the critical ones?
	Long-term performance can often be linked directly to key decision points. Are these clearly defined and are decision criteria specified and understood?
The value and priority of each activity or sub-process is not known	Is the contribution to the customer of each and every activity understood?
	Do you understand why all activities take place in the way they do?

Are the processes well managed?

Issue	Supplementary questions
Roles and responsibilities in the process are not defined or understood	Does everybody understand what they are supposed to do?
	Is there any duplication of roles, or are there any gaps?
There are insufficient resources allocated to the important processes	Do key processes sometimes stop due to lack of resources?
	Are the necessary budgets, facilities and materials available as and when required?
There is no effective management of the processes (functional management only exists)	Is anybody actually looking at the performance of the overall process, as opposed to just managing their piece?

Here is an example of a cross-functional process which is central to success but frequently left in functional pigeon-holes.

CASE STUDY

Straightening out the bid process

In many companies which sell complex solutions, there is bound to be a process which makes sure that what is being proposed in any given case will be deliverable and profitable. Frequently bids are completed at the last moment or even later when a plea has to be made to the customer for extra time.

It is often the case in such a situation that although all the functions are involved, no one is looking at the whole aspect of the bid process.

Identifying the pitfalls in knowledge transfer

Issue	Supplementary questions
Trends are not being picked up from the external or competitive environments (technology, customer expectations, competitor performance etc)	Is your organisation reactive?
	Do plans constantly change, and are projects sometimes cancelled half-way through?

Issue	Supplementary questions
The mechanism for transferring knowledge is picking up the wrong data, at the wrong times – typically because it is historically available or easy!	Does your organisation have a lot of data which seems to be the wrong data at the wrong time?
What information does exist is not analysed effectively, or is being picked up too late to allow proactivity	Is the available information in a format which allows easy analysis? Are reports really used to manage operations proactively?
Some information exists but it is spread across functional units, or is retained in people's heads only (when they leave so does their knowledge!)	Does your organisation have mechanisms for capturing useful information and making it available to people as and when they require it? Is individual and organisational learning an integral part of the culture?
Knowledge of customers, end-users and the supplier base is limited	How well are customers and suppliers really understood throughout the whole organisation? Is it clear which customers are the most important?
Meetings are managed ineffectively, and internal communications are disjointed	Do meetings have clear objectives, involve the right people and no more? Are meetings managed on time and to a prepared agenda? Is there a widely agreed process for managing meetings?
Technology is insufficient to meet information needs	How effectively is technology utilised throughout the organisation? Does technology make completion of tasks quicker, easier and more accurate?

Issue	Supplementary questions
No training or education in 'information management' is provided	Do staff understand the principles of continuous learning?
	Have people received any formal education in the gathering, organising and analysing of data?
The organisation does not learn from its successes and failures – nobody asks whether we did well or badly!	Are projects and activities formally closed out on completion so that people learn for the next time?
	Is there a 'blame' culture which inhibits the honest debate of successes and failures?
People do not learn from each other as an 'information is power' culture predominates	Do people make decisions for personal reasons rather than for the benefit of the organisation?
	Do people willingly volunteer information if they think it might help, or do they always wait to be asked?
Management reports either provide too much, too little or inaccurate information	Are reports so thick and bulky that few people read them until forced?
	Are reports inaccurate and therefore not trusted for making real decisions?
There is no central area for the gathering, organising and displaying of key information	Is critical information so dispersed that it takes forever to retrieve anything useful?
	Is there a single point for communicating information for education or decision-making purposes?

If the processes within the organisation do not give the real performance information managers need, they will spend time doing it for themselves.

DIY performance monitoring

A second line sales manager had in her head four key ratios. Actual sales and deliveries compared to budget, actual costs of her operation compared to budget and number of customer complaints. Each month she got about an inch of computer output purporting to give her this information.

In fact it took the best part of a weekend to add to and manipulate the figures first of all to tell her where she was and secondly in order to input changes to the data she had been given.

Identifying the pitfalls in people

Issue	Supplementary questions
People are viewed as being somewhat 'different' or external to the organisation	Are people viewed as a prime resource or something which can be bought in as required?
	Is the role of people in formulating strategy and designing processes clearly defined and understood?
Expectations about performance standards are not defined – no vision of what success will look like has been articulated	Do target standards exist for every activity?
Performance targets are not understood or seen as realistic	Have people been actively involved in setting the targets?
	Is the rationale behind the setting of targets understood by everyone involved?
People do not possess the skills or capabilities to perform the tasks expected of them	Are the skills and knowledge needs for each activity defined?
	Are people systematically assessed against the requirements for the job, and then given support and training where appropriate?

Issue	Supplementary questions
There is no clear succession planning and the wrong people are asked to do the wrong jobs	Are people sometimes given jobs simply because they happened to be there at the time?
	Do people get jobs because of who they know rather than what they know?
People do not have access to the necessary resources (money, time, information, facilities etc) to perform tasks effectively	Are people sometimes blamed for poor performance when in fact they had insufficient resources to do the task?
Rewards are not balanced (positive behaviours receiving positive rewards and vice versa)	Is the focus in the organisation balanced between short- and long-term objectives?
Rewards are set from the organisational perspective without considering individual preferences	Are the objectives and aspirations of individuals known and considered when setting objectives?
Performance feedback is not provided to people in a relevant, accurate, timely and specific way	Do people receive feedback on how they have performed?
	Does this feedback help people to do the job better next time?
The organisational culture is confused (guiding principles are not defined or adhered to)	Are the values and beliefs of the organisation clearly articulated and linked to the performance of the organisation?
	Are the values real or aspirational?
	Do people use the values for real decision making or are they perceived by people as a PR exercise?
Management style is inappropriate (too tightly controlled or too loose)	Are activities too tightly defined and suppressing or too loosely defined and unclear?
	Are managers seen as being outsiders?
	Is there an us and them culture?
There is no balance between the alignment of people to specific objectives and the empowerment of people to get on with the job	Where people have the necessary knowledge and expertise, are they allowed to get on with the job without constant interference?

Crisis meeting at Europower

To illustrate a number of the key symptoms of organisational confusion, we visit part of a crisis meeting of the Power Generating Division of Europower. Far from being a sensitive organisation, Europower managers have perfected the art of turning a crisis into an unending drama.

The concern

To describe what happened at the oil-fired power station, known as the Mulger Station, as a concern is an understatement. It is a disaster. As part of the long-term growth in electricity generation capacity, Europower had purchased a new turbine for Mulger. The project to install took six months and was completed on time and pretty much within budget. In fact it was shortly after the bonuses for completing on time were handed out at a celebration party which senior managers attended mob-handed that the 'incident' occurred.

A bolt worked loose from its seating, dropped into the turbine, broke into millions of shards and wrecked much of the machine. The following afternoon the Power Generating Division (PGD) Board met.

Amongst those present were:

Joop van Daylaan   Managing Director
Claus Raes   Director of Human Resources
Michelle Surtain   Director of Coal-powered Stations
Paco Diaz   Director of Marketing
Ian MacDonald   Director of Finance.

A significant absentee was Panos Goumez, Director Oil-fired Stations. The location was a conference room at Head Office.

Joop   Well, there is no chance I'm afraid that we will get round to any of the topics which were on the original note I sent you. We have to look at Mulger and decide what needs to be done. Until we hear from Panos we are somewhat in the dark. Is anyone aware of how long it will take to correct the problem or how much it is going to cost? I don't really think so.

Ian   Could I just say Joop that those of us who have been on the generating side for a while knew that this was going to happen.

Claus   Eh? That's just the problem, we had no idea this was going to happen.

Ian   No, no I don't mean the actual incident, I mean that we all knew that eventually these new reward structures provided by the last bunch of consultants would make people take risks which would cost us a fortune.

Michelle   How do you know they took a risk? I mean, life's a risk anyway, so certainly powering up massive modern turbines is bound to have some risk. But I've always thought how frustrating it must be for you people in finance knowing exactly what needs to be done whilst we poor engineers run around making such a mess of things.

Ian   Sorry, sorry, sorry. All I meant is that the installation team has plainly gone for the bonuses available for completing on time and ignored something or other in the process. I won't say any more, but in the days before clever consultants, people used to complete things on time because it was part of their job, and if something unexpected happened everyone knew it was better to go late than take a risk.

Secretary interrupting the meeting   I'm sorry to interrupt, but the man from the *Das Figaro* newspaper is on the phone again saying that he needs to talk to Joop urgently.

Joop   Tell him I'll call him back. Look we cannot make any progress on exactly what happened until Panos gets back from Mulger. I told him to be back by now but, would you believe, he stayed overnight down there to buy them all a drink since they are all so utterly down.

Ian   I'm sorry Joop but that will not do. There has been a major disaster down there. Panos should be deciding who is going to lose their job, not buying them drinks. If the incentives are there for good performance then we also need the stick for failure.

Michelle   You can't call it failure yet. We do not know what happened. Having said that, the thing that worries me is that we have already installed one of these units at Arachaig and that went fine.

Joop   Why didn't we have someone from Arachaig working on this one?

Claus   We tried, but the unions put up such demands for expenses, overtime and bonuses that it just was not possible. It's crazy but it was just as though we were installing the first one twice.

Secretary interrupting again   I'm sorry Joop, I've got the Department of Energy on the phone, they've heard a rumour about Mulger and want to know what's happening.

Joop   Look, tell them I am still investigating, and that I will report to the Minister when I see him tonight. Actually, I'm half inclined to tell the Minister it's all his fault. If he had given us the investment money when we said we needed it this would not have been such a disaster. Look everyone, let's keep some focus on this meeting please. What are we doing to maintain supply, and how will we handle customer problems if we cannot maintain supply? Michelle.

Michelle   We're keeping going quite well due to two circumstances. Firstly the weather is unusually warm and peak loads are not too high. Secondly we have postponed the commissioning of the new unit at Preyent and as a result we can keep that in continuous production.

Joop   How long is that weather going to last?

Michelle   Good point, I'll get someone to look at that.

Claus   You do know that the Preyent solution is costing us a fortune do you? I can't imagine how much. They were expecting to go down to a skeleton staff, so people are cancelling holidays and we are conceding massive overtime and special payments to keep the station up and running. And to be honest, I think it will get worse once the people there realise just what a difficult situation we are in.

Ian   Yep, they'll put the knife in no doubt. How feasible is it for this to be a long-term solution? There must be something else we can do.

Joop   OK, we need a meeting of Michelle, Panos and myself to decide what is the way forward from here. We had better involve the Grid people, although heaven knows I am not looking forward to seeing their faces gloating across the table, just after we got them on the hop about the handling of the storm. Now what about the customers? Paco?

Paco   Well we have it pretty well under wraps, and as long as we can keep it there we should be all right. I've already had a call, though, from Universal Steel saying that they had heard a rumour etc and did we realise that they are in the middle of a long process which will cost millions if it is interrupted. Its probably a bluff, but we don't really know what the impact on them will be.

From our domestic customers' point of view, a breach in supply would be ghastly. What with the price increase they know we have asked for and the business about top managers' salaries the politics of this one will be dreadful. We've got to keep it under wraps.

Secretary interrupts again   I'm sorry to interrupt, but the man from *Das Figaro* says that as you will not talk to him he is going to run a story with the headline 'Dropped clanger at Europower wrecks turbine, millions may be without electricity'.

Joop (as Panos enters) Oh my God, tell him I will be able to brief him in five minutes. Panos, thank goodness, tell us what happened.

Panos Well the Station Manager did, I'm afraid, have some warning. There was a computer printout which showed a very, very small amount of vibration within the unit.

Joop So what did he do?

Panos Er, nothing, he decided that it was very unlikely that an event like this could possibly happen.

Ian Told you so, he went for the bonuses. 'Sod safety first, let's get the money.'

Joop Right, that does it. Claus, I want the resignation of the Mulger Station Manager on my desk by 5.30 this evening. At least that is one positive thing I can tell the Minister.

To summarise the situation which Europower is in. It does not really understand the impact of this crisis in terms of what it will cost to fix or how long it will take. It does not understand what impact it will have on its largest customer or whether its competitors will be able to exploit the situation. It does not know what to say to its shareholder, the Minister, because it does not really know what caused this thing to happen.

We need now to go through the processes involved in creating organisational sensitivity, and at the end of the book reflect how this crisis might have been handled.

'It's not how you play the game, it's who you get to take the blame.'

Frustrated account manager, also an international sportsman

THE RESTRICTIVE IMPACT OF FUNCTIONAL THINKING

The instinct to 'belong'
hinders cross-functional
sensitivity.

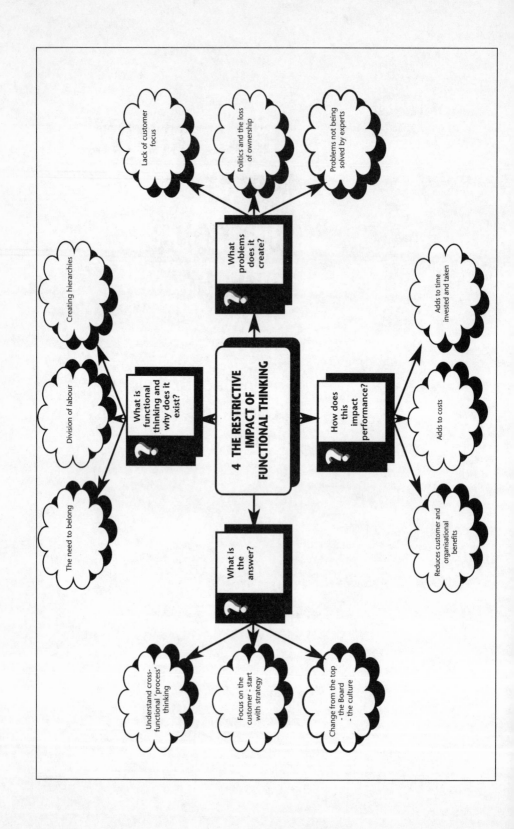

4 THE RESTRICTIVE IMPACT OF FUNCTIONAL THINKING

What is functional thinking and why does it exist?
- Creating hierarchies
- Division of labour
- The need to belong

What problems does it create?
- Lack of customer focus
- Politics and the loss of ownership
- Problems not being solved by experts

How does this impact performance?
- Adds to time invested and taken
- Adds to costs
- Reduces customer and organisational benefits

What is the answer?
- Understand cross-functional 'process' thinking
- Focus on the customer - start with strategy
- Change from the top
  - the Board
  - the culture

A basic human need is to know exactly where we belong or fit. A functional group of like-minded people satisfies this need. It is easier than thinking about what drives performance for the whole organisation – process or cross-functional sensitivity.

After reading this chapter, readers will be able to state how functional thinking restricts an organisation from its performance potential in time, cost and benefits to the customer. They will also be able to state the starting point for creating cross-functional 'process' thinking in their organisation, group or team.

What is functional thinking and why does it exist?

Division of labour neatly divides people by their expertise or capabilities. This mind-set is reinforced throughout our formative years in education, particularly technical or vocational training at college. This has historically been based around specialisms. Even nowadays when there are many business degree courses available, their teaching is essentially based around 'functions' such as finance, marketing, operations, planning etc.

In recruiting from the graduate pool, organisations send teams of personnel people on the annual 'milk round' to find new people to fill positions in the organisation by function. The opening pitches tend to be about the organisation's salesforce or research arm, for example, rather than about the organisation's final deliverable to the customer, from idea inception to actual delivery.

The first cut of the desirability of hiring someone tends to start from where he or she will 'fit' into the organisation. Having decided that, then appropriate line managers will do the final interviewing to make their selection. Before the graduate has started to work for the organisation, he or she is already feeling part of a specialised, and special, function in the organisation. They have listened to line managers extolling the virtues of their part of the piece. Esprit de corps is not about the corporation but about the line function.

Traditional view of an organisation

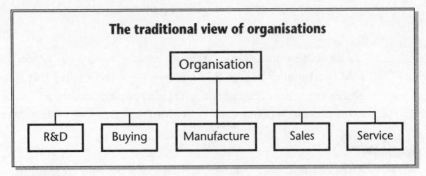

FIGURE 4.1

If you ask managers to describe what their organisation looks like, most start by drawing their organisation chart as in this figure. They can then describe the responsibilities of each of their people and delineate the part of the delivery process which concerns them. This functional thinking and deliberate encouragement of pride in the department results in colleagues in other functions being viewed as 'outsiders'. 'It's a communication problem' is a popular cry. The complaint is that sales don't talk to the research people, who in turn don't talk to the manufacturing people, who do not consult the service department. They all believe that the output of their own particular area of expertise is the end in itself, rather than providing part of the means to the ultimate goal of customer satisfaction.

This hierarchical structure becomes a god, or a demon if you happen to be the customer. A large organisation we know well traditionally starts all internal presentations with words 'My name is so-and-so, and I am a grade 5, or 6 or 7, in the such-and-such department'.

If used badly, electronic mail can actually add to this desire to stay in one's own department.

CASE STUDY

Slashing the gordian knot of e-mail-based functional thinking

A Sales Director in a garment firm started to receive a growing number of e-mail copies about a particularly large delivery of product on what had begun as a reasonable timescale, but had degenerated into a very tight one. She watched the problem escalate through the functional lines as the buck was passed and the blame laid, sometimes subtly sometimes not. She could see the problem being chucked over the protective walls of the leading players.

When the number of copies of each message reached 20 and one level below the holding company Board, she stepped in. Each individual was instructed to attend a meeting with the Sales Director and given the impression that they would be alone. In fact she invited them all for the same time.

She promised them three things: coffee when they had agreed to find a way forward together, food when they had an agreed analysis of the situation as it then was and release from the room when, and only when, they had a satisfactory plan offering the best customer satisfaction available.

They solved the problem.

It is easy to see how functional thinking has come to be a dominant feature of the culture of most organisations. The results of this are a series of disparate and self-generating problems.

What problems does functional thinking create?

The simply stated problem is that in a heavily function-oriented organisation there is no real focus on the customer. The customer does not merit a mention in the organisation charts which are promulgated inside and outside the organisation. This results in an inward-looking culture not one focused on the satisfaction of customer needs.

In a heavily function-oriented organisation there is no real focus on the customer.

The first problem is the measurement of performance which focuses on the function. It is actually possible for all the functions to perform optimally and to plan, while at the same time the organisation overall fails to meet customer expectations in the short or long term. If the performance measures are not customer focused, then the activities will not be customer focused.

At best the salespeople are the only people in the organisation trying to see the whole project as a deliverable to the customer. (Even this can lead to problems, as salespeople travel miles to pick up a cable from the factory, or go out and buy service from someone else just to get the job done.)

At worst not even the salespeople can get away from their arms-length functional view of other parts of the organisation. In this case no one has ownership of the customer order. As the order flows through the organisation there are by definition hand offs as it moves from one function to the next. This results in a loss of time as the order 'sits on the shelf' going from one in-tray, or receiving system to another and each delay causes a further loss of understanding, or even remembering, what is going on. Each hand off leads to increasing loss of ownership.

Depending on the industry this lack of ownership will cause severe or less severe problems. In an industry which is being pushed by competition to drive itself by 'time-to-market' criteria the problem can be fatal. Time-to-market focus requires concurrent or simultaneous engineering where cross-functional teams work together.

Perhaps the most serious problem of all which comes with functional thinking is the creation of powerbases and internal politics. Some management power can be used very positively. The power to reward, in terms of money or career, is a positive motivator to getting things done. The stick, as well as the carrot can be equally effective. 'If you do not do this your reputation, or even your job, will become insecure'.

Functional thinking tends to lead to an overabundance of 'expert' power, normally a veto power to stop things happening. Expert power in a functionally thinking organisation can only be destructive.

Expert power in a functionally thinking organisation can only be destructive.

If managers can concentrate on their own function without being responsible for ultimate outputs to customers, they can set up and hoard expert power. At the beginning of the planning cycle functional managers will fight to obtain scarce resources, knowing that what the group they run produces is the sole measure of success. This results in power plays between managers and trade-offs or compromises driven by reasons which are neither customer-oriented nor to do with the business.

This is particularly true when there are experts involved.

CASE STUDY

So expert, they could not live in an organisation

A group of software writers came up with a solution to a plant maintenance requirement so good that the Board realised that the software itself was saleable as part of the solution they offered to their customers. The writers were put into a specially created department and charged with producing a generic version of the software which could be sold profitably in volume.

They were very dedicated and very functionally oriented. Management were driven mad by changes to the software specification which their people were trying to sell being made by the experts who were by their own lights and measures producing the most elegant and function-rich solution to the problem. The fact that they were disappointing customers and infuriating their colleagues in no way diverted them from this quest or mission.

In the end, the organisation spun the individuals off into a separate company, sold them half of it and started to get what they wanted by themselves becoming the experts' customer.

The strange bedfellow of this misdirection of expert power into politics is that a functionally thinking organisation tends to have to escalate problems up several levels of management before a solution is found. In effect the problem is not being solved by the experts but by general management whose merit in making the decision is only that of being responsible for all the functional areas concerned. This is a major waste of time, distracts senior management attention from priority areas and involves significantly more people in the solution of problems than is really necessary.

This escalation procedure also causes people at the grass roots level to lose confidence in their ability to, on their own, solve problems and get things done. In the end it produces an escalation mentality which slowly but surely delegates decision making up the way.

The only time when functions come together is at Board meetings where the purpose of discussions should be strategic. However, due to the preponderance of functional thinking and the other pitfalls discussed in Chapter 3, Boards do not get round to strategic matters, and the meetings quickly become a forum for resolving problems and competing for resources.

How does functional thinking impact on performance?

All the illustrations of the restrictive impact of functional thinking we have looked at so far end up with an impact on the three key performance measures of cost, time and benefits to the customer.

Two further cases point out that not only is the impact direct, but it is also indirect in significantly curtailing management's ability to manage, or at least to recognise and work on the key issues of the organisation as seen by the people at the grass roots.

Look at this company losing out because it could not put together a key plan across functions.

CASE STUDY

Missing the bus

A manufacturer of public transport buses had maintained a healthy market share of the local authority requirement for single- and double-decker buses. Its managers foresaw a period of dramatic change as the bus companies became deregulated and small niche operators started to compete with the newly privatised companies emerging from their comfortable monopoly.

The chief requirements for the new environment were new products to meet the demand for smaller urban vehicles, and new markets in the new operators. Management also recognised that its export effort, a small player in the global market, should have new injections of time and money to combat the inevitable loss of market share in the home country.

Management brought in new marketing people and created a major account salesforce to tackle the burgeoning number of operators in the field.

Unfortunately, it failed to do this on a cross-functional basis.

The impact was severe, in that the organisation lost the window of time which it had to get its act together before the new environment really struck.

The marketing people produced marketing plans and then presented them to the design and build departments as set in concrete. Manufacturing could not possibly make all the changes which marketing believed were necessary in the timescale they feared. Instead of even trying they dismissed the plans as impractical and made few changes to the products being built which, after all, still had steady if unspectacular sales.

The account managers produced their plans as a result of discussions with their customers. They made no allowance for variations on what their customers wanted, insisting that any other plan would result in no sales to that client. They even produced plans which contained actions for departments, such as marketing, who had not even been represented at the planning meetings.

Senior management was lulled into a false sense of security as it saw these ambitious plans being tabled. It could hardly believe subsequently that the plans were being produced in isolation.

Cost – Looked at realistically, almost all the planning effort of some two years was a complete waste of money.

Time – By the time it became apparent that something radical was necessary to make change happen, it was too late to match the competitive offering in a number of areas.

Benefits to the customer – The company found itself unable to supply its current and targeted customers with the products they wanted.

A simple cross-functional meeting can produce dramatic results.

CASE STUDY

Starting the process of eliminating functional thinking

Do we work for the same organisation?

A change initiative in one organisation entailed the running of training workshops and the modification to systems. On the first workshop, the senior manager attended with a staff from different areas and layers in the organisation. To make the workshop more applicable to the participants, real organisational issues were discussed, covering what was going wrong, and what could be improved. At the end of the second day, the senior manager commented to the group that he was completely unaware of most of the issues that had been raised, and that he would start to resolve them immediately on his return. Clearly he was shaken as to how little he knew of his own operation or of the concerns of his staff – even though he had only one layer of management between him and most of the workshop participants.

To start the process of getting away from functional thinking to cross-functional thinking is a cultural problem as well as a process problem.

Producing a plan to eliminate functional thinking

The rest of this book suggests how managers can create a new culture within a whole organisation or more narrowly within their sphere of interest.

Start from the top

Boards are historically structured around the functions. So long as this remains, functions and political power bases will persist. The senior managers need first to recognise that there is a problem, and then commit to changing it by firstly recognising that their job titles are part of the problem.

Get the strategy right first

The starting point of all changes and of efficient management rests with strategy. Deciding what products are provided to which markets

> *To start the process of getting away from functional thinking to cross-functional thinking is a cultural problem as well as a process problem.*

forces the organisation to be outward-looking. Internal perspectives cannot drive long-term perspectives no matter what industry or market. Understanding what drives performance, a key strategic question, forces internal managers to understand how they contribute. This in turn makes them realise that to contribute they are dependent on their colleagues in other functions. First they need to recognise the need for interdependence and then act on it.

Current and future customers must drive strategy but they must also drive everything the organisation does.

Change the culture

Even where the rationale for working across boundaries is clear, the reality is often that functional thinking will still predominate. The reasons for this are multiple and are covered in more detail in Chapter 9.

Getting each individual manager to adopt the new process-oriented thinking requires that a number of questions are addressed.

 Checklist

➡ **What is required of me and is it realistic?**

➡ **What skills are necessary for success and do I have them?**

➡ **What resources and information are needed to work this way?**

➡ **How will I know if it's working?**

➡ **What is in it for me?**

A principal reason for functional thinking comes back to power bases and politics with a small 'p'. Functional thinking implies expertise. Information and expertise is one of the natural sources of individual power within organisations. People will typically resist any reduction in their power base, whether it is the right thing for the organisation or not. In this regard the most important question to be addressed above is the last one – 'What's in it for me?'

PART 3

CONCEPTS

What new management skills are required?

'Before you plan where you are going and how to get there, make sure you know exactly where you are now.'

Chinese proverb

CUSTOMER-
FOCUSED
ANALYSIS

How to ensure that the
final arbiter of success, the
customer, drives the whole
plan.

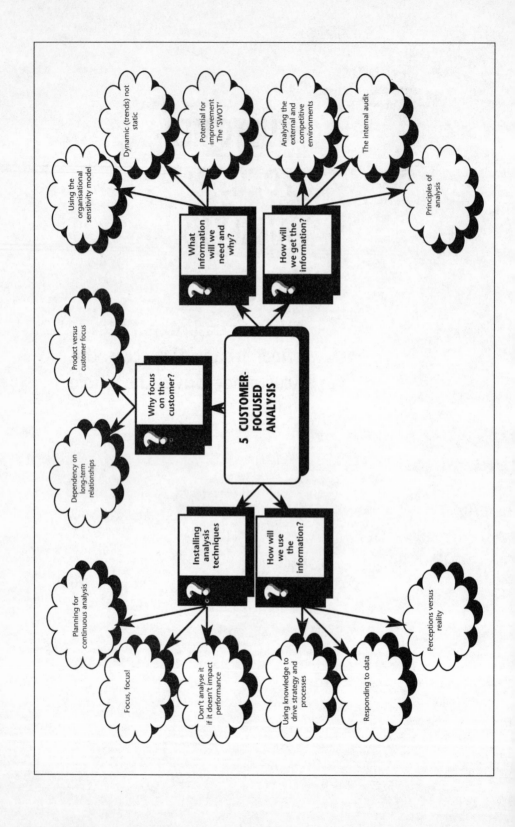

All plans and improvements start from an analysis of the current situation. This statement is, in fact, incomplete. The situation is continuously changing, so the sensitivity model needs to allow for continuous analysis.

By the end of this chapter readers will have identified the information they need before starting the process of creating organisational sensitivity, understood how to gather the information in a customer-focused manner and thought about what processes will be required to keep a continuous flow of information into the organisation as the environment changes.

Why focus on the customer?

If it were easy to do, all organisations would run with a model which focused on the customer. For reasons of history and human behaviour it is not easy. We will start with a rehearsal of why we need to focus at all times on the customer.

Dependency on long-term relationships

For any organisation, group or individual, the starting point of all strategic planning and process management activity is to understand the answer to a fundamental question:

➲ 'How will we continue to be the preferred provider of specified products and services to current and future customers?'

The question sounds simple, but many organisations have literally ceased to exist because either:

➡ they no longer provide customers with what they want

➡ they no longer outperform their competitors

➡ their source of competitive advantage has become irrelevant.

The net result would be: liquidation for the organisation; outsourcing for the group; redundancy for the individual!

Few organisations can afford to ignore customer expectations and needs. In all but monopoly situations this will hold true. If we accept that ultimately everything that we do is to provide outputs to customers, then any ultimate determinant of short- and long-term success must relate to the satisfaction of customers' needs and expectations. Where customers have real choice of supplier, then the relationship is fundamental to perception of customer satisfaction – a strong relationship can often overcome mediocre or poor performance in the short term. This premise increasingly holds true for internal customer-supplier relationships as more and more organisations will actively consider ridding themselves of any elements of their operations that they feel can be performed more effectively by an external unit – a term affectionately known as 'outsourcing'.

Product focus versus customer focus

The history and origins of many organisations lie in their specialisation and expertise in the design and production of products and services. Their people have been appointed because of their unique skills or expertise. For most organisations this was reflected in an internal division of labour (the functions discussed in the previous chapter), reinforcing the focus on technical, product or service expertise. In their own area they knew best!

This inward-looking focus reflected the sincere opinion of the drivers of the organisation who were following a line of development logic which, while excellent in its own way, was not sensitive to external factors which impacted their customers.

Make sure you know who the customer is

Before setting out the principles and processes of external analysis, it is important to agree on who the customer actually is. Many organisations get mixed up between the people, often experts, who choose and buy products and services and the managers of the organisation. In fact these experts are rarely the customer. The customer is the end-user for consumer products, and the senior management of other organisations in the case of products, or benefits, being delivered to other organisations. We have seen in the example in Chapter 1 how the communications company switched its focus from the network operator to the network user. In this case the consumer has become the end-user even of the infrastructure of the network. Knowing who the customer is, is vital in any long-term relationship.

Equally in internal customer relationships, it is important to know who is your customer and to make sure that you recognise the customer at a high enough level.

The simple motto is 'Sell high, sell wide'. Failing to do so is fraught with risk.

If you wait for the detailed specification, you will fight on someone else's battleground

A firm of chartered surveyors had a good and profitable long-term relationship with a major organisation in the aerospace business. It had, over the years, received instructions for all their services, from estate agency to property portfolio management. Unfortunately, its main contact was with the Technical Manager who ran the Central Property Department.

From this person the company received instructions to act for many of the subsidiaries of the organisation.

At the time there was a major debate going on at Head Office level over home-working. The Board was considering a number of possible strategic possibilities for moving many employees out of offices into a situation where, supported by new technology, they worked from home.

The issues were largely ones of productivity, morale, culture change and training, but there was, of course a significant impact on property. They would be getting rid of a number of offices, and buying or leasing new buildings which lent themselves to the new environment of offices which catered for few permanent residents and many visitors.

A competitor of the normal firm had got an introduction to the Chief Executive and was proving very helpful with suggestions for how the buildings portfolio might look in the new environment. The competitor was, in effect, offering strategic advice for little or no short-term return.

Eventually decisions were made and a series of moves and relocations were handed down in detail to the Property Manager. The new competitor was in such a position of power in knowing exactly what the real customer, the Board, wanted that it was a relatively simple task to tackle the Property Manager and get most of the instructions to act and make fees.

The analysis starts, therefore, with real customers and their needs. Now we need to gather information to get the hard and soft data which allows the strategic planning process to begin.

What information will we need and why?

The organisational sensitivity model

If the model represents all of the dynamic drivers of performance, then it will also provide the clues as to what we need to analyse. Looking outside the organisation, analysis should focus on the external environment, the competitive environment and on customers. This allows us to understand what is 'prodding the jelly'.

Analysis should focus on the external environment, the competitive environment and on customers.

Understanding this alone is not sufficient. The organisation also needs to understand how healthy it is in itself. Therefore, an audit of internal aspects of the organisation should also be conducted covering all processes, knowledge and people. See Figure 2.5 on page 53.

The information requirement is therefore very broad, and its gathering is a never-ending task. In the next section we will give some guidelines for getting the appropriate information, but before that we need to look at the type of information needed and suggest in outline how we are going to use it. In the first place we want to gather dynamic information, and in the second to gather it in such a way as to allow us to prepare a plan for taking advantage of any potential for improvement.

Dynamic (trends) not static

All forms of analysis provide a simple 'snap-shot' of the picture as it looks like today. Whilst in itself this can be valuable, it is vital to take the appropriate action in response. This can only be achieved if the trend is fully understood. A 10 per cent underachievement on productivity is always of concern. However, if for the previous 5 months the figure was a 50 per cent underachievement, then the latest figure would probably be looked at favourably!

In many ways this trend is more important than the absolute figure. It can be difficult sometimes for the finance department to agree with this statement. They have a mission to get to the real and detailed numbers behind an organisation, but planners often need only rough figures as long as they are calculated the same way for each time period.

Potential for improvement

Data in itself, even the right data, still has to be interpreted. The key question to ask is 'So what?' What are the implications to us – both good and bad, and what is the potential for improvement if we counter a threat or exploit an opportunity? The acid test of any analysis should be the identification of the potential for improvement over the 'Do nothing' or status quo. This may be measured in both positive or negative terms in that sometimes the analysis highlights an opportunity to be exploited, and other times it highlights a critical weakness that needs to be addressed. Actions resulting from such analysis are therefore either exploiting or defending situations.

The analysis technique which we use for sorting out our knowledge is called SWOT analysis – **strengths, weaknesses, opportunities and threats**.

This is a simple technique, as so many good ones are, for helping a planning team decide what it needs to do.

Unfortunately, like all techniques it can be implemented well and therefore also badly. Further guidance on good SWOT analysis follows, so suffice it to say at this point that a comprehensive, well-documented SWOT analysis makes the next part of the planning process more straightforward.

The objective of SWOT analysis is not simply to describe the environment, rather it is to describe the environment in a way which helps us to understand what we need to do.

Before we go further into the interpretation of the data which has been gathered, we must return to the question of how to get the information in the first place.

How will we get the information?

Starting with stakeholders

A good starting point for information gathering is to identify all those groups and people that have an involvement or are impacted by the activities of the organisation or group. These are commonly called 'stakeholders' as they have some stake in the success or failure of the organisation.

Such a list will provide a useful checklist for the analysis, and it will be used throughout all the resulting change as activities are planned to deal with the threats and weaknesses identified in the analysis. Any key player who is not in favour could kill the project.

Don't forget the key players!

When starting a change initiative the opportunities for improvement should always be assessed. The overall target is then to achieve 100 per cent of the opportunities for improvement. The reality is that for a variety of reasons 100 per cent is rarely, if ever, achieved. The difference between the two represents the unrealised potential. Does this mean that if there is always going to be unrealised potential, that we should not undertake change projects? No, it simply means that we should reflect on the typical reasons for unrealised potential and ensure that actions are taken to prevent them from occurring. Due to the distributed nature of power within organisations, even though a change project may have the support of certain senior managers, if all the key 'stakeholders' have not been actively taken into consideration or involved then they may actively oppose the project. At one technology company, one of the functional directors opposed a project, and only some 30 per cent of the potential was realised as a result.

As a starting point the following groups might be on the list:

External stakeholders	Internal stakeholders
Shareholders	Directors
Owners	Senior managers
Customers	Middle managers
Suppliers	Operational staff
Competitors	Support staff
Society	Unions
Government	Functional staff
Legislators	Team members
Advisory groups	Other specialists
Press	Colleagues

External environment analysis

Analysis of the external environment can be structured using the headings from Figure 5.1.

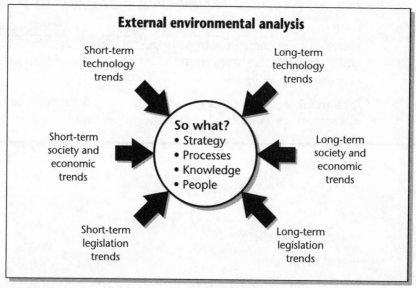

FIGURE 5.1

In each case, the manager should be looking for:

➡ trends

➡ an assessment of whether the trend represents a threat, an opportunity or both

➡ a sense of priority for each trend (this can be measured in terms of impact and urgency).

The trend identifies events or changes in the external environment that may require any element within the organisation to respond – either reactively or proactively in the case of a 'forecast trend'.

The assessment of whether the trend represents a threat, opportunity or both is answering the 'So what?' question. Do we need to worry about it and why? Answering the 'So what?' questions gives a much more detailed level of understanding of the environment in which the organisation or team is competing and encourages the manager to reflect on what really drives organisational performance.

Finally, assuming that several trends are uncovered which may impact the organisation, each must be assessed to set priority on how big a threat or opportunity each represents – the potential for improvement, and how quickly action needs to be taken. This setting of priorities is a vital activity if the manager is not to be overcome by the abundant opportunities to change, and the requirement to generate cash flow by continuing to get orders out of the door!

Understanding the dynamic shown above is not complicated, and this exercise is best completed by bringing together a number of interested and diverse people drawn from the list of stakeholders, and brainstorming using the model for structure.

Each manager or planning group needs to decide in detail how the external trends are going to affect them. Here are some examples.

Technology trends that can have an impact on the organisation include:

➡ mainframe to PC computing

➡ Internet and intranet developments

➡ video-conferencing

➡ database marketing.

Society and economy relates to trends in these areas:

➡ rate of inflation

➡ exchange rates

➡ ageing population.

Legislation includes:

➡ change of government

➡ European Acts

➡ professional standards

➡ ISO 9000.

Looking at both the short and the long term encourages creative thinking. Often the short term can be identified through analysis of current events and through the reading of trade journals etc. However, thinking about the longer term forces the assessment of what is possible, rather than what is likely. This often requires the group to think in a different way, adopting a different 'mind-set', and is therefore both more challenging and more exciting.

Customer and competitor audit

A similar dynamic exists for the assessment of the industry or market in which an organisation competes.

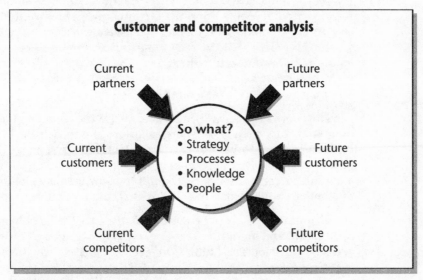

FIGURE 5.2

As with the analysis of the external environment, trends in each of the six areas should be assessed, and then the impact or implications to the organisation or team assessed – the 'So what?' question.

Breaking customers into current and future, highlights that customers and customer groups change. In, for example, consolidating industries, where there are fewer and larger firms, the ones remaining will probably have to change radically the way products and services are sold. In declining industries, such, as coal-generated power, the trend was that future customers would have to come from a different industry.

Product and service delivery is becoming increasingly dependent on relationships with suppliers, corporate parents, joint ventures – we will call all of these partners. Their relative strength, position, and strategies will change over time, and if we are dependent for our livelihood on a relationship with another organisation, either now or in the future, we need to analyse them as much as the competition.

Breaking partners into current and future highlights that partners as well as customers change! Particularly in any endeavour which has brand new characteristics, you are likely to find some unusual alliances.

109

CASE STUDY

Multi-media needs talent as well as technology

It is worth remembering that when the movie camera and film were created, the only thing the technologists who invented it could think of doing with it was to film Vaudeville variety acts on stage. This meant that the real opportunities of film were ignored. It was not until writers and directors started to come up with completely new ideas for the new medium that film's potential started to be exploited.

Similarly, new alliances will be created to use the creative potential of multi-media. Already there are collusions and groups of companies being formed to encourage journalists and advertising people to work with the technologists who are providing infrastructure and authoring products to allow the development of multi-media applications and their global communications aspects.

These groups are likely to be difficult to manage. The combination of a brilliant and innovative real-time programmer with a brilliant and innovative journalist both managed by a brilliant and innovative entrepreneur is explosive in its potential for success or disaster.

The final source of information at this stage is the competition which will also change, with future competition looking very different from today. British Airways, for example, identified video-conferencing companies as a source of major competition for the business traveller sector in the future. You can see reflections of this in almost all the major business airlines as they strengthen their offerings in communications terms and in allowing the executive to make better and better use of his or her time in the air.

At this stage you have to think laterally and allow that unusual or innovative ideas may in the end have merit.

CASE STUDY

This is the first look at the environment, make sure it is comprehensive

A group of design engineers was trying to improve the design and quality of car components. It became apparent after a while that there was a lot of guesswork and assumptions going into their analysis. A manager referred to this rather 'cavalier' approach using the term 'SWAG', sophisticated wide-angled guess! In coming to decisions about what to do, some of the more esoteric ideas were dropped, but some survived demonstrating the need to go for the SWAG.

Before we leave gathering information from external sources, take some time to ensure that the customers you are focused on when, in Chapter 6, you do your product market plan are the right ones. Make sure you focus on the customer base offering the best potential.

Customer attribute analysis

The focus of any customer analysis should always be conducted within the knowledge of how important each customer or customer group is in terms of overall impact on the organisation or the team. Focusing on customers allows the identification of relationships – any successful supplier-customer relationship exists between people in organisations, not the organisations themselves. These relationships will drive some of the strategy and most of the tactics of handling the customer. Focusing on customer groups is also beneficial as it allows identification of groupings of customers (based on common attribute requirements) and therefore makes the targeting of potential customers within target groups easier to achieve. It also, perhaps more importantly, tells us what not to target.

The Pareto principle can be used in this area to devastating effect. This often paints a very different picture from that expected.

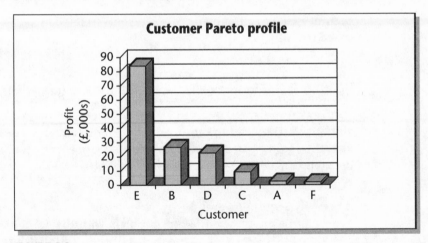

FIGURE 5.3

In order to arrive at this graph we have had to break down our customers into groups by shared attribute. What these attributes are will be driven by the nature of the deliverable and the market.

Next we choose a measure of the relative value of each customer grouping. In this case we have chosen profit as the dominant measure. However, there are others and it may be better for some organisations to see amount of product or service delivered to the customer groups as the measure of value. Then we draw the graph.

The Pareto principle tells us to expect that something like 80 per cent of our sales will come from 20 per cent of our customers. What this graph shows is the principle in operation. We now know that customer groups A and F between them provide less than 2 per cent of our profits. To make matters worse, in all probability we have calculated that profitability using standard costing techniques. Such techniques will have used the same relative measure for allocation of fixed costs to customers in the A and F group as were used for customer group E. The reality is much more likely to be that groups A and F were much more costly. It is, therefore, a more than reasonable assumption that we are making a loss in actual fact on these two customer groups.

So, why are we still selling to them? The answer to this question may be that the customers are strategic, and that in time they will be as profitable as the current profitable groups. Management teams the world over use strategic as an excuse for not turning to a market segment and saying 'Sorry, but we do not want your business'. And such an attitude can lead to further investment and further loss.

Sometimes it takes a traumatic turn of events to force managers to get out of a bad situation.

CASE STUDY

Wait until the founder dies, then kill off the lossmakers

A family business was founded on selling street lighting to local authorities. The division remained a huge one for many years. In time the second generation of the founder family presided over the company while it made shrewd moves into other markets and eventually into many other products.

It grew by acquisition and the lighting group remained an important profit earner. The only problem with the lighting division was that the traditional local authority customer group had become only marginally profitable and that was using a very favourable measure of costs. It was obvious to all the managers involved that the time had come to say 'Thanks but no thanks'. It was not however until the demise of the founding family that the professional managers could cut the operation, so emotional and significant was the original market.

This holding on for 'strategic' reasons is very common and needs to be rigorously examined. Almost all organisations err on the side of sticking with something for too long, very few err by chopping something which was eventually proved to have had strategic value. The argument will always rage, however, because some groups of customers are indeed strategic. If we applied the Pareto principle continuously, we would end up with only one customer.

Having asked the question 'Who are our best customers?' we now need to look at why they buy from us.

Analysis of the basis of decision

Customers do not only make their purchase decisions based on price. The reality is that there will probably be a dozen or so 'attributes' of the product and services which will influence their choice where they have one, and will certainly influence their perception of satisfaction. Analysis of the basis of decision is a technique used in competitive solution selling and can be very revealing if carried out at an organisational level. Modern jargon calls it 'customer value analysis'. The technique identifies the attributes against which products and services are assessed, and their relative importance to the customer in making their purchase decision. This applies for both an external and an internal customer–supplier relationship. This analysis should not only be in absolute terms, but in comparison to competition where it exists.

Customers do not only make their purchase decisions based on price.

To summarise, the four steps of raising the matrix are:

➡ product and service attributes identified

➡ attribute importance identified for each customer group

➡ current performance level identified

➡ best competitor performance level identified.

This analysis makes up a two-dimensional matrix which plots product and service attributes (under the generic headings of benefits, cost and timeliness) against customers. For each customer the evaluation of the organisation or team's performance should also be assessed against the target required by the customer. A similar estimate is then made for the likely performance of the competition. You can analyse individual competitors or if you are striving to be 'world class' you can analyse the best performer against each criteria. Where customers will be buying different products and services against a different set of product and service attributes, then a separate analysis should be conducted for each.

The following example demonstrates a simple customer attribute analysis where a score out of ten is assigned to each attribute. The scores placed in the customer's target column must be generated with the help of the customer and their relative scores will reflect their relative influence in the selection process.

Customer attribute analysis

	Us	Best competitor	Customer Group A	Customer Group B	Customer Group C
Product or service attributes			Target	Target	Target
Benefit: eg units per hour	10	6	10	4	2
Benefit: eg functionality	7	7	2	8	10
Benefit: eg reliability	7	8	4	10	8
Cost: eg low purchase price	4	7	9	5	3
Cost: eg low running costs	6	3	7	2	3
Timeliness: eg availability	2	10	2	5	9

The use of such an analytic matrix should not be seen as too scientific. It can, however, be useful to take the maths a step further than this by using weighted averages as is frequently done in planning major sales campaigns. Numbers are used to reflect customer thinking and to aid management decision making not replace it. So what thoughts does this matrix suggest? The list below are some thought starters which would need to be validated more thoroughly with customers in each of the groupings. But it does highlight the radically different needs of different customer groups. (It has been assumed that the organisation sells products to external customers, but the analysis technique is valid for all internal and external groups.)

Possible reasons for the different customer values

➡ The requirements of the three customer groups imply that they have very different needs in terms of the product or service being offered.

➡ Customer A is focusing on productivity and may well be working in a 'commodity' industry as functionality is not important but price is. They are also not worried about lead times, and time-to-market may be less of an issue.

➡ Customer B is very risk averse and will pay more for the guarantee of success. Functionality is important but productivity is less important implying that they probably compete in a differentiated market.

➡ Customer C values functionality highly, reflecting a need to differentiate, but productivity is valued very little implying a high-value low-turnover operation. On the other hand, availability is clearly important which may mean that purchase is determined by an ability to meet a particular 'window of opportunity' in the market.

➡ Looking internally, we appear to be strong in productivity and OK in terms of both functionality and reliability. On the other hand our availability is very poor, and we are perceived by the market as being both expensive to buy and not cheap to run.

➡ If we compare ourselves with our competition we can see that we outperform the best in the areas of productivity and running costs. This will give us some insights as to how we may choose to market ourselves, but we will need to attack different customer groups in different ways – customer groups B and C do not value these attributes highly.

A simple example of these different criteria could be the attitude of double glazing manufacturers to their suppliers of computerised cutting machines. One may be differentiating itself by the number of shapes available, another is looking at the product as a commodity to be sold as a wholesaler and a third may have a significant pressure due to a short window of opportunity to attend an exhibition.

By now a team using this process of external analysis will have a series of statements of its strengths and weaknesses written in a form which enables the team to see the way ahead. Having made sure that the plan is being driven by the customers it intends to focus on, the team can look inwards to discover its current ability to service these customers.

The internal audit

Internal analysis is really trying to find strengths and weaknesses which will either assist or block any effort to improve. This final step

115

will allow the knowledge gained to be summed up into a full-blown SWOT analysis (strengths, weaknesses, opportunities and threats). Do not forget the alternative name for this process, the 'So-wot analysis'. Make sure that the statements contain at least the germ of an idea for correcting a weakness or exploiting an opportunity.

Completing the SWOT analysis

A starting point for the internal audit would be to use the organisational sensitivity model (Figure 2.5) and the 'pitfalls' checklists given in Chapter 3. How many of these apply and what is their impact on performance?

Secondly, analysis around groupings will indicate the degree of balance within the organisation or team. At an organisational level this will focus on the functions or divisions depending on the organisational structure. Indeed it is probable that each function or division will get together to produce a SWOT analysis for their ability to support the customer-focused plan.

Just as we have seen the need to recognise what businesses we are not in, so it is important to recognise at this stage what we do not know.

CASE STUDY

Europower: identifying what we do not know

At Europower managers decided that every SWOT analysis should have a series of statements under the heading 'We do not know'. This proved very useful, as some groups who felt ignorant of some fact or risk, assumed that somewhere else in the organisation this knowledge would be held. It frequently occurred that this was not the case, and the combination of all the 'We do not know' lists gave a fairly comprehensive view of where the organisation was operating with poor or non-existent information.

The simplicity of the technique was its strength.

At the team level this may get right down to the capabilities of individuals, but for it to succeed it must be seen as positive and non-judgemental. To achieve this the culture will need to be supportive – this is covered in more depth in the final chapter.

Personal capabilities or deficiencies are emotional but have to be faced.

The title describes the job not necessarily the person in it

A major provider of systems solutions to the IT industry was structured around its projects. It was no surprise, therefore that they had many people within the organisation whose title was that of 'project manager.' Because of this, discussion on their use of the organisational sensitivity model to review their business, did not begin with an examination of their skills and capabilities in project management. When they came to activity planning, however, they quickly realised the need for project management training for some 60 of their senior project managers. A job title did not necessarily mean competency. Make no assumptions at the analysis stage.

Finally, internal 'activity' data can be used to highlight areas of focus. These are often assumed, but it is not until hard data is presented to people that they will accept that their 'view of the world' has changed somewhat over the last few years! When looking at hard data, remember the trend rule. It is more important to understand the trend than the absolute figures. Something which feels as though it is working can sometimes be shown to be faulty if a trend is examined.

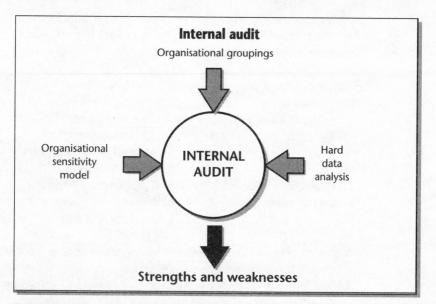

FIGURE 5.4

117

Portfolio analysis

Portfolio analysis allows the evaluation of products and services as a portfolio rather than in isolation. Each is 'mapped' on to a two-dimensional matrix.

The power of portfolio analysis is that it forces managers to reflect on what makes a market an attractive one for them to be in, and what is their relative level of performance compared with the competition.

For each axis 'market attractiveness' and 'competitive position', the cross-functional team should develop criteria which their products and services can be evaluated against. Often these criteria will not be equally important and so as a refinement, the criteria can be weighted.

Make a list of the attributes of market attractiveness and competitive differentiators, score each of your products or product groupings and plot them on a two-dimensional matrix.

Each product or service can be plotted on the matrix to show their relative position. This form of analysis can be used to assess a total 'portfolio' of present product and service groups. Equally it can be used to assess relative performance against the competition.

CASE STUDY

Assessing the competitive position

A leading manufacturer of computer-driven machinery used the following list of criteria. The numbers reflect the relative importance of each attribute.

Competitive position	Market attractiveness
10 Market share	10 Growth of market
8 Product quality	10 Level of competition
8 Price competitiveness	8 Industry capacity
6 Costs	6 Stage of business lifecycle
5 Efficiency	6 Inflation
5 Financial resources	3 Government subsidies
3 Management skills	2 Raw material costs
2 Service levels	1 Location

The management team used a simple 'brainstorming' technique to answer the following two questions and develop its set of criteria: What will impact our competitive level of performance? What will determine whether a market is attractive to us?

It was then able to analyse all its products and those of its competitors. It gained significant insight into how it needed to drop some products and significantly reposition others. Perhaps of greatest value, however, was the increased and shared understanding it now had about its business.

Again much of the value of such analysis lies in the thinking, not the outputs. As usual the integrity of the analysis is dependent on the usefulness of the knowledge which goes into it. It is quality not quantity that counts.

CASE STUDY

Are you getting a lot of data rather than a little of the right data?

This good example of misinformation is from a large manufacturing company. That there was an abundance of historical data available could probably be explained by the fact that the current and previous managing directors were both from accounting backgrounds. This is probably a little unfair, however, as many manufacturing companies suffer from the same problem with their monthly reports.

On a monthly basis, the management team received approximately 30 pages full of numbers showing individual product line profitability. This initially sounds reasonable – shouldn't the organisation focus on profit? The answer is yes, but what they were actually doing was anything but *focus* on *profit*. Nine hundred individual product line profit figures is hardly a narrow focus! The Pareto principle held true here in as far as 80 per cent of the total profit came from 20 per cent of the products. Unfortunately, in their reports there was no way of telling which products constituted this 80 per cent, or which were of more importance for long-term strategic reasons.

Secondly, and perhaps of more concern, was the use of a standard costing system for allocation of fixed costs or overheads. This method had been used for many years as a way of spreading the cost of overheads across the total anticipated sales of products for the year. This method is valid for accounting for stock consumption annually, but it fails to take account of the 'complexity costs' associated with individual products or customers. When accounting data is used for making management decisions, it frequently results in the sale of unprofitable products to unprofitable customers. The data that this management team received on a monthly basis had nothing to do with focus or *true* profit. Unfortunately, however, it did consume an enormous amount of technology and management time! This is hard to correct, but the starting point is the customer-focused analysis described in this chapter.

It is important that all the people involved in the analysis are trained or have a good understanding of the techniques of environmental analysis. Good analysis techniques require that each member of staff understands what really drives performance in the organisation – this knowledge alone is likely to result in activities being conducted in a way which is more aligned to organisational objectives.

Secondly, the people with the information are those that are closest to the customer or that are carrying out operational activities. People often have a wealth of information, but because they either don't recognise its value, or there is no formal mechanism for gathering it, it gets lost, forgotten, or walks out of the door when they leave.

Principles of analysis

Good analysis techniques require the agreement of all concerned to some disciplines.

Specific measures and indicators

The broader the analysis data is, the less useful it is. To say that 'market dynamics have changed' is not particularly useful. However, to say that customers are becoming more focused on the 'total cost of ownership' for products allows the organisation to refocus its activities from sales through to product development.

Good analysis techniques require the agreement of all concerned to some disciplines.

Cross-reference sources of information

Often information can be unreliable. Recognising this fact means that data should always be cross-referenced wherever practical. This helps to avoid bias and making a response which is in some way inappropriate for the situation. For example, verbal feedback from an account manager might be backed up by an article published in a journal. Two cross-referenced sources of data increase the probability of relevance and accuracy.

Technology versus personal approach

Information systems and technology can be used to collect data. This often provides a useful verification technique for the data, but should be treated with a certain amount of caution. Technology should never replace quality thinking. Furthermore, when information is received, it is often the 'way' in which it is said or expressed that is important. It is said that 85 per cent of human communication is done through 'body language'. This perhaps explains why organisations that come to rely heavily on their e-mail system often lose the personal feel to their culture and way of working.

Look for both the positive and the negative

Too often analysis is seen as a means of apportioning blame. If this is to be overcome, it must be carried out in a non-judgemental way, and should always be seen as a way to correct things that are 'broken' and to look for creative opportunities for improvement.

Initial and ongoing analysis

Conducting a detailed analysis is hard work. This is often due to the fact that this activity has been done badly, if at all, in the past. Once the value from a one-off analysis has been identified, organisations often build in activities into their way of working. If such an approach can be transferred to all members of staff, this can radically change the proactive nature of the whole organisation. We will need to follow this through into the action plans which come after the analysis phase. If the team monitors the action plan as a dynamic document which is an integral part of how they carry out their function, better data for updating the analysis will result as a by-product. The team needs to ensure that it never again has to start from scratch to do a comprehensive SWOT.

CASE STUDY

Europower: regular swotting at Europower

Once all the functional and some cross-functional teams had completed their SWOT analysis, a process was put in place by which each team revisited and updated their SWOT at least twice a year. This was by no means the only time the team looked at their original analysis, that happened at each planning review meeting, but was a backstop to make sure that no analysis could become so out of date that only starting again would do.

Europower also trained facilitators from the training department who monitored the quality of the analysis data and policed the updating procedure.

Time period for monitoring

A key question of how often certain information should be gathered. Unfortunately, there is no one right or wrong answer to this as it depends on how fast things change. Monitoring too often results in 'analysis paralysis', but not monitoring enough results in concerns becoming crises unnecessarily. See Figure 5.5.

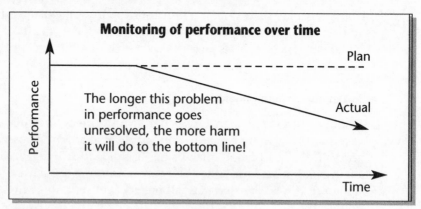

FIGURE 5.5

How will we use the information?

Much of the rest of this book concerns using this gathering exercise as a starting point for creating organisational sensitivity, but it is worth looking at a few pointers on good technique in turning data into a plan for action.

Perception versus reality

The appropriate response depends whether the data is real or perceived. For example, a customer may state that the quality of our products is inferior to that of a major competitor. If this situation is real, then the response may well be targeted at product and process improvement. However, it the situation is perceived, then the response may lie in a changed sales and marketing approach. Getting this wrong either way will result in cost expenditure with no improvement in performance.

Identify deviations and causes

Ideally, the data gathered will not only identify what the concerns or opportunities are, but it will also highlight the reasons why. This question is fundamental to ensuring that appropriate action is taken. Understanding that market share is 10 per cent off plan is one thing, but how can it be resolved? It could be due to a number of factors ranging from competitive product features to the weather. To fix a concern or to capitalise on an opportunity requires understanding of cause. This will be covered in more detail in later chapters, but at this stage managers should reflect on how to change data-gathering mechanisms and ways of presentation to ensure that cause is also identified if possible. It is often much easier to do this as the data is gathered.

Be aware – if you want to delight the customer, it costs!

Overperforming against customer expectations was all the rage a number of years ago. Unfortunately, many organisations adopted this as a cultural norm without thinking through the potential adverse consequences. Customers will typically pay for what they think they are getting. This can be measured in performance levels against key attributes as defined earlier in this chapter. Typically, to overperform against attributes such as product performance, service responsiveness etc will require additional resources and funding, it therefore costs. If this gives the organisation a genuine advantage in the marketplace then this may be justified.

Unfortunately, overperformance is often not valued by customers and so little advantage accrues. Furthermore, not only have additional costs been incurred, but customer expectations are often raised for the next time, we have therefore only created a rod for our own backs.

We need to be sure that if we are going to exceed customer expectations and 'delight them', then we can do it time and time again

We need to be sure that if we are going to exceed customer expectations and 'delight them', then we can do it time and time again, and that it will give us some real advantage in the marketplace.

Reaction versus overreaction

When faced with apparent crises, the temptation is to get on and fix it. A more cautious approach would be to first make sure that the set of figures just received, or the angry telephone call from a customer, are representative of the real situation. An experienced and respected engineer can make the occasional mistake, or the best salesperson can miss a sale once in a while, but it doesn't necessarily mean that the whole approach should be changed.

It is necessary to react to data to resolve concerns or capitalise on opportunities, but overreaction can often make the situation worse. We must not become slaves to data rather we must first understand it and then stop and think.

Using knowledge to drive strategy and processes

Ultimately, we gather data in order to increase the probability that we are doing the right things in the right way, but if we are not, then the data will be used to initiate and guide change. Hence, customer-focused analysis is the first element in achieving organisational sensitivity – recognising the need for change. The second part, changing, will be achieved through changing the 'what' to ensure that we are doing the right things, and the 'how' to ensure that we are doing things right! This will therefore take us into the first two elements of the organisational sensitivity model – strategy and processes.

Customer-focused analysis is the first element in achieving organisational sensitivity

Installing analysis techniques

The putting in place of good information-monitoring techniques along with methods of analysing the results needs time and effort. In many ways what is not needed is as important a consideration as what is actually needed. And the process is continuous. As the environment changes the organisation which is sensitive to its external surroundings will detect changes early through its processes for gathering information.

'If it aint broke, don't fix it' applies to information gathering but in a slightly different way.

Do not analyse it if it does not impact performance

Too much time, effort and duplication of effort is wasted gathering data that does not help the organisation or team to improve its performance. We have examined the reasons for this in earlier chapters, but that is no reason why it should continue. A review of continuous analysis and monitoring activities should typically result in different and new data being collected, but just as critical is that unnecessary data gathering should be identified and stopped.

Focus, focus!

There is too much information available when you start to look for it and so an effective analysis will take into consideration what information is actually required, 'knowledge', and what resources are available to get it. This requires a high degree of prioritisation and focus! As information often has a degree of bias, information from a variety of sources should be used. This will require strong relationships internally and externally – again focusing on the most significant customers, suppliers etc.

Planning for continuous analysis

Get the team to brainstorm their information requirements using the following structure.

➡ **What information do I really require?**

➡ **How will I get it?**

➡ **How will I know that it is what I want?**

➡ **What will it mean?**

➡ **How will I use it?**

Finally, identify what skills the team needs to conduct analysis effectively: market research? customer value analysis? questioning? report writing and presentation? Make sure the team is trained to use the necessary techniques.

Customer-focused analysis

KEY POINTS

Take a few minutes to reflect on each of these.

➡ Long-term performance depends on long-term relationships with key customer groups.

➡ The culture of the organisation should be external, focusing on the customer.

➡ Data should be gathered from a variety of external and internal sources.

➡ Analysis should be dynamic and ongoing – not a one-off exercise.

➡ Identification of 'stakeholders' is a necessary first step.

➡ Customers choose suppliers against explicit and implicit attributes.

➡ 'Robust' required data, or knowledge, drives the selection of strategy and process design.

➡ Data gathering must be focused and planned.

SELF-ASSESSMENT

Rate your organisation or unit on a scale of 1 to 5.

1   Do you know the top five external major trends currently impacting your organisation? ☐

2   Do you know what their impact is likely to be and how quickly it will happen? ☐

3   Do you know who your major competitors are and how good they are? ☐

4   Do you know who your most important customers are? ☐

5   Do you know why your most important customers choose to use your products and services? ☐

6   Do you know how appropriate your processes are to the needs of your customers? ☐

7   Do you know how effective your processes are? ☐

8   Do you know how effective your knowledge-sharing mechanisms are? ☐

9   Do you know how capable and motivated your staff are? ☐

10 Do you have too much or insufficient data? ☐

ACTION PLAN

Where you scored badly in your self-assessment, identify what
actions you will take to improve your performance.

What?	Who?	When?
1		
2		
3		
4		
5		

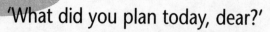

'What did you plan today, dear?'

Mrs Robert Townsend to her husband when he was Director of Planning

CHAPTER

6

WHOLE ENVIRONMENT THINKING: 'STRATEGY'

Defining what products and services will be provided to which markets and customers.

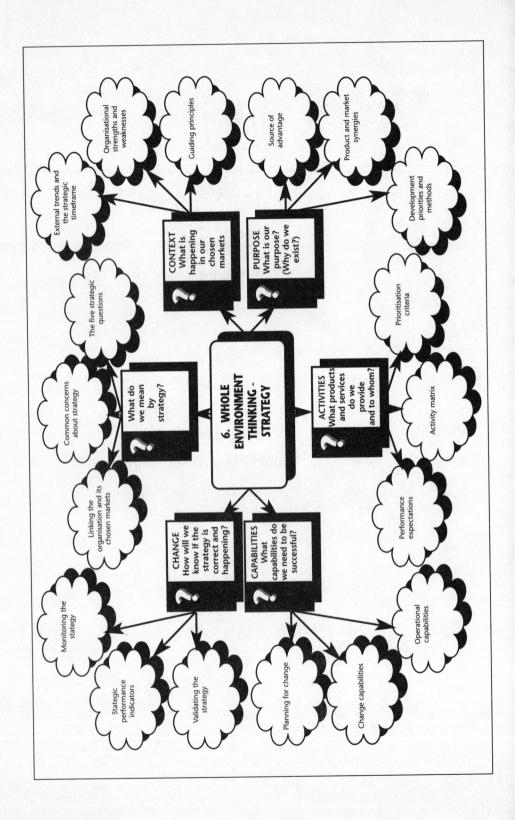

The first key to organisational sensitivity is to have a strategy which is agreed by everyone and communicated in an appropriate way to all concerned. The output of strategic thinking is a dynamic plan which people have to understand and follow in order to be able to carry out their jobs effectively.

At the end of this chapter readers will be in a position to produce a strategic framework for the management of the organisation, group or team for which they are planning.

What do we mean by strategy?

Many academic writers have contributed significantly to the development of analytical tools and concepts in the field of strategy. Most would still find great difficulty in developing real strategic frameworks which not only address key external threats and opportunities, but also gain the commitment of those essential for its implementation.

The concepts presented in this chapter are based on experience of what can be made to work. Furthermore, the approaches suggested have been used successfully across many industry sectors from telecommunications and office products to government and charitable institutions.

The semantics of the word 'strategy' can take teams an entire planning session to discuss. A major problem when working with groups is that everybody has a different definition of the word 'strategy': mission, where we are going, objectives, values, the what, the how, plans etc. We will start by defining what *strategy* is and then explain the route to producing a strategic framework.

Linking the organisation and its chosen markets

Strategy is at the heart of the model (see Figure 6.1), linking today with tomorrow, and linking the external environment with the processes, knowledge and people of the organisation. Strategy is the

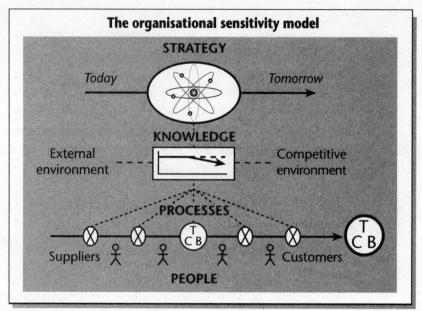

FIGURE 6.1

'what' question – the processes will be the 'how'. What we are going to achieve is strategy: how we are going to achieve it is the basis for the processes.

Strategic concepts can be applied at the organisation, group or individual level. Effective organisations ensure that the concepts are used at all three levels. First the organisation's strategy is developed and used as the framework within which to develop group strategies. Individual strategies are all about career and personal development planning.

In fact, strategy can only be confirmed when the team responsible for its implementation is involved with its definition. To help define strategies at organisational and group levels professional planners are sometimes used. However, the role of professional planners combines facilitation – assisting the teams to produce their strategy – and administration – drawing the plans together to ensure consistency and that the process continues. The role of professional planner **cannot** be to produce the strategic plan. Where this occurs in organisations, you can be sure there will be a huge gap between what the Board thinks is happening and what *is* actually happening.

So, if each team or group of teams is prepared to put the brainstorming effort in, this chapter attempts to present the idea of a 'framework' which:

➡ clarifies the underlying organisational values

➡ defines the scope of products and markets

➡ bridges the gap between the present and the future

➡ guides operational decision making.

The strategy will not be a 'plan' which is set in concrete once every five years, but will be a dynamic and responsive framework. Once a longer term strategy is agreed, short-term rolling plans can be developed. Whilst the strategic framework will never be less than three years, the operating plans will rarely exceed three years. This demonstrates again the difference between the questions 'Where do we want to be?' and 'How are we going to get there?'

Common concerns about strategy

'There is no strategy.' Strange though it may seem, many organisations attempt to succeed and grow without a definition of what is trying to be achieved being agreed and communicated. Normally this is because so much management time is going into fire-fighting the operational problems of the day, that management teams and even Boards do not find the time to think strategically. This is potentially catastrophic and means that the Board can hardly be said to be operating with good corporate governance. After all, if the Board is not there to plan a strategy why do we need it at all?

Another reason for the lack of a good strategic framework is that the Board has never been educated in strategic thinking and yet that is its sole remit when meeting as a Board. At Europower they used a simple discipline to overcome this problem.

CASE STUDY

Strategic discipline at Europower

In order to correct the fire-fighting problem, the management teams who ran the production and distribution businesses put in two simple disciplines. First, Board meetings, which lasted one day, were broken into two parts separated by lunch. During the morning the managers considered operational performance and remedial actions relating to the problems of the day. In the afternoon, they moved on to the strategic framework, having delegated unfinished actions from the morning to sub-teams or individuals.

Each member of the team took responsibility for one part of the strategic framework and reported on this. Incidentally, members decided to take the agenda in a different order each time to make sure that the same items were not always handled at the ends of meetings.

Secondly, reports or other documents concerning the strategic items had to be with the secretary one week before the meeting. This meant that they could be circulated, and everyone could read and absorb the detail which they felt they needed, prior to the meeting. This avoided another common problem – people trying to read and absorb something for the first time and comment on it immediately.

If no clearly defined process for formulating and implementing strategy exists, plans tend to be a conglomeration of functional 'plans'. If such a process is defined, the organisation can use it to make sure that the people with the knowledge of customers and operations, or whose commitment is necessary for implementation, are involved in the formulation of the strategic framework.

Sometimes an assumption is made that if the environment is dynamic it is not worth while formulating strategy. 'What is the point in planning, it will only change?' In fact the opposite is true, in that in chaotic environments, organisations need effective strategic 'frameworks' with which to assess the impact of any potential threat or opportunity in a fast and flexible way.

Having ensured that management teams have a forum for planning on a regular basis, we can turn our attention to the questions they need to answer.

 Five strategic questions

➡ What is happening in our chosen markets?

➡ What is our purpose (or why do we exist)?

➡ What products and services do we provide, and to whom?

➡ What capabilities do we need to be successful?

➡ How will we know if the strategy is correct and happening?

Context

What is happening in our chosen markets?

Before making strategic choices, it is necessary to understand the constraints placed upon us by the outside world, by our own capabilities, and by our beliefs.

External trends and a strategic timeframe

An effective analysis of the external, competitive and internal environments, as described in Chapter 5, is a vital first stage in developing or challenging strategy. One decision before starting the analysis is the time period to consider.

Every decision has a time period associated with it. If we buy a computer to last one year as opposed to ten years, we are likely to make a fundamentally different choice. The same applies for strategic decision making.

➲ Strategic timeframes should not be set by the financial or reporting yearly cycle, but should be dictated by the rate of change in the external environment.

Some of the shortest timeframes, at approximately two years, are adopted by software companies. Heavy industries, such as steel production, plan for 25 years due to the necessary investment in low-cost production machinery. A church whose plan we recently saw had a timeframe of 50 years as the fundamental needs of society that it was trying to address had not changed in centuries.

The comment above still holds, however. Whilst the picture of what the organisation will look like can be envisaged over such periods, management teams find it difficult to deal with actions which look ahead more than three years.

Organisational strengths and weaknesses

Strengths and weaknesses should be viewed within the context of the external trends, and hence we will end up with a customer-oriented SWOT analysis as the basic driver of the strategy.

The organisation should also reflect on its strategic history – what has it done in the past? This will give useful clues as to what might be possible in the future, and provide guidelines as to what approach will be taken towards risk, investment or rates of return etc.

137

Guiding principles

Most organisations have publicised value statements. For most these are 'marketing fluff' which achieve little if anything for the organisation. Yet the principles which will guide strategic and operational decision making should be based on the beliefs that the owners and management team have with regard to what is ethically sound (for example, anti-tobacco), or what factors are necessary for success in their chosen markets.

If the principles are 'aspirational' as opposed to 'real' then it is likely that people will see through them. Recently, many annual reports have included a value stated as: 'Our people are our strength'. Further on in the same document, directors describe how they have downsized by making 20 per cent of the workforce redundant. With admirers like these who needs detractors.

To test guiding principles, look for supporting evidence for each guiding principle in turn. If there is no evidence, then actions will need to be taken to make the guiding principle real or it has to be dropped. Here is how a food company handled the issue of guiding principles.

CASE STUDY

Guiding principles in frozen food

To illustrate the strategic framework we will use the example of a company in the frozen foods business. The level of the plan is 'Organisation' and the overall owner of the plan is the Chief Executive.

The *strategic timeframe* will be five years, although it is anticipated that significant changes will have been made within three.

Guiding principles reflect the underlying values of the company and are validated by evidence. Here are two examples.

➡ One *guiding principle* is that we need to be one of the lowest cost producers of bulk ice cream in order to survive, and the *evidence* is that we educate all staff in cost management techniques. We also continuously reduce complexity of products and markets.

➡ Another *guiding principle* is that we will not be a branded company, and there are two pieces of supporting evidence for this. We currently supply 80 per cent own label, and there is no price premium for branded products.

We will be returning to this food company example throughout this chapter.

What is our purpose (why do we exist)?

It sounds obvious that we need to understand why we exist as an entity but this understanding is often lost in time, or forgotten in the day-to-day heat of battle. As has already been said, for any organisation, group or individual, the starting point of all strategic planning and process management activity is to understand the answer to a fundamental question:

➲ 'How will we continue to be the preferred provider of specified products and services to current and future customers?'

What is needed is a model for competitive advantage which is applicable for both commercial and not-for-profit organisations (see Figure 6.2)

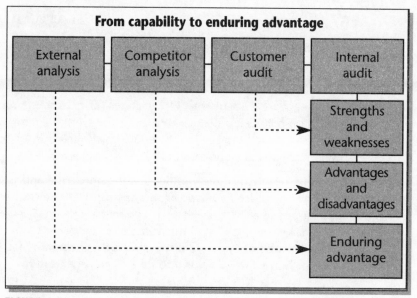

FIGURE 6.2

We will explore this model in more detail in the following pages.

Working towards the sustainable source of advantage

Organisations have many resources and capabilities. Often when asked what an organisation's long-term source of advantage is, people throughout the organisation will refer to these capabilities. Unfortunately, however, this often reflects their affection for the capability rather than a clear understanding of how it enables the organisation to sustain its performance in the marketplace. Capabilities will only provide organisations with strengths if they enable the organisation to provide its customers with something they want! (This is perhaps the difference between features and benefits.) If this is not the case, and retention of the capability consumes resources, then the capability is by definition a weakness as it diverts scarce resources away from those other capabilities that have a direct and positive impact on the customer.

Step one

Step one in the process of identifying competitive advantage is to recognise those capabilities which can be turned into customer benefits. It does not matter how clever the capabilities are, you cannot bend a customer's situation to match your capabilities.

CASE STUDY

Consultants with a one-track mind

Nowhere is the problem of believing that a capability is a strength whilst not understanding how it provides benefits to the customer more evident than in the consultancy business. Once a consultant has an unquestionable deep ability in a narrow field, he or she will start to see that strength as the solution to all client problems or opportunities.

A consultant who is deeply imbued with knowledge and faith in, for example, neuro-linguistic programming (NLP), will find applications of NLP at every turn. The management of such people is very difficult, and it is sometimes better to apply the rule which we have already discussed: such a person needs to be on his or her own as opposed to part of an organisation.

Step two

Unfortunately, having strengths is not necessarily enough. Once we have identified that we have a strength (a capability that provides value or benefits to the customer), the temptation is to go out and tell the marketplace. What we often do is create an awareness amongst customers that what we are advertising is something that they should take into consideration when making their purchasing decisions. However, if we have competitors that also provide these benefits but do so at a superior level of price performance, then we will still not win the business. So step two needs to take all of the strengths and determine which ones are provided at a competitive level.

The final step

The final step is to take all sources of advantage today and think about the long-term picture. Success today does not guarantee success tomorrow. We only need to reflect on the companies used as exemplars in Peter's and Waterman's book, *In Search of Excellence* (Harper & Row, 1982). In a number of cases the examples of excellence proved to be short-lived. The sources of competitive advantage that can be sustained into the future are the ones that will keep the organisation profitable.

The model is not prescriptive or absolute, but the discipline of completing each stage of the analysis and reflecting on its implications will help to avoid unnecessary liquidations, outsourced functions or redundancies.

The model also provides a snapshot. Whilst it is looking at trends, the exercise of analysis should be repeated on an ongoing basis, providing the manager with monthly information reports which can be translated into meaningful knowledge, allowing flexibility and 'proactive responsiveness' to trends before they become crises.

To continue the food company story.

CASE STUDY

Source of advantage for the frozen food manufacturer

Our **statement of purpose** is to provide quality, non-branded frozen food products to major retailers, and our **competitive advantage** lies in our ability to provide a superior level of service as measured by response times and order flexibility, whilst matching the pricing policies of our competitors.

Product and market synergies

Before selecting specific products and services, it is important to understand what their common characteristics are. Synergies exist where capabilities, or characteristics of capabilities, can be used to service more than one customer group, or offer a variety of products and services. If there are no 'synergies' between them, the implication

141

is that the organisation or group will have to have a complex (and inefficient) set of capabilities to provide them all to the same high standard. Understanding what the synergies are facilitaties the future selection of new products and markets.

At this stage, the organisation should also specify what types of products and services it will not provide, and what types of markets it will not serve. Too much time, effort and resources are wasted in an organisation chasing sales that ultimately prove unprofitable or unattractive even if they are won.

CASE STUDY

Frozen foods choice of products and markets – some examples

In terms of *markets*, we will focus on grocery multiple retailers, target the top four by size of revenue and number of outlets. We will not focus on locally based retailers.

We will supply bulk or high-volume *products* with a focus 'ice cream'. We will not offer prepared meals.

We have now understood our method for getting sustainable advantage and our strengths in delivering benefits to the customer. It is now time to look into the future.

Development priorities and methods

Looking into the future, the organisation has a number of alternatives for development which can best be surmised using an Ansoff matrix (see Figure 6.3).

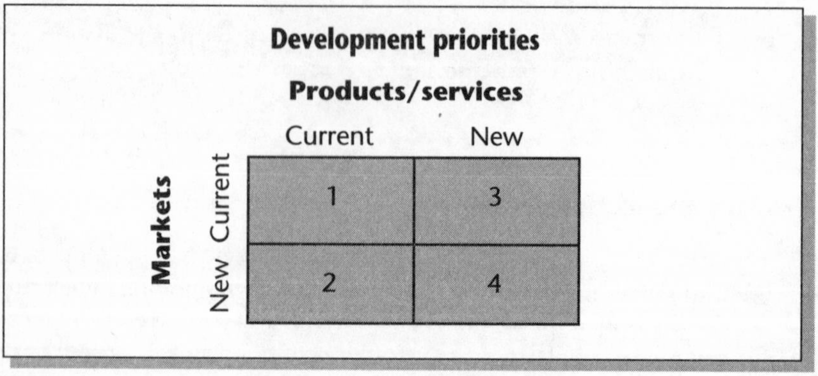

FIGURE 6.3

142

➡ **Cell 1** This represents three alternatives: withdrawing from the market; sustaining the current provision of products and services to current markets; or increasing the market share or penetration of current markets using existing products and services. Withdrawal may not be pleasant, but if it is required, it had best be done in a planned way!

➡ **Cell 2** This represents the provision of current products and services to new markets however the markets are currently segmented.

➡ **Cell 3** This represents the provision of new products and services to current markets.

➡ **Cell 4** This represents the provision of new products and services to new markets. This is known as *diversification* and, as for success, it requires a significant effort in research and development of sourcing, and sales and markets. Moving into one unknown area is difficult, but to attempt two simultaneously has proved too difficult for many of the world's multi-nationals.

Where development in either direction has been identified, then the organisation still has a number of further choices based around:

➡ internal versus external (make or buy)

➡ acquisition, joint venture, partnership, licensing etc.

Indeed, the thinking still needs to flow freely at this stage. If the plan is to be creative, it must not be held back by, for example, what already exists.

CASE STUDY

Predominant thrust for new business in frozen foods

Primary focus in year one will be to resolve current operational problems and to focus on the core business.

By the end of year one we will have re-emphasised resources for the 'Top four' customer groups.

By the end of year three we will provide new products within defined characteristics to meet the needs of the 'Top four' customer groups.

The way ahead clear – it is time, in planning terms, to make some decisions on what products you are going to sell. Probably the most important activity so far, this exercise in a sensitive organisation has to be done at all levels, and agreed by all the line managers concerned.

What products and services do we provide, and to whom?

In deciding what products and services to offer, or what markets and customers to focus on, the organisation should identify what criteria drive performance.

Prioritisation of criteria

Some criteria will be mandatory, such as complying with legislation, others will be more subjective, maximising profitability for example, but there is no clear-cut division. Additionally, the subjective criteria are not all equally important and should therefore be weighted. A simple scale of 1 to 10 will probably sort out the priorities. Critical decision-making techniques are discussed in more detail in Chapter 10.

CASE STUDY

Criteria for emphasis in frozen foods

We will use, amongst others, the following *criteria* to prioritise product/market cells and to allocate resources.

➡ Must fit with strategy.

➡ Must be able to meet all legal and safety requirements.

➡ Must be consistent with guiding principles.

On a weighted basis:

Potential for profit	10
Allows flexibility and speed of response	10
In-house capacity to meet demand	2

This list of criteria will be used in the formulation of strategy to help prioritise product-market combinations in the activity matrix that follows. However, once identified, they should be circulated to everybody in the organisation as they can be used to assess every decision made in all functions and at all levels.

Activity matrix

The activity matrix is a two-dimensional matrix which maps product and service 'groupings' against market segments or groupings.

To achieve the matrix, the first step is to segment each category into logical groupings which should be able to contain 100 per cent of all current and future product-market combinations. In this way, it is possible to plot the current picture against the future picture, and thereby show the degree of change in the organisation's operations over the period of the analysis.

Grouping should recognise the difference in the capability needs or financing requirements, or degree of change in both products and markets. Some markets have different servicing requirements due to geographic location, size, complexity, channel etc, and some products have different requirements as measured by technology, stage of lifecycle, manufacturing needs, etc.

A simple example at this point would help to show the value of such a matrix (see Figure 6.4).

Activity matrix

Products/services

Markets	Group A	Group B
Group A	H>L	M>L
Group B	M>H	0>M

FIGURE 6.4

In each cell, the current emphasis (graded H = high, M = medium, L = low and 0 = zero) is shown on the left, with the future emphasis on the right. A completed matrix should contain a maximum of 100 cells at a strategic level, and there should be no more than 25 per cent as high emphasis as this may reflect a lack of focus.

A number of observations can be drawn from Figure 6.4.

➡ Market group A is more important than group B but this will be reversed in the future.

➡ Both product groups A and B are important now and in the future.

➡ Significant sales and marketing activity will be required to develop the sales of product group B to market group B.

➡ Resource commitment (people, effort, finance) will be moved from market group A to market group B.

For each product market cell, where the organisation has identified either high or medium future emphasis, the key success factors should be clearly understood. This is sometimes called the 'basis of competition' as the attributes used by customers when making purchasing decisions represent the *bases* on which organisations compete for business

We can see how the specification of the prioritisation criteria will reflect elements of their strategy. For example, the reliance on flexibility and speed of response as their main source of advantage.

Performance expectations

Emphasis areas within the matrix are identified using the HML classifications, reflecting the current and anticipated levels of activity in each cell, and hence the name 'activity matrix'.

At the strategic level the use of HML is probably sufficient but for planning purposes more work is required.

The letters H, M and L can and should be translated into hard and tangible performance data – revenue, profit, budget, people, capital equipment investment etc – whatever is meaningful for the organisation.

This 'planning' activity can be performed by analysis or functional experts, but the information should come back to the Board as it provides an excellent first 'validation' of its strategic thinking. The 'mix' is also important as it will show the overall percentage coming from one product grouping, or from a particular market grouping. This gives the organisation an insight into risk or dependency on selective areas.

The mix and degree of change in the mix over time can also be used for each function to evaluate the appropriateness of how budgets are allocated.

Once figures have been placed in each cell 'from the bottom up' this will provide an aggregation which should be consistent with overall performance expectations. The food company example could be summarised as follows.

Growth and return expectations in frozen foods

Within three years we will take our:

➡ turnover from £36 million to £70 million

➡ profits from £0.8 million to £4.0 million, and

➡ number of employees from 400 to 640.

Capabilities

What capabilities do we need to be successful?

The need for change can best be seen in the simple schematic shown in Figure 6.5.

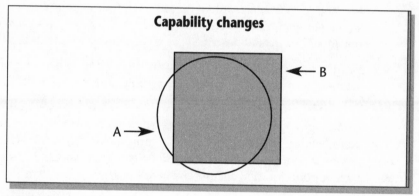

FIGURE 6.5

Figure 6.5 represents the organisation moving from the circle to the square shape over the period of its strategic timeframe. As it does so, it must recognise that in the future, the capabilities identified as 'A' – this may be a manufacturing line, a skills set, a layer of management or simply the company car park – may no longer be required. Success in the future will, in part, be dependent on the organisation's ability to remove capabilities it no longer requires because while they still exist, they **will** consume resources, and they **will** lose organisational focus.

We can also see that there are some resources – represented by the area 'B' which the organisation will need to acquire or develop in the future. This requires a commitment of time and resources to make it happen. These areas need to be identified from the strategic framework and a plan developed for their attainment.

147

Operational capabilities

Strategy often results in changes to the products and markets (what is provided externally to the organisation or group), which in turn need to have a ripple effect resulting in changes internally. One place to look for necessary changes will be the activity matrix. Areas of significant change within the matrix will result in the need for changed activities or emphasis.

The type of activity can be identified at a broad level by comparing where the emphasis is now to where it needs to be in the future. For example, moving from low current emphasis to high future emphasis will require, 'investment' in the cell. Conversely, lowering future emphasis results in a form of 'withdrawal'.

It should not be assumed that cells with no apparent change will not require any effort, such cells should be 'supported'.

Within the matrix, there will be some areas which the organisation feel are outside its 'strategic intent' but if a significant opportunity arose, it would consider them. Such cells should not have significant investment, but should be treated 'reactively' as and when such a situation arises.

Finally, cells which do not apply (this may occur depending on the segmentation), can be shaded out as they play no real part in the development of the matrix.

Understanding what activity type is required on a cell by cell basis allows consolidation across the matrix to identify areas where the current organisational capabilities are not sufficient. These should be listed in a table for prioritisation against all change projects (once identified).

Change capabilities

Changes do not simply result from changes to the activity matrix, but could also result from other areas of the organisation. Again the organisational sensitivity model can be used, focusing in turn on each element: processes, knowledge and people. An alternative approach is often to use the functional grouping but we have already seen the pitfalls in strengthening the functional mind-set.

The planning team needs, at this stage, to review each element of the strategic framework in turn (from the external trends, organisational weaknesses, guiding principles etc), and ask the question: 'What changes are required to our processes, knowledge and people?'

Again, all needs for change should be listed in the same table as above for prioritisation.

Planning for change

The capability needs identified above will form the basis of the implementation of the strategy, or aligning the 'organisation to its environment'.

A simple table with the following headings is sufficient:

➡ **Statement of need** – a brief statement stating what needs to be achieved.

➡ **Priority** – defined by the 'impact' the project will have on performance, and the 'urgency' of resolution (simply using HML is sufficient).

➡ **Who?** – broken into who will take responsibility, and who else needs to be involved for success (this represents an opportunity to utilise cross-functional teams).

➡ **When?** – stating when the project should be completed (this should reflect the level of urgency identified).

Ref:	Statement of need	Impact	Urgency	Who responsible	Who involved	When
001	Create a cross-functional management information system	High	Medium	IS Director	Full Board	<16 wks
002	etc.					

Change

How will we know if the strategy is correct and happening?

Validating the strategy

Following these processes to develop a strategic framework is, as we have seen, a top down and bottom up approach. The final step in the development of the document is to get the inputs from and commitment to the strategy by all concerned in its implementation.

There are two prime reasons for validating the strategy. The first is to confirm that it is the right strategy, and the second is to obtain a high level of commitment to its implementation through the active involvement of others.

The strategy is often formulated by a select team. Whilst these people typically have the greatest knowledge and understanding of the organisation and its markets, the strategy should be validated with others, those that are closest to customers or 'the eyes and ears' of the organisation. Everybody has a role to play in strategy:

 ## The SAFE test

The strategy must pass four 'hurdles', the SAFE test.

➡ *Suitability* – Is it the most appropriate strategy for this organisation competing for these customers against these competitors in this environment? In other words, will it proactively maintain a high level of 'strategic fit' between the organisation and its environment?

➡ *Acceptability* – Considering all the list of stakeholders, particularly the customer, will the strategy be acceptable to them, in other words, will people be willing to support it?

➡ *Feasibility* – An ambitious strategy is all very well, but can we make it happen? Have we got the necessary resources, time and budget, in other words, do we have the necessary capabilities?

➡ *Endurance* – In view of the changes and the rate of change, will this strategy also be right for tomorrow as it is for today? If not, then can we change at the same speed?

To plan for this two-way dialogue, a communication matrix (see Figure 6.6 overleaf) should be drawn up confirming who needs to be involved, what information they should receive or need to provide, and how it will be conducted.

Strategic performance indicators

Even once the strategic framework is complete and has been tested for validity against the criteria, it does not mean to say that the senior team can sit back.

 One of two pitfalls needs to be avoided:

➡ the external environment changes, making the strategy sub-optimal

➡ the actions necessary to implement the strategy don't happen.

A communication matrix			
	Full strategy	Summary document	Guiding principles
Internal			
Senior managers	Presentation and personal copies	Copies	
Implementation team	Personal copies and facilitated workshop	Copies	
All staff		Presentation and two-way discussion	Noticeboards
External			
Customers		One-on-one meetings with account managers	
Shareholders		Presentation at AGM and annual report	

FIGURE 6.6

The senior management team needs to focus on the knowledge it has that will indicate the existence of one or both of these pitfalls.

Whilst some indicators of performance will be obvious: revenue growth, profitability, customer satisfaction etc, some require a little more thought. Indeed you may have to dig quite deep to get to the really important indicator, as in this case.

CASE STUDY

Don't let the overall performance hide a significant point of focus

A typical strategic performance indicator for an organisation that is dependent on its people is the staff turnover level. Whilst this indicator can be misleading due to changes in the underlying market conditions, it often has some merit. One organisation that competed in the design and development of software solutions for the telecommunications industry reflected on its strategy. It specifically identified that its source of advantage lay in its ability to produce 'feature-rich' products ahead of the competition.

The organisation then reflected on what capabilities it had that directly impacted on its ability to deliver against this identified source of advantage – their software design engineers. The identification of a strategic performance indicator then became clear:

turnover rate of their software design engineers!

This gave the organisation a totally different picture to the one it previously had which provided general turnover rates, where individual problems had been hidden in the bigger picture. It enabled the senior team to focus on a few, but the correct, indicators of current and future success.

Performance indicators are covered in a lot more detail in later chapters. At this stage, the point is to reflect on what indicators we really need to avoid the two major pitfalls. We should be starting to focus on the difference between what information has been historically available, and what information we really need to run the business – 'knowledge'. This is where we see the links between the 'strategy' and the 'knowledge' elements of the model being reinforced.

Monitoring the strategy

Strategic performance indicators should be coming in on a regular basis. For many organisations, they arrive monthly in time for regular management meetings. The meeting agendas must change to reflect the new strategy, and the indicators must be used. This is the point at which the team must commit to making the strategy happen and using it on a day-to-day basis. The alternative is that the strategy will simply be another report to be put on the shelf to gather dust.

The same principles of 'customer-focused analysis' apply to the monitoring of the strategy. Whilst the initial analysis may have been a one-off, the key indicators should be 'systematised' to make it as easy as possible to obtain the data.

Focus of the monitoring should not be on covering all of the headings, but to concentrate on the indicators that are failing to meet targets set – deviation reporting. Time for the senior managers is tight, and must therefore stay focused only on those items that require their combined attention.

Monitoring activities will therefore include:

➡ scenario planning where an external monitor picks up a forecast change in the external environment which needs to be assessed

➡ strategic 'issue resolution' where under (or over) performance needs to be analysed to identify cause, and actions to correct or exploit the situation agreed.

Finally, no matter how good the initial framework was, it will change. It must not be seen as a plan set in concrete as this will destroy all flexibility and responsiveness. Some deviations, once analysed, will indicate that the strategy needs changing (see Figure 6.7): in which case change it. This is where politics or functional thinking must not interfere with identifying the need for change, and taking the appropriate action – 'organisational sensitivity'.

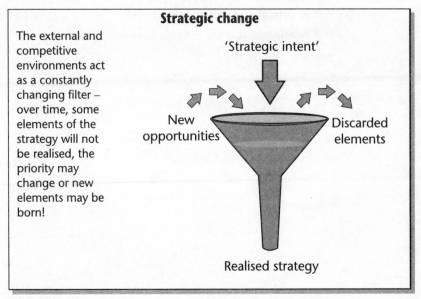

FIGURE 6.7

If the strategy is to remain current, it will have to change. It is vital that:

➡ new opportunities are constantly evaluated

➡ inappropriate products or markets are dropped, and

➡ the 'realised' strategy is the SAFEst.

Whole environment thinking: 'strategy'

KEY POINTS

Take a few minutes to reflect on each of these.

➡ Strategy should clarify organisation values, define the scope of products and markets, bridge the gap between the present and the future, and guide operational decision making.

➡ The five strategic questions are:
  – what is happening in our chosen markets?

  – what is our purpose (why do we exist)?

  – what products and services do we provide, and to whom?

  – what capabilities do we need to be successful?

  – how will we know if the strategy is correct and happening?

➡ Before implementing a new strategy, it should pass four hurdles:

  – is it **suitable**?

  – is it **acceptable** to all stakeholders?

  – is it **feasible** – can we make it happen?

  – will it be **enduring**?

(S-A-F-E)

SELF-ASSESSMENT

Rate your organisation or unit on a scale of 1 to 5.

1 Do you balance your short- and long-term perspectives? ☐

2 Do you know what your 'strategic timeframe' is? ☐

3 Do you have clearly articulated guiding principles? ☐

4 Are these adhered to or are they aspirational? ☐

5 Do you understand what keeps you in existence today? ☐

6 Do you understand what will keep you in existence tomorrow? ☐

7 Do you have synergies between the products and services offered, and between all markets served? ☐

8 Are these synergies exploited fully? ☐

9 Do you know which are the most important products and services for today? ☐

10 What about tomorrow? ☐

11 Do you know which are the most important markets for today? ☐

12 What about tomorrow? ☐

13 Do you know what capabilities will be required for success in the future, and do you have them? ☐

14 If not then do you have a plan to obtain or develop them? ☐

15 Do you know what key performance indicators will tell you whether the strategy is happening and whether it is successful? ☐

16 Does your strategy pass the SAFE test? (Is it the most suitable, is it acceptable to all stakeholders, is it feasible, and will it be enduring?) ☐

ACTION PLAN

Where you scored badly in your self-assessment, identify what actions you will take to improve your performance.

What?	Who?	When?
1		
2		
3		
4		
5		

'I am not determining a point of law;
I am restoring tranquillity.'

Edmund Burke

CHAPTER

HOLISTIC PROCESS MANAGEMENT

Looking at the processes
which turn inputs into
outputs as a whole chain
of events.

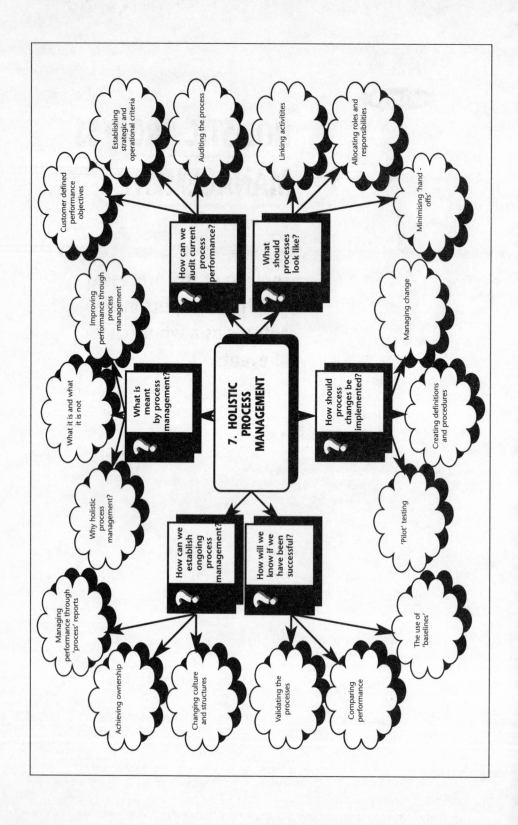

ust as functional thinking is counterproductive, so looking at individual processes out of the context of the whole organisation reduces the organisation's effectiveness and sensitivity.

At the end of this chapter readers will be able to use a non-traditional view of processes, create process owners and teams and use them to develop, improve and maintain cross-functional processes.

What is meant by process management?

As all activities can be seen as being part of a process, process management requires managers to examine each and every process on a continuing basis. Seeking improvements in processes by applying some guidelines and techniques is an activity we refer to as process management.

Why holistic process management?

We have seen that strategy is the 'what' and that processes, not functions, are the 'how'. We have also defined processes as the means by which products and services are provided to customers. We now need to see processes as requiring a 'holistic' view. We must not see any part of any process in isolation just as one function can not deliver time, cost and benefits in isolation.

'Holistic' means combining all activities that take inputs (whether raw materials, information, specifications etc) and translating them into outputs (products or services). This holistic view is sometimes referred to as the 'value chain'; the 'core processes' identify all the principle activities conducted within the organisation that add value to inputs as perceived by customers, be they internal or external. This concept of added value is a useful one as it forces people to think critically about what value each activity adds to customers.

Part of the reason for holistic process management relates to earlier discussions about why functional management is not the answer.

What it is and what it is not

Processes can simply be defined as 'a series of interconnected activities achieving specified performance objectives'. Perhaps a clearer way of explaining processes and process thinking is to draw a number of comparisons. People are often very wary of processes due to their lack of real understanding or their perception that it somehow relates to people responsible for 'quality' and is not generally applicable. The presentation of processes can also be poor, causing people to see them as pure bureaucracy. This is particularly true in, for example, the case of a takeover.

CASE STUDY

Being taken over remains a shock if new processes are implemented insensitively

A firm of caterers won a contract for a large sports facility. The staff of the facility went through a very difficult period of uncertainty while they discovered whether or not they would keep their jobs. Even after this uncertainty was removed, and the staff who remained tried to settle down in the new environment the management team maintained low staff morale by hitting people with a load of new standard processes.

Asked how they were getting on some two months into the contract, they replied that all that had changed was that they were required to fill in a load of new paperwork at the same time as trying to do their jobs.

They saw their jobs as a separate activity.

The fact is that every repeat activity performed by each employee of an organisation is conducted within a process. The effective and efficient design of that process, therefore, has a direct impact on the performance and delivery of individuals working within the process.

Process not procedure

Processes define and 'map' activities and their inter-relationship. They should not appear as large heavy documents defining exactly 'how' each activity should be conducted.

Enabling not enforcing

Procedures are often used to ensure compliance. The fundamental purpose of processes is different and therefore they should have significantly different cultural implications. Processes should identify what resources people need to perform each of the tasks, and should therefore be 'enablers' of performance.

There is a cultural and performance monitoring problem here, where, for example, safety procedures lengthen the amount of time an activity takes. If the sole measure is productivity then there is a risk that safety procedures will not be followed unless the culture encourages it. As we will see the technique of workers making decisions can solve such a situation, as opposed to enforcing and policing by Head Office.

Proactive (active) not reactive (passive)

Activities should be planned in advance and actively managed where possible. Lack of clarity in how processes 'work' results in reactive or unpredictable environments.

Prioritised not random

Not all activities are equally important. The process should clearly identify which are critical, and which can be dropped in a crisis.

Responsibility not abdication

Activities are performed by people, so clear understanding of responsibilities is essential if duplication or gaps are to be avoided.

Clarity not chaotic

Understanding of 'how things work' is often unclear, resulting in difficulty for training of new hires, or ensuring consistency of outputs to customers – not a good idea. Processes help to ensure a consistent approach based on 'best practice', (or at least ensuring that the organisation learnt from what it did well/badly last time)

Improving performance through process management

The following principles can be used to assist with the design of business processes. They should not be used as 'absolutes', but merely as guidelines for consideration. The degree of influence will be dictated by the specific make-up of the market, industry and company.

➡ It is often possible to **combine several jobs into one**. Given that their industrial relations allow it, managers can expand jobs to cover many tasks, this is sometimes known as horizontal compression. Where managers find opportunities for doing this they frequently avoid hand offs and misunderstandings by having a single point of responsibility. Other benefits are found in reduced administration overheads.

As well as being more rewarding for the people involved, combining jobs also encourages creative ways to reduce cycle times and costs, and of course with fewer people to monitor control is simpler. Make sure that there are process owners responsible for the whole process from end to end, and use the concept of process teams which are groups of people who have all the necessary skills and authority to get the job done.

➡ Look also for **vertical compression of jobs** where workers make decisions. In this delayering environment decision making becomes *part* of the work – previously performed by managers. Examples of the many benefits of doing this are fewer delays, lower overhead costs, better customer response and greater empowerment of the people performing the tasks.

➡ Try to ensure that the steps in the process are **performed in the natural order**, so that work is sequenced by what *needs* to follow what – not a linear sequence. This leads to reduced cycle times and less reworking.

The move towards building quality into the operation rather than leaving it to the end is a good example of this.

➡ In most industries processes need to have **multiple versions**. Single processes are plainly best suited for mass production for mass markets. Different situations will require a process to be executed in different ways. Unfortunately, the technology used in many organisations dramatically reduces flexibility. Because computing started with mainframes and the economics dictated that systems were centralised, many large companies still suffer. The syndrome is that systems meant to satisfy a large user base end up satisfying none.

➡ Many organisations have improved their processes by making sure that **work is performed where it makes most sense**. In this context they avoid organising work around functional specialists, and pieces of work that are currently performed by independent units are integrated. Work is allocated not by function, but by the role the person is fulfilling.

You frequently find that the customer of a process can often perform all or some of the process. Internally this concept eliminates hand offs and overheads. This concept is initially alien to many people, but active involvement of customers will help build very strong and lasting relationships. Those who have thought it worth a try have never gone back to the old way.

➡ Another technique is to **reduce checks and controls**. Controls are used only where they make sense rather than frequent checking and control which rarely add value. You can also avoid the costs associated with tight control systems.

➡ By reducing the number of external contact points that a process has it becomes possible to **minimise reconciliation**. Each time a product or service is passed to an external group, a detailed reconciliation is required. Each will cost in terms of time and money.

➡ The concept of a **process owner** provides a single point of contact. This gives a useful 'buffer' between the customer and complex/core processes. Note, however, that the owner needs access to all the information available to all those working the process.

➡ We will discuss the importance of fluid structures later on but at this stage it is worth mentioning the importance of an appropriate **mix of centralised and decentralised structures**. Both centralised and decentralised structures have advantages.

How can we audit current process performance?

Improving effectiveness in a business starts from an analysis of where we are now.

As always, improving effectiveness in a business starts from an analysis of where we are now. In terms of improving the processes in a business the starting point is an audit of current processes.

Auditing the process

Any audit should start by specifying process boundaries – this is particularly important when the process under audit cuts across several functions.

The following questions should be asked and answered:

➡ What is the name of the process?

➡ What is the 'purpose' of the process

➡ Who are the major 'stakeholders'?

➡ What are the principle outputs and who are the principle customers (whether internal or external)?

165

➡ What emphasis is given on which outputs (products and services) and customers? If there is a bottleneck, who gets priority?

Two key questions can then be asked of the 'bounded' process. We must assess the current situation – 'How can we do things better?' and assess future process needs – 'How should we change what we do?' These two questions need to be asked in both operational and strategic areas. In fact, while question one is often asked first, logically we should deal with 'How should we change what we do?' before we start on the quest to improve things.

Question one will be achieved through the following activities:

➡ establishing process performance objectives, indicators and targets (ask the customers)

➡ confirmation of performance feasibility (possibly benchmark competition) – 'Is what the customer wants actually possible and realistic?'

➡ assess current performance (this information will be used as a 'baseline' against which to measure future performance improvement and to assess the size of the gap)

➡ map current process (what activities are conducted by whom and in what order?)

➡ critique the process (where is the process ineffective, what are the major concerns, where do activities fall on an 'activity value map'?)

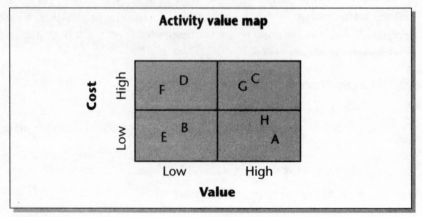

FIGURE 7.1

The activity value map (see Figure 7.1) plots activities conducted within a process against two axes. One represents 'costs' as measured in time or budget consumed. The other represents 'value' as defined by the customer, for example, how would each activity contribute to meeting each customer-defined performance target or 'attribute' needs?

Question two will be answered by reflecting back on the strategy developed in Chapter 6.

Comparing the future organisational 'state' with its current state will identify a potential need for change even though current performance looks good. Assess this state against the established criteria:

➡ strategic performance indicators

➡ source of competitive advantage

➡ product–market mix and emphasis

➡ future capability requirements.

In considering the strategic needs for change, and the operational needs for efficiency, the following checklist may be useful.

 Some useful questions

Value added:

➡ **What is the impact of each activity on process objectives (customer benefits, cost and time)?**

Task efficiency:

➡ **What tasks can be eliminated?**

➡ **What tasks can the customer be asked to do?**

➡ **What tasks can be outsourced?**

➡ **Can complex tasks be broken into simple tasks?**

➡ **What tasks can be performed simultaneously?**

(A useful indicator of time efficiency is to analyse the time of 'value added' activity versus total elapsed time.)

Wastage:

➡ **What goes wrong at the end of each step? What is the impact?**

➡ **How many hand offs are there?**

➡ **What goes wrong at the end of each hand off? What is the impact?**

➡ **How can hand offs be eliminated?**

➡ **Where is there rework? How can it be eliminated?**

Opportunities for design improvement:

➡ How can the process be redesigned?

➡ How can automation and IT help to improve benefits, cost or time attributes?

Impact of changes:

➡ How will people's roles and responsibilities be affected?

➡ How will people's attitude be affected?

What should processes look like?

The traditional view of process design tends to inhibit rather than encourage organisational sensitivity. With this in mind we need to re-assess the way we design and implement the new processes required by the audit of the current position.

The traditional view

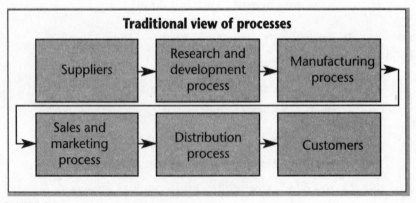

FIGURE 7.2

The traditional view, as shown in Figure 7.2, illustrates the inter-relationships between activities linking suppliers to customers. However, it is still predominantly based around functional groupings and has several potential problems.

➡ The linear view from left to right hides the fact that many processes are 'iterative' and will not necessarily pass through an area just once. It also places the customer at the end of the chain. But in reality customers will often have an impact or involvement in almost all major activities within the process, which is not visible in this diagram.

➡ The use of a single line also represents a great simplification. It makes it look as though there is a single customer point of contact. With customers, whether internal or external, there are often many points of contact, from technical contacts, through financial contacts to contacts at strategic level.

➡ By using this functional view of an organisation the groupings do not emphasise the predominant activity that takes place at that point in the process. Functional 'titles' are used rather than a description of what actually takes place. This point may sound trivial, but titles can have an enormous impact on culture.

➡ The linear view of processes tends to miss out planning (or thinking). Many activities are missing. Whilst some activities, such as planning, may not be perceived to be adding value, without them the core processes just do not work.

➡ The traditional view suggests that all products use the same process, ignoring the guideline that multi-processes are more likely to be effective. Whilst a process should reflect the best way of performing any particular activity, one design will often not cater for a wide diversity of products, services and customers. Hence decisions will be taken during the process which will determine which activities are necessary for a given situation.

➡ Finally, this way of looking at things does not reflect the organisation's source of advantage. We need a different view.

An alternative view

Because our argument is that all processes should be driven by their purpose as opposed to a template, we can only illustrate the alternative view with an example. Here is one of a machine installation process for a manufacturer of machine tools. See Figure 7.3.

This form of process map has many advantages. First of all we can ensure that the customer drives the process by making clear customer involvement at all stages. Each customer interface can be actively managed. It needs to be as each time an organisation or group interfaces with its customer it will have an impact on the long-term relationship.

169

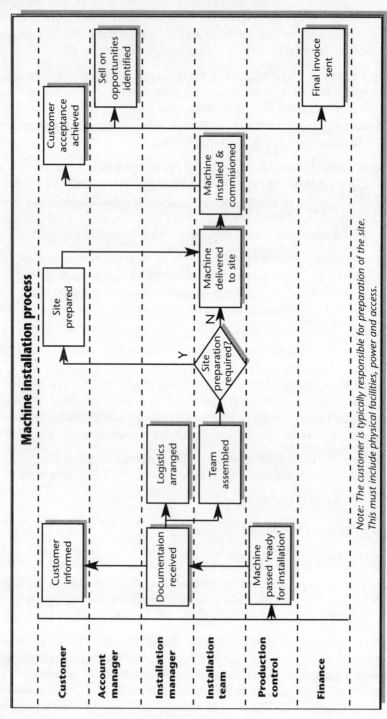

Machine installation process

| Customer | Account manager | Installation manager | Installation team | Production control | Finance |

Note: The customer is typically responsible for preparation of the site. This must include physical facilities, power and access.

FIGURE 7.3

Roles and responsibilities are clear as the map shows activities **and** roles. Vertical lines show where the management of the customer order is 'handed off' from one person or group to another. Experience has shown that it is at these points of hand offs, the 'vertical lines', that problems occur. Meanwhile horizontal lines reflect that two connecting activities are being completed by the same person or group, and so less control should be required.

The shadowed boxes identify the high-value points within the process. Whilst all activities should be important, some should be monitored and managed more closely than others.

Notes at the bottom of the map allow words of explanation to be added, so that as well as helping in the initial design of the process, this technique can be used for ongoing education and induction for new staff.

Perhaps the greatest value overall is that this form of mapping bridges functional roles and responsibilities with process activities. A major barrier to getting people to adopt a more cross-functional process perspective is that we all have a need to see where we belong. With this form of mapping, people can find their role down the left axis and look horizontally along at the activities which they are responsible for – where they fit.

Looked at this way, it becomes easier to identify and allocate roles and responsibilities.

Allocating roles and responsibilities

Once the focus is switched towards an understanding of how work actually gets carried out, it is often surprising for some people to realise that functional groups appear everywhere. This reinforces the point made earlier that functional groupings are the wrong basis for taking a holistic view on an organisation. For example, the account manager, sitting within the sales and marketing 'function', clearly has a key role to play in the installation process. Without this form of critical evaluation, the real need can be missed and opportunities, such as 'sell-ons', simply never appear.

Once the process has been defined, then the question can be asked 'What is the most appropriate organisational structure?' Thus we can see how strategy should drive process and how process design should drive structure.

It is almost impossible to ensure that an organisation has the most appropriate structure until it really understands its processes and understands how work is best conducted. In response to organisational crises many organisations restructure and it is not surprising that such efforts often cause enormous confusion for little benefit. Interestingly, the same organisations are likely to be restructuring again within a two-year period. See Figure 7.4.

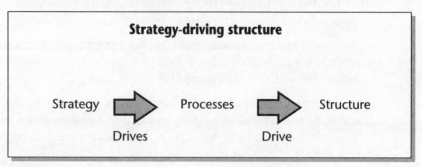

FIGURE 7.4

Minimising hand offs

Hand offs occur, as we have seen when roles and responsibilities are unclear or where agreement to activity is lacking. This way of designing processes will tend to minimise the number of hand offs between individuals and groups.

The implications of this for the customer can be significant as it should result in increased benefits, reduced costs and time (perhaps of greatest interest in today's time-driven markets).

The implications of this for the organisation should also be significant, but to really impact bottom-line performance the organisation will have to commit itself and aim high to achieve changes in how it works. Some of the implications may be:

➡ multi-skilling and reduced traditional demarcation

➡ changed performance reward systems to be based on team and process measures rather than individual and functional.

How should process changes be implemented?

The redesign of some or all of the processes involved in delivering benefits to the customer will bring change. Much has been written on the management of change, so here we present no more than the bones of the process.

Managing change

Changing processes is the same as introducing any change into an organisation – it must be managed proactively.

Minimum requirements of the change plan should include:

> *Changing processes is the same as introducing any change into an organisation – it must be managed proactively.*

➡ **objectives to be achieved**

➡ **a list of all stakeholders impacted by the changes**

➡ **a list of tasks to be completed and resource requirements**

➡ **clear responsibilities and involvement**

➡ **completion dates for each change activity**

➡ **detailed risk and opportunity analysis.**

Similar questions will occur again when we consider putting technology to work in Chapter 13.

Creating definitions and procedures

Changes must be communicated so that those involved in the process will understand the new way of working. Clear definitions of new tasks and procedures can sometimes help with this, but beware the tomb of documents syndrome. The involvement of the people whose lives you are going to change needs to happen early in the process and continuously.

'Pilot' testing

No matter how well the new processes have been planned they should be tested against the same hurdles of suitability, acceptability feasibility and endurance.

The worst possible outcome is not that the new process will have no impact but that the new process will make things worse. This happens on many process improvement projects if they are not thought through.

The answer is to plan thoroughly and then conduct a pilot test. This can be done in two phases. Firstly the 'dry run' which tests the new design using historical data – 'What would have happened if we had done it this way for the last batch?' Secondly, a 'wet run' will test an order or contract by running in through the old and new processes in parallel. In this way a direct comparison can be made.

Pilot testing is also a vital step in gaining the understanding and commitment of others to the new processes. To begin with Europower tried to implement the wholesale process change.

Europower: trying to swallow the whole elephant

The Board of the Electricity Distribution Division decided to experiment with a popular technique of the moment – 'business re-engineering'. They chose as the starting project the delivery of new connections to new customers. This was a broad project involving everyone from planners to suppliers of wooden poles to credit checking etc.

The culture of the company tended to avoid pilot testing on the grounds that its job was to deliver a similar service to all its customers. The new processes worked reasonably well, except that an important part of customer charging was done at the wrong rate. The cost of this ran into millions, some ten times what it would have cost if they had used a pilot to test the process.

How will we know if we have been successful?

It is most important to validate the difference each new process has made to the organisation. Not only does this give learning messages for future changes, but perhaps more importantly it gives proof statements to doubters of the new way of looking at things.

The use of 'baselines'

It is all too easy to make changes without really knowing whether things have improved. If, for example, the objective of the changes is to improve time-to-market, then it is vital that the current level of performance is defined and agreed before starting

This should have been an integral part of the audit process, but once the changes have been made, the baselines provide the means for evaluating performance improvement

Comparing performance

Not all process changes will result in immediate benefits or improvements. Some have the dual impact of making life easier whilst at the same time, causing a certain amount of confusion resulting from the changed state. It will sometimes be necessary to give the new way of working time to have an impact. It is like learning to change your grip at tennis. Initially it feels strange and your game deteriorates, but over time it should result in improved performance. The timescale over which performance improvement is validated is crucial.

Validating the processes

Performance improvement is not enough unless it results in some tangible benefit for internal and external customers.

Ultimately, of course, the design of the process must be validated by the customer. Performance improvement is not enough unless it results in some tangible benefit for internal and external customers. They must be involved in the validation process, and should probably take part in the pilot.

How can we establish ongoing process management?

Assuming the organisation has experimented with this new way of designing processes, organisational sensitivity then depends on this becoming a never-ending way of seeking and implementing performance improvement.

Changing culture and structure

Culture is an integral part of all processes and activities and can therefore not be ignored. Elements of culture relate to the degree of autonomy or risk taking. Such elements can be specified by managers once it is understood what culture will be required to be successful in a particular area. It has been known for a long time that certain jobs required tight control whilst in other jobs there is a high degree of room for individuality and flare.

Other elements of the culture relate to the values and beliefs of the organisation and its strategy. These are often more difficult to change, and will in fact often affect the initial design of the processes themselves (strategy-driving processes). The final chapter of this book deals with cultural transformation.

175

Alternative structures can be reviewed against predefined criteria, but will essentially be driven by the design of the processes. Sometimes the rate at which structures can be changed will be dependent on the historical structural development. This can mean that even once the ideal structure has been identified, it may take several years to work towards the 'ideal'. The rate of change is also affected by the willingness of people to accept it and management's desire and ability to make things happen.

Achieving ownership

Designing cross-functional processes will achieve nothing unless ownership and effective management of the processes themselves is achieved within the line operations. This requires much more of a team focus than exists in most functionally based organisations. All processes should have specified 'process owners' and cross-functional 'process review teams'.

Movement towards management of processes in place of functions will often be actively resisted as it results in changes to power bases, and it involves change. These emotions exist and are very real – they must be explicitly recognised and planned for. Ultimately, these people must be judged at the end of the year for how effectively the processes have performed. We need a definition of process owners and process review teams.

Process owners

The process owner is a senior person with responsibility and accountability for the end-to-end performance of a process. The role entails designing the process, monitoring and modifying the process whenever necessary, and taking responsibility for the performance of the process.

Typical ongoing activities include:

➡ monitoring customer requirements

➡ benchmarking for opportunities for improvement

➡ measuring process performance

➡ modifying the design when needed

➡ selecting people to perform the process

➡ motivating those who work within the process

➡ providing the resources that are needed, when they are needed.

Process owners are senior managers, well respected and well connected, and will therefore have a high degree of authority across functions. They must be able to lead by example, to make things happen, and to be creative and process-minded.

Process review teams

Process review teams should contain between six and ten people on a part-time basis. Approximately 75 per cent should be selected from within the process and 25 per cent from outside. The insiders will bring detailed knowledge of the business and customers, intuition and experience, credibility and opinion leadership, and the necessary authority. The outsiders will bring specialist techniques, imagination and creativity, objectivity and risk taking, and an ability to **not** get too close to the issues.

The teams should be drawn from different levels and skills, and should be multi-functional in nature. The participation of customers and suppliers is required on a situation-specific basis, and there is a need for occasional involvement of specialists.

Managing performance through 'process' reports

Finally, once the cross-functional processes have been defined, making them work requires that the performance of the processes are monitored on a regular (monthly) basis. Owners of the process and those responsible for their effectiveness must be held accountable for their performance.

Process performance reporting is covered in detail in the next chapter.

Holistic process management

KEY POINTS

Take a few minutes to reflect on each of these.

➡ Organisation processes should be defined, communicated and understood.

➡ All activities performed within organisations are performed in processes – whether core or support.

➡ Processes are not the same as procedures, processes management should be enabling not enforcing, process design should encourage proactivity not reactivity, activities should be prioritised, responsibilities should be clearly defined and processes should provide clarity as to how work is actually performed.

➡ Principles of process design include:

- the combination of several jobs into one
- the vertical compression of jobs
- the performance of tasks in their natural order and place
- reduced number of checks and controls, minimised number of reconciliations
- clear process ownership from end to end.

➡ Process maps should define:

- a clear purpose
- hand-offs from one group to another
- high-value activities
- key decision points
- how and when the customer is involved.

➡ Active process ownership and management is required for effective and efficient cross-functional performance. Process review teams must regularly monitor and improve process performance.

SELF-ASSESSMENT

Rate your organisation or unit on a scale of 1 to 5.

1   Are all organisational processes defined and 'mapped'?   ☐

2   Are process management skills given to all key employees?   ☐

3   Are the processes communicated to and understood by all those involved in their execution?   ☐

4   Could processes be redesigned to incorporate some of the principles of process design stated above?   ☐

5   Can the processes be made to be more efficient for today's needs – greater customer benefits, reduced time, reduced cost?   ☐

6   How appropriate will the processes be in the future? Consider the strategy.   ☐

7   Do you know which activities have the greatest impact on the customer and on performance?   ☐

8   Do you know which activities have the greatest impact in terms of time and cost?   ☐

9   Are all the hand offs from one group or individual to another identified?   ☐

10 Could the number be reduced?   ☐

11 Are there clearly defined indicators and targets for acceptable levels of performance for all hand offs to internal or external customers?   ☐

12 Are roles and responsibilities clearly defined and understood?   ☐

13 Is the role of 'process owner' specified?   ☐

14 Is there a 'process review team' for all core processes?   ☐

ACTION PLAN

Where you scored badly in your self-assessment, identify what
actions you will take to improve your performance.

What?	Who?	When?
1		
2		
3		
4		
5		

'I do not see the signal.'

Horatio, Viscount Nelson

CHAPTER

8

DEFINING
INTERNAL
'PROCESS'
PERFORMANCE
INDICATORS

Tracking the improving
processes through agreed
key indicators.

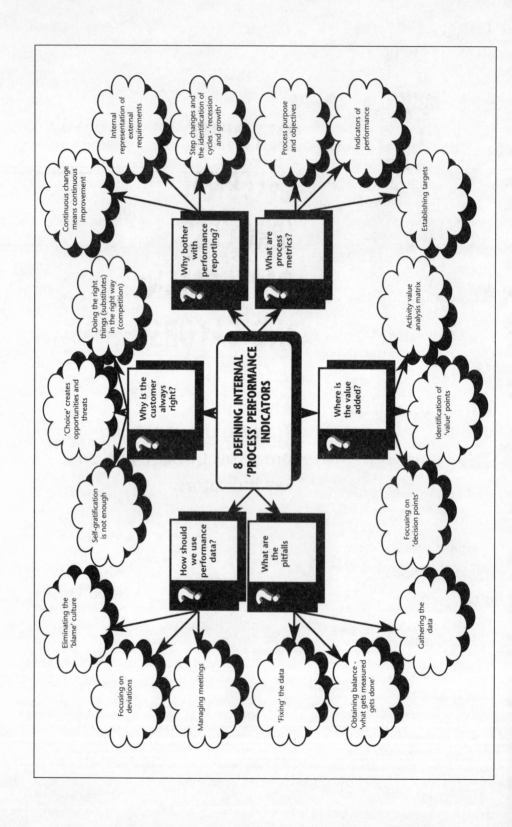

8 DEFINING INTERNAL 'PROCESS' PERFORMANCE INDICATORS

Why is the customer always right?

'Choice' creates opportunities and threats

Self-gratification is not enough

Doing the right things (substitutes) in the right way (competition)

Why bother with performance reporting?

Continuous change means continuous improvement

Internal representation of external requirements

Step changes and the identification of cycles - 'recession and growth'

What are process metrics?

Process purpose and objectives

Indicators of performance

Establishing targets

Activity value analysis matrix

Where is the value added?

Identification of 'value' points

Focusing on 'decision points'

How should we use performance data?

What are the pitfalls

Eliminating the 'blame' culture

Focusing on deviations

Managing meetings

'Fixing' the data

Obtaining balance - 'what gets measured gets done'

Gathering the data

Once process teams and owners have reviewed processes and planned them cross-functionally, they need to define the objectives of the new processes and use key indicators to track progress. Managers now understand that excellent indicators of how an organisation is performing can mean the difference between seeing the cliff coming and changing direction before you get there, or having change dictated to you as the organisation accelerates to disaster.

At the end of this chapter, readers will be able to define the objectives of redesigned processes, attach specific indicators of progress and define the critical areas and risks of the processes.

Why is the customer always right?

In this chapter we will discuss the use of indicators to ensure that an organisation is sensitive, both to its functional and cross-functional groupings, but also to the external environment. As usual this external environment is dominated by the customer. We will also take the Europower case and trace its progress as it implements the processes we have talked about so far to become customer-focused and sensitive.

Self-gratification is not enough

If we refer back to the product versus customer focus debate, our indicators can tell us that we are still the best producers of black and white televisions, but if we are not producing what our customers want, our indicators must tell us.

Once a cross-functional process has been designed, it is tempting to focus inwardly on the process. Just as the process must be designed from the customer perspective (whether internal or external), the indicators must focus on the outputs of the process as perceived by customers. Internal indicators will still be useful, but only as a predictor of long-term or future performance.

It is easy to allow personal targets to interfere with what the customer actually wants.

It is easy to allow personal targets to interfere with what the customer actually wants, as this case shows.

CASE STUDY

Driving hard at the wrong target

A successful manufacturing company for office products needed to set strategy and decide on a new direction in the face of dramatic changes in the way their products were being bought. Unfortunately no clear performance metrics existed. The Board members all said they knew what was driving the business.

After the first few sessions of working towards their new strategy, several major decisions failed to achieve the expected benefits. As the situation continued, it became clear that some major actions needed for long-term survival were being 'ducked.' In fact the only criteria being used for decisions was their likely impact on the personal pension policies of the Board members. This explained the reluctance to avoid establishing clear performance indicators, and also explained why, a year later, the company had gradually slipped into crisis.

'Choice' creates opportunities and threats

In monopoly situations, there is less need to worry about performance indicators except those agreed with the regulators. Poor performance is to all intents and purposes irrelevant as a lack of any comparison probably means it goes unnoticed and there is not a lot most customers can do about it.

Real choice in a market presents an organisation with real threats, as competition attempts to take market share, and real opportunities as new markets are opened up.

Nowhere is a change of market status more clear than a government-inspired move from a monopoly provider to the provision of choice. This dramatically impacts market forces. This is precisely what happened to Europower. At the end of this chapter we will illustrate the situation arrived at so far in the Europower case.

Doing the right things (substitutes) in the right way (competition)

Indicators will need to identify two aspects of performance, that we are doing the right things, and that we are doing things in the right way.

Not doing the right things opens us up to loss of future business from products and services that are effectively substitutes to our current offering. Remember the British Airways example where to meet the needs of the business traveller, it was necessary to pick up on the fact that the basic need, albeit in the future, might be satisfied by a different type of service altogether. We must know about that.

Not doing things in the right way means that we will be more expensive, slower and offer customers fewer benefits than our competition, a recipe for disaster.

Why bother with performance reporting?

Continuous change means continuous improvement

Even if the organisation currently satisfies the exact needs and expectations of its targeted markets, there is no guarantee that this will be the case tomorrow. Market dynamics are so complicated, and depend on so many factors, that very quickly requirements will have changed, possibly resulting in a degree of strategic drift. And this process is happening all the time.

Awareness of the direction and rate of change is vital in planning preventive or corrective action.

Awareness of the direction and rate of change is vital in planning preventive or corrective action. It can be very difficult for market leaders, or organisations with a unique offering, to accept this fact, and in many of them an inability to change arises. At its simplest an element of arrogance creeps in, 'We know best what our customers want'. The fact is that success today does not guarantee success tomorrow.

Internal representation of external requirements

Reflecting external requirements through internal indicators helps to create a culture of focusing on the customer. It is important that departments or groups do not do this in isolation, but that they work together. Remember the Europower account manager and his immediate requirement to talk to the main supplier.

Hence the starting point for indicators should be at the top, where the organisation as a whole asks what indicators should be used to assess performance against short- and long-term customer requirements. Thus, a 'hierarchy of performance indicators' is established where organisational indicators are simply a consolidation from each group or process making up the whole organisation.

This hierarchy ensures a cascading of objectives to ensure cross-functional harmony, irrespective of how far they have moved to a cross-function process culture, and helps to align the organisation to its markets. See Figure 8.1.

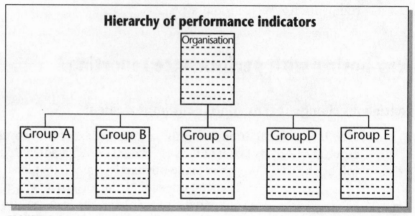

FIGURE 8.1

Furthermore, single indicators in isolation can be meaningless. It is only as a complete set that we can see the overall picture, and what behaviour is desirable. Measuring, for example, revenue in isolation of profit only encourages sales personnel to go out and 'buy' sales, by discounting prices to increase revenues, even though the margin will suffer. Do not underestimate the difficulties of achieving this, it requires real cross-functional co-operation.

Step changes and the identification of cycles – 'recession and growth'

As well as identifying particular areas of concern, the indicators should also point to underlying trends, such as the chaotic swing from growth to recession mentioned in Chapter 1. If your customer is sensitive to his or her environment, he or she will get early indications from customers and so on.

In other words, the indicators should also point to identification of the cause for any problem, current or future, where possible.

What are process performance indicators?

After the organisation has produced its comprehensive list of processes, identified owners and members of the process team it can produce the cross-functional process maps talked about earlier. Process indicators provide the basis for managers to set targets for the process and monitor the team's achievements. They will be set in a suitable timeframe and monitored regularly.

For each process we need to understand the purpose and objectives of the process, agree on the indicators and put targets against them.

Process purpose and objectives

To identify performance indicators we must start with a clear understanding of the purpose of each process, just why does it exist?

In achieving its primary purpose, there will be specific performance objectives. These can be broken into the generic attribute areas of benefits, cost and time. There is also a fourth category of performance objectives which can best be described as performance 'enabling' objectives.

Objectives relating to benefits reflect desired benefits to the organisation, such as profit, revenue and market share figures, while objectives relating to cost reflect minimisation of various operating costs within the process. Finally objectives relating to time may include the minimising of 'time-to-market', or 'wait times'.

Performance 'enabling' objectives reflect those aspects of the organisation which will potentially have a large impact in the future, such as staff turnover, customer satisfaction or investment levels.

These examples reinforce the need for the complete set of objectives to be viewed as a group and to be mutually supportive. For example. reducing process costs could easily be achieved through the elimination of certain activities, however, these very activities may be the ones that significantly reduce time-to-market. A complete fit of performance objectives throughout the organisation is almost a definition of organisational sensitivity.

The compete list of performance objectives should fit on a maximum of a single sheet of A4, and are typically a total of 12–15 for each process which teams are going to monitor.

Indicators of performance

Once objectives have been identified, each must be turned into some hard and tangible 'indicator'. 'What will indicate whether we are achieving our objectives?' For example, an objective for a manufacturer of cars could be to 'maximise quality'. The indicator for this objective could be 'the number of defects per vehicle', assuming that that was a relevant indicator of quality.

Sometimes, in order to get to something meaningful, several indicators are required for a single objectives. For example, an objective to 'maximise financial performance' may have three indicators which in combination give the management team the information they require – 'annual revenue, net operating profit, return on capital employed'.

Establishing targets

The progression from the purpose of the process, through the objectives to be achieved by the process to the definition of what will indicate performance levels is a logical one. The final step in the assessment of performance must be to ask what standard or 'target' would be an acceptable or desired level of performance.

People must understand what success will look like. The clearer this is, the more likely it is that it will happen. For each indicator a target level of performance must be identified which should be both challenging and realistic.

The car manufacturer may have a current level of 5 defects per 100 vehicles, and may set a target of 2 defects per 100 vehicles. Again when you are evaluating targets you can apply the standard SAFE test for suitability, acceptability, feasibility and endurance.

The suitability of targets is best obtained by looking at customer needs and expectations and discussing them with the customer, and by reviewing competitor levels of performance.

Objective	Indicator	Target
Maximise car quality	Number of defects per vehicle	<2 per 100 vehicle

Where is the added value?

Indicators will tend to focus on the outputs from the process, but not exclusively. High-risk or high-value areas within the processes might also justify closer attention.

Activity value analysis matrix

The work on activity-value mapping in Chapter 7 will help to identify those higher value areas. Indicators related to high-value activities will often forewarn the manager of future process performance problems. In this context internal indicators are often performance enablers, for example percentage of business derived from new clients.

Identification of the value points

With a process, and even focusing on higher value activities, there will be one or two activities which are fundamental to their potential to impact performance. These are often termed 'value points' and will already have been identified in the cross-functional process map.

As was discussed, vertical lines also represent areas of risk where one function is handing over to another. The risk for hand off or delay can be reduced by identifying internal process indicators which monitor progress at these key points.

Focusing on decision points

In the same way that any one process will have only a very small number of 'value' points, there are often only a very small number of key decisions within the process that may have a dramatic impact on the output.

Many modern management and motivational 'gurus' suggest that success in life is fundamentally determined by a very small number of decisions that we make. The trick is to recognise these key decisions in advance and pay particular attention to them.

For many activities and decisions, poor performance will have little overall effect, while for others, it might mean the difference between success and failure. It is vital to know the difference and to focus greater attention on those points of high leverage. Use of internal process performance indicators as part of the A4 report is one very effective way of doing this.

It is a fact that encouraging managers to identify higher value activities, value points and decision points can transform the way managers think about processes, and eventually lead to enormous improvement in the implementation of processes.

What are the pitfalls?

Getting a list of appropriate objectives and indicators is not a trivial pursuit, it needs effort and the will to see things through. It is, though, a vital part of creating organisational sensitivity.

Gathering the data

Defining process performance indicators is difficult enough, especially as most organisations start with an existing system in place. It is worth while to point out some of the difficulties in doing it.

Data gathering in itself can add significant complexity to an overworked manager or workforce. There must be a balance drawn between the value of the information and the cost of getting it. Many organisations have recognised the inadequacies of their financial reporting systems, but these same organisations have tried and subsequently rejected the use of activity-based costing systems due to the potential enormity of producing the monitoring and information gathering systems.

Often technology can be used to help with the data gathering, but this must, as usual, be treated with a certain amount of caution. Managers must still apply the 'common sense' rule. 'Does this data really make sense?' Often where a major problem has been identified, its conclusions should be validated by a second source before remedial action is confirmed. Reflecting the principles of 'customer-focused analysis', process performance indicators are a specific way of constantly analysing the performance of internal aspects of the organisation.

A key rule is the KIS rule – keep it simple! If an indicator exists or can be obtained easily, even if it is not 100 per cent ideal, it may be good enough to trigger further investigation if there is a problem. In this case the additional cost of making the indicator 'ideal' is not worth while.

The net result of critically evaluating the use of performance indicators should be to reduce the total amount of information gathered. In most organisations, the majority of information is the wrong information. Hence, as well as establishing some new indicators, many of the old ones should be stopped. Many managers

In most organisations, the majority of information is the wrong information.

have a certain comfort zone in watching their favourite old indicators, but really if they are no longer relevant then they should be stopped. If you have too many indicators, they will detract from the ones that are really important.

Obtaining balance – 'what gets measured gets done'

Whilst the indicators are really being used to monitor performance, we must recognise that they will also drive behaviour, and will therefore, in themselves influence performance. In many cases the phrase 'what gets measured gets done' holds true.

Thus if you focus on a particular indicator, suddenly performance against that indicator starts to improve. It is therefore **vital** that indicators are mutually supportive as it is all too easy to make the situation worse by driving the wrong behaviour.

'Fixing' the data

The flip side of the fact that indicators will drive behaviour, is that it will also drive potentially negative behaviour to 'fix' the data.

For example, managers can stop investing in maintenance to improve short-term cash flow, but sooner or later the lack of maintenance will have a dramatic adverse impact on performance.

Mutually supportive indicators will help to discourage or prevent such behaviour, where an individual can only fix one indicator at the expense of another. Perhaps the question of sustainability will prove the most useful test here.

Managers must also avoid the trap of this next case. Here the new business culture has got to the stage where managers will only accept a forecast of success, whatever the real circumstances.

CASE STUDY

Heads the organisation loses, tails it loses

An experienced account manager, very much a farmer in sales jargon, was talking to a colleague salesman who was responsible for finding new business, very much an aggressive hunter. The hunter was interested in some of the points the other salesman was making, and asked him to look at his monthly sales forecast to see if he could help to evaluate his opportunities.

> It became apparent very quickly that most of the forecast was overly optimistic. In order to achieve even half of the forecast orders, the hunter was going to need terrific luck. 'Alan, if you put a forecast like this in you could get fired,' murmured the account manager. 'No, no Ken, if I do *not* put a forecast like this in, I *will* get fired.'

The culture in this case encourages people to take huge risks with their estimates of future performance. It will lead to a huge amount of variation in results, as the people doing the job try to juggle with what is really feasible and what their managers want to hear.

How should we use performance data?

The cross-functional teams who own the processes will need to meet from time to time. Keeping the number of meetings down, and keeping them short is one of the benefits of using process indicators.

Another is the elimination of the blame culture. If the processes are going to maximise profitability, or eliminate defects for example, there are going to be occasions when they fail. The culture of apportioning blame is not consistent with the sensitive organisation.

Managing meetings

One of the first things that must change once new process performance indicators have been specified are meetings. Firstly, of course, meetings will increasingly be of a cross-functional nature. This helps to reinforce the team and cross-functional process approach and hence help to break down some of the power bases.

Secondly, the agenda for the meetings should focus very much on the A4 report. Meetings that have the performance figures mixed in with a lot of other business lose focus. Process performance is so important that for such meetings there should only be one item on the agenda. Another reason for this is that attendance is mandatory, so the meeting should only have on the agenda items which are of interest to every person attending.

The required information or knowledge should be visible at such meetings. For many organisations this requires the establishment of a central knowledge centre which will be covered in more detail in Chapter 12.

Focusing on deviations

We have said that any team should be able to limit their monthly reports to a maximum of a single sheet of A4. One of the primary reasons for this is that each member of the team will at least look at them before attending a review meeting, and critically evaluate their processes and their role in them. It also gives focus. Too many managers use a shotgun approach in the hope that if they monitor enough things then one may give them what they need.

One of the reasons why managers are uncomfortable with the single page approach, is that they have not formulated their strategy and designed their cross-functional processes effectively and do not therefore really understand how their organisation works or what indicators to focus on. Another is that they do not use 'deviation reporting'.

Deviation reporting presumes that managers have developed a detailed plan of their operations, and set the right targets for the right indicators. If this is the case, then managers should not waste time reviewing performance data on a regular basis if all indicators are within targets.

They should use the reports to identify only those areas which have gone 'off-track', ie outside the targets, and then focus their time on those areas. In this way the specific meeting agenda is set by performance. If there are no deviations there should be no meeting. (If something is not broken then why fix it, or waste time examining it? We don't check the starter motor on our cars if the engine starts when we turn the key.)

Eliminating the 'blame' culture

Finally, a chapter on performance reporting should not be closed without a comment on culture. Reporting should not be for the purpose of apportioning blame. If people feel that it is, then the managers have a problem with style and culture. A blame-apportioning culture is oppressive in all elements of organisational performance and mitigates heavily against organisational sensitivity.

A certain amount of controlled risk taking will be required if an organisation is to progress.

The culture should be one of looking forward to solutions. A certain amount of controlled risk taking will be required if an organisation is to progress, and it is to be expected that some targets will be missed some of the time. This will be covered in detail in the final chapter of this book.

As a postscript to this chapter here is a short summary of the progress of Europower's project to achieve organisational sensitivity using the techniques discussed so far.

CASE STUDY

Europower: the first stages of progress towards organisational sensitivity and competitiveness

The current owners of Europower have told the company to be prepared to face real competition within five years. This gives an excellent *strategic timeframe*.

We will follow the managers of the division responsible for distribution and supply to the market. Using this timeframe, management carries out a detailed external and internal analysis producing a comprehensive *SWOT analysis* for all appropriate groupings. This enables the division, called Customer Distribution Division (CDD), to recognise where competition is most likely to come and what the competitive strategy is likely to be. They put disciplines in place to maintain this analysis and to measure continuously the trends in the industry and general benchmarks of performance.

It is difficult at this time to do the next step which is state their *guiding principles* and the evidence for them. The fact is that the current basic beliefs will in many cases be inappropriate in the new environment. Current guiding principles include, for example, acting as a service to the community. In the new world this will still to some extent hold true, but the competitive battle ground will refocus this basic belief. Other beliefs include total job security, and strict demarcation of the craftspeople and others. While Europower is not going to become a hire and fire company overnight, it knows that competitiveness cannot be achieved without a significant change to these beliefs. They decide to come back to the basic beliefs once the plan has made more progress.

Their *source of advantage* lies in their ability to deliver good quality electricity to the whole marketplace right now, and maintain that supply by their ability to respond fast to crises such as major storm damage. Their *statement of purpose* in summary is to maintain the historical source of advantage in the new competitive environment arriving in three years' time. This is such a radical change that it will be the principle driver of their strategy.

For the purpose of this study we will simplify the *market* into three segments. The first is a small number of massive users of electricity, manufacturers of steel, chemicals and cars. This market is important for strategic reasons, for example they operate 24 hours a day, as well as having a good potential for profit. Notice that it is even at this stage only a potential for profit. Such companies have no choice of electricity supplier, but they do have a choice of whether to keep and/or expand their operations in Europower's country or not. The loss of a major manufacturer would be unsatisfactory from the shareholders' point of view, when you remember that the vast majority of Europower's customers not only get an electricity bill but they also get a vote.

The second market segment is the biggest. It is all the customers who live in urban areas, close enough together to allow a company to make a sensible profit by selling them power. The third segment includes remote farmhouses at the top of hills which are difficult to access. Only regulatory protection keeps these sites as customers and there is no doubt that no competitor in its right mind would target such an unprofitable type of customer.

As to *product* let us concentrate only on the provision of electricity, which in any case provides more than 95 per cent of this division's revenues. The Group Board will have done a similar exercise to give a framework of priorities to all the divisions.

The thrust for *new business* is to take current products to an expanding industrial base, and to a slowly increasing domestic market. The expectation is for some growth in this market due to a small increase in population and a steady move towards a lower ratio of people to habitations.

The management can now write a five-year *plan for revenues and return.* It is aware that they also need as a crucial measure the changing ratio of employees to sales, but for the reasons above are unable at this stage to put numbers to that. It will return to it.

The *activity matrix* shows a determination to develop the first two segments of the customer base, and sustain the third whilst trying to reduce the resources allocated to it. Once again numbers for sales and profits are put into the activity matrix.

There is a problem in completing the step which delivers the matrix for *building capabilities*, in that shareholder agreement has to be gained for any investment plans. Thus the management team puts priorities and plans together for those capabilities which it can control, and produces other plans which require investment along with ideas on how to get shareholder agreement.

As part of a wide-ranging consultation process with all the people concerned in the implementation of the plan, a *communications matrix* is built which ensures that the plan is made known at the right level.

Implementation of the plan will be achieved by getting functional strategies in a consistent format using the same process as built the strategic framework. *Process teams* are put in place for the high-priority tasks, and *process owners* identified. *Validation of the strategy* was predominantly aimed at the shareholders, in this case the government, trying to get their agreement at each significant step.

We will take one example of a process team further. It was very important to look at the process by which the company delivered product and services to the top market segment of very high-volume users. Almost every role within the organisation had something to do with this process, so appointing an *owner* was difficult. The real owner who had sufficient authority was actually the Marketing Director, or even the Chief Executive if you took into account the Power Generating Division (PGD) which was the main supplier to the CDD. This was remedied by appointing account managers to take ownership of this process.

Defining process performance indicators came next. Managers could have taken an industry view of these by looking around the world at best practices and benchmarks. This produces some sort of result, but it is unfocused and difficult to keep up to date. Much better is to concentrate on the customer. At what price could a new competitor sell to the individual customers concerned? By identifying from the SWOT analysis who this was most likely to be, the account manager was able to make an estimate of what the price would need to be in five years' time. Taking estimates for sales growth and the benchmark for return on investment identified in the strategic framework, he could calculate the required margin and their price. He could now see that there was a problem. The price they would require to charge these key customers to make the return was much more than the price which a competitor could or would offer.

The supplier, PGD, were involved at this stage and a five-year improvement in the costs of providing all the services agreed.

The customer had driven the strategy, the strategy had driven the processes and customer-focused performance measures were agreed and could be monitored.

Defining internal process performance indicators

KEY POINTS

Take a few minutes to reflect on each of these.

➡ The customer is always right – choice creates opportunities and threats.

➡ Continuous change externally means there is a need for continuous improvement internally.

➡ Every organisation has scarce resources – processes consume resources – a clear purpose and set of objectives is required to ensure that every activity performed within the organisation adds value.

➡ Performance indicators should focus on providing the right information to the right people in the right format at the right time.

➡ Performance indicators are not used to apportion blame, but to identify areas where action is required to correct a problem or exploit an opportunity.

SELF-ASSESSMENT

Rate your organisation or unit on a scale of 1 to 5.

1 Is the purpose of each process specified? ☐

2 Are there clearly defined objectives for every process? ☐

3 For each process objective are there indicators of
   performance and agreed target levels of performance? ☐

4 Is there too much of the wrong information being
   produced? ☐

5 Is the right information in the right format given to the
   right people at the right time? ☐

6 Can all of the performance indicators be fitted clearly
   onto a single sheet of A4 paper? ☐

7 Do all 'value' and 'decision' points have performance
   indicators? ☐

8 Are these monitored systematically? ☐

9 Are the performance indicators used as the primary means
   of assessing performance and the need for change? ☐

10 Do the right people attend meetings? ☐

11 Is there a clear agenda? ☐

12 Does the meeting focus on deviations? ☐

13 Does information get used as a source of power? ☐

14 Is the information that is provided accurate? ☐

15 Is there a blame culture? ☐

16 Are the performance indicators linked directly with job
   definitions and individual evaluations? ☐

ACTION PLAN

Where you scored badly in your self-assessment, identify what actions you will take to improve your performance.

What?	Who?	When?
1		
2		
3		
4		
5		

'Superfluity comes sooner by white hair,
but competence lives longer.'

Shakespeare, *The Merchant of Venice*

MODIFYING THE PERFORMANCE ENVIRONMENT AND CREATING FLUID STRUCTURES

The processes are only as effective as the people implementing them are competent, motivated and correctly structured.

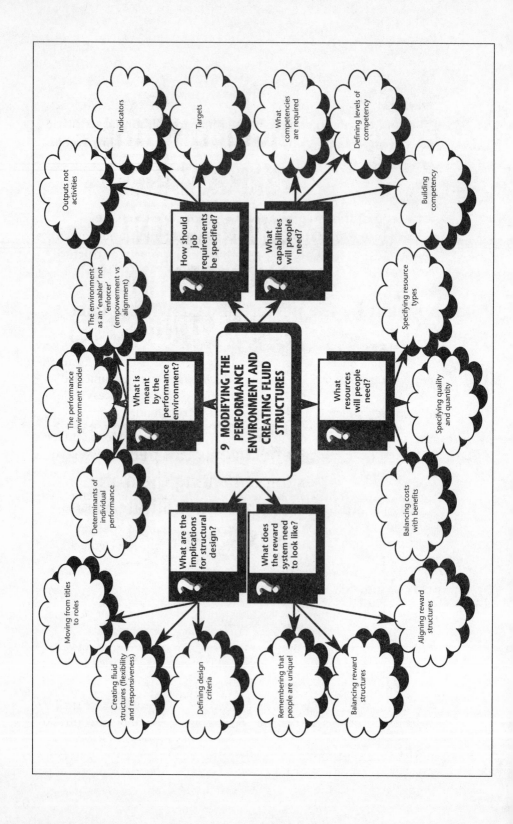

9 MODIFYING THE PERFORMANCE ENVIRONMENT AND CREATING FLUID STRUCTURES

What is meant by the performance environment?
- The performance environment model
- The environment as an 'enabler' not 'enforcer' (empowerment vs alignment)
- Determinants of individual performance

How should job requirements be specified?
- Outputs not activities
- Indicators
- Targets

What capabilities will people need?
- What competencies are required
- Defining levels of competency
- Building competency

What resources will people need?
- Specifying resource types
- Specifying quality and quantity
- Balancing costs with benefits

What are the implications for structural design?
- Moving from titles to roles
- Creating fluid structures (flexibility and responsiveness)
- Defining design criteria

What does the reward system need to look like?
- Remembering that people are unique!
- Balancing reward structures
- Aligning reward structures

G etting people to engage in creating organisational sensitivity is as important as any part of the process. And many would say the most difficult.

At the end of this chapter, readers will be able to create performance expectations, specify job requirements and build the competence of the people involved in an appropriate structure.

What is meant by the performance environment?

We have tried to show the gradual building of organisational sensitivity as following a process which is more logical, or virtual, than linear. The starting point is an agreed **strategy** which has been communicated around the organisation. This strategy then drives the **process** review and redesign which is done along cross-functional lines.

Process owners and process teams then require **knowledge** to set targets for process performance and monitor progress towards those targets.

We now turn to the fourth and final building block in the organisational sensitivity model – **people**. The model then attempts to show how the melding together of these elements is what truly achieves sensitivity. You cannot have any element or even any part of any element outside the holistic view of the organisation. See Figure 9.1.

Determinants of individual performance

People performance on the job is determined by both their personal psyche and by the 'performance environment'. Managers can influence people behaviour, and thereby their performance, by focusing on either area. Few managers, however, are trained to assess the psyche of their staff.

We will focus on the performance environment because, as we shall see, each element of the performance environment is within the control of the manager. We will introduce a model for assessing the factors that impact human performance in any particular circumstance.

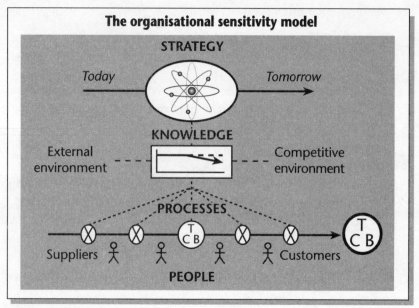

FIGURE 9.1

Typically, when managers are asked to express a preference for dealing with technical or people problems, most reply 'technical'. This is largely because this is their area of expertise, but also because people are 'different' and 'difficult'. Different, because every person is absolutely unique, and therefore, generalisations are often prone to failure in specific circumstances, difficult because people are not rational or predictable (although groups, such as process teams are often seen to be more predictable).

When faced with a 'people problem' the typical response is to find someone to blame. However, whilst individuals are sometimes deliberately unhelpful, the reason for the performance deficiency is typically found in the performance environment and not in the individual themselves. In analysing people problems, the starting point is therefore to gather the facts in a structured 'non-emotional' way, focusing on the specific behaviour that we are concerned about. This can be done either reactively, once a problem has occurred, or proactively if a change is planned.

A further difficulty with people problems is that there is often 'multiple cause' and inconsistency of observed behaviour simply because people are people. Therefore when looking for possible causes, we should focus on the four elements of the performance environment detailed below, all of which have an impact on people's **ability** or **willingness** to do a good job.

The performance environment model

We have broken the performance environment into four distinct but inter-related elements:

➡ requirements

➡ capabilities

➡ resources

➡ rewards. See Figure 9.2.

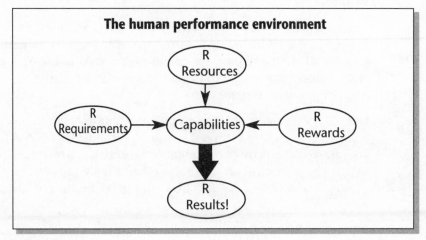

The human performance environment

FIGURE 9.2

Requirements

The starting point is to ensure that it is clearly understood what the desired output is. Without knowing what is required it is impossible to know whether people are doing a good job or a bad job. Performance requirements should be clearly defined, communicated and understood by those performing the tasks, and should be seen as reasonable. The same principles will apply here as applied in setting performance indicators in the previous chapter. The same principles, but now applied at a job or task level.

> **Without knowing what is required it is impossible to know whether people are doing a good job or a bad job.**

Capabilities

Having defined performance expectations, it is then necessary to ensure that we have the right people with the right skills and knowledge doing the task. If people are to be truly 'empowered' it is not sufficient to delegate responsibility for tasks – they must be given the capability to do a good job or else it will result in frustration and failure.

Resources

Skills and knowledge alone are not enough. Successful completion of tasks is often dependent on having the right resources such as facilities, equipment, information, materials and budget.

Rewards

Finally, whilst we now understand what is required, and have the right people with the right resources, this still does not guarantee that people will use the resources to complete the tasks to the best of their ability. Since people need to be motivated and committed, we need to review the reward systems.

Each of the elements of the performance environment model can be seen to act as a chain in that it is only as strong as its weakest link. We can see that if any one element is 'broken' it is likely that the task will not be performed satisfactorily. What is more important for many managers to realise is that it is likely not to be the fault of the person doing the job.

We will explore each of these elements in more detail throughout the rest of this chapter

The environment as an 'enabler' not 'enforcer'

Specifying jobs can often be seen as a means of controlling the way work is performed. Some organisations use very 'tight' controls so that work is specified and almost all activities performed follow some strict procedure. Other organisations view themselves as having a more 'empowered' workforce where people are allowed to get on with their jobs.

The reality is that for different situations, the degree of alignment or empowerment will be different. The reality is that there must always be a balance. Another angle on the safety dilemma at Europower will help to explain this balance.

Europower: do you empower or enforce safety?

Europower Head Office ensured that its procedures fell within its own and European Union standards for safety. These standards were promulgated to the people in the field. Unfortunately safety measures added to the time taken to do a job. They were thus frequently ignored by the workforce, who were motivated to get jobs done fast.

What should we do? Do we empower local management to keep a tight control on tasks involving often-ignored safety precautions? Or should we by inspection enforce the rules?

Perhaps we should put a 'not less than' timescale rather than the more usual 'not more than.'

In fact the problem is a cultural one. Two existing cultures are in conflict with the safety performance environment. The first is job security, meaning that there is no sanction on a persistent rule breaker. The second is the freedom held at the front end to respond fast to crisis situations.

Well, nobody said that life was easy!

How should job requirements be specified?

Outputs not activities

The focus should always be on the outputs from tasks, not the activities. If there is a problem with the outputs, then we should look at the activities in order to find the causes. Specifying outputs focuses on achieving 'alignment'. 'Empowerment' is assisted by being not too specific with the activities.

This can be linked directly to the cross-functional process maps, where the vertical lines, representing hand offs, are all places where there is an output from one person or group to the next. Alignment between what customers require and what suppliers provide must be achieved at all hand offs whether these are between groups inside the organisation or involve external people.

The focus is without doubt on outputs. Once, however, these have been clearly articulated, it may also be advisable to define what

209

activities contribute to success. This should be based on the opinion of experts, including those who actually carry out the activities, and recorded so that new hires can learn from experts simply by referring to documented notes long after the expert has left.

Whether or not activities are also specified will depend on the task, since some jobs have, for example, activities defined as legal procedures. In this case at Europower, it is seen to be necessary to monitor activity which can conflict with the achievement of an operational target.

CASE STUDY

Europower: work done and empowerment

A good example of this enabler, not enforcer, occurs at Europower. There is a measure passed down to all the generating stations called 'availability'. This measures the amount of time during any period when the station was available 'to go on the bars' and be used as a source of power. People talked about 90 per cent availability and increasing.

Senior managers considered this a most significant performance measure, and linked it into the bonus scheme. There was a problem.

One of the ways of putting availability up is to do less routine maintenance. This will tend to increase availability but disguise a potential problem. Eventually the lack of maintenance will cause a major problem and down time.

There was a need to put in another performance indicator which was outputs or work achieved by groups and individuals in terms of routine maintenance.

Indicators and targets

Indicators and target levels of performance are established in exactly the same way as specified for performance reports in the previous chapter.

What capabilities will people need?

Too many plans and processes die because the people involved in implementation do not have the skills to carry out their role. Managers tend to use hunch and instinct in this area, rather than giving it a proper analysis as they would if the process was more project oriented.

What capabilities?

Understanding what outputs and specific levels of performance are required enables the identification of the capabilities required for success. We often hear of changes to job specifications made without the recognition that you need to give people the necessary skills to the do the new job.

It can be a two-edged sword. For example, it is a good idea to train people for their first management role before they are made managers. In fact the training is often done after the person has been in the job for some time. This is not least because the moment you have trained people for a more senior role, they are demanding to know when they are going to be given a new opportunity.

Skill or capability areas can be broken down under three headings:

➡ **content** – where specific knowledge is supplied to enable a person to do a job

➡ **process** – where people are trained in skills of a generally applicable nature, such as project management

➡ **people** – which is the development of the whole spectrum of personal, relationship and people management skills.

Most skills training in organisations is in fact based on content. Historically, every time a new product or service was introduced, people would be given a product- or service-specific training programme. Nowadays, progressive management teams have understood firstly that effective performance is as much related to process skills, as it is to knowledge of the product, and secondly that ever-increasing product and service complexity is making it virtually impossible for anyone to have even a passing knowledge of everything an organisation provides. Figure 9.3 (overleaf) shows a useful checklist describing a general approach to training and curriculum planning. Such a list is at once imposing, and at the same time frightening. Do not forget that everybody will not require all of the skills tomorrow.

Defining levels of competency

For each job or role, there will be an ideal profile since everybody does not need all the skills. The analysis is complete when you categorise the levels of competence required. An effective way of doing this is by using a four-point letter scale.

➡ 0 = zero. No competence required, or this skill is inappropriate for this particular job.

211

General approach to training and planning		
Content	**Process**	**People**
Organisation induction	Strategy formulation	Recruitment and selection
Team induction	Business planning	Appraisal and coaching
Health and safety	Problem solving	Delegation and involvement
Investors in People	Decision making	Performance management
	Project management	Meetings management
Job specific 1	Quality management	Presentation and report writing
Job specific 2	Cost management	Relationship building
"	Knowledge management	Mentoring and coaching
"	Process design and mapping	Personal development planning
"	Risk management	Communications
"	Change management	Personal organisation or time management

FIGURE 9.3

➡ A = awareness. People need to be aware that the competence is required in a process in which they are involved without having to have the competence themselves.

➡ C = competent. People can perform the job without any need for supervision.

➡ E = expert. People not only have the competence but can teach it to others and improve the job or processes where opportunity exists.

Managers need to exercise some caution when considering job titles. A job title does not define absolute skills levels in itself. Increasingly, people work in teams where the team must have the appropriate balance in terms of capabilities. For example, in a team that is managing a major change project, it is unlikely that everybody in the team needs to be an expert in the use of their recently purchased project management software, but at least one of the team does.

Building competency

The starting point for building competency is to define the gap between what level a person currently is at, and what is required for successful performance against their current or future role. If the above profile has been created for all jobs, the size of the gap should be identified through discussions with the manager.

The size of the gap reflects the potential impact if the person is not developed in the way they require.

There are many ways of closing the gaps. Training, using internal or external resources, self-development, mentoring, etc or any combination. There is no absolute rule, and progress may depend on the availability of specialists. When you use the mentoring approach, for example, make sure that the mentor is at least competent. A mentor who is simply 'aware' may do more harm than good.

Increasingly technology is being used to assist with on-the-job training through the use of CD-ROMs and interactive learning videos. However it is done, learning is achieved as much through feedback as anything else and an integral part of the development process should include feedback from a respected mentor.

Once this activity has been completed for the whole team or organisation, a central training and development plan can be created to map the closing of the gaps. This will also take into consideration, the priority of each of the areas and jobs, and the availability of the necessary resources and budgets.

The other use of the capability profile is to help with recruitment, and career and succession planning. Ensuring that people coming into jobs are prepared beforehand can make them much more effective much faster.

What resources will people need?

To recap where we are. We have made sure that the strategy is driving the processes, identified and reviewed the key processes on a cross-functional basis, made sure the knowledge is available to monitor these key processes and are working on ensuring that the people have the competencies required for their part in the process. We now need to look briefly at the allocation of resources to the people involved in the processes.

There will always be requests for more resources than are available. Managers can always think of new ways of spending money, often to very good effect. Senior management will on a regular basis look at the requests and make judgements based on their potential impact on performance. By now this should be made easier by the fact that the process owners have identified the objectives of the process and its key performance indicators in a specific way.

Organisational sensitivity and cross-functional planning should have made the resource allocation process less like a win or lose battle with the rest of the organisation. The resources are being allocated to the process not the function, although for reporting purposes they will probably sit inside one function or another.

Specifying resource types

Eventually managers will allocate budgets to process owners. These budgets are the sum of the costs of the resources which can be broken into:

➡ people (skills and knowledge)

➡ facilities

➡ equipment

➡ materials.

Where access to a rare or unique resource is identified it represents an area of risk, as it increases the probability that this resource will at some stage not be available when required.

Finally, as well as looking for additional resources, it is likely that some resources that are currently consumed or are tied up are no longer required. A change in the way work is carried out should not always result in the need for additional resources.

Specifying quality and quantity

We have said that the key to understanding added value is the concept that inputs plus process equals outputs. This means that for each of the resources it is not enough to specify a description, but also an accurate statement of quantity and quality.

This may result in a need for a detailed performance specification (as would be needed for a computer) and detailed statements of when the resource will be required. This last is particularly important in the case of shared resources such as training facilities.

Balancing costs with benefits

If you ask a manager to think about what will make a task easier to perform he or she will produce a long list of resource needs. It must be recognised, however, that some resources are 'mandatory' in that the task cannot be performed without them, but others can be made up by additional effort, energy and possibly resources in other areas.

It is important to reflect on what is actually required rather than creating a 'wish list'. The only real way of doing this is to have a strong process and discipline of cost justification. This should be relatively straightforward if the value of the process is quantified. Managers can then compare the value added with the cost of obtaining and using the resource.

The counter-argument to this is that the resource is required for a process which is strategic to the organisation. This can first of all be checked against the strategic framework defined earlier and then re-examined to see if the intangible or impossible to quantify benefits actually stack up. Managers' instincts for something needing to be done are often right, but should always be tested against more mundane processes of cost–benefit analysis.

What does the reward system need to look like?

The most elegant processes in the world will only work if people are in some way rewarded for implementing them successfully. They will continue to fail also if failure does not cause some form of pain on behalf of the person who has not performed.

Aligning reward structures

Rewarding people is about motivation. Once they have the capabilities and resources to do what is required, they need sufficient motivation to employ their resources to greatest effect. Once a task is completed the reward can be financial and non-financial.

'Alignment' means ensuring that people are rewarded for completing tasks in a way that maximises the benefit to the organisation. This implies an understanding of what the organisation is trying to do and therefore links directly to the strategy. Without a clear and appropriate strategy, aligning reward structures is virtually impossible, and is 'hit and miss' at the best of times.

The starting point of this strategy-reward structure's 'dynamic' will be the strategy for the organisation. This will then be 'cascaded' through the organisation through the objectives for each of the groups to the people performing the tasks. Recognising this relationship causes us to realise that changing strategy will result in a need to change not only every element of the organisation model, but every element of the performance environment. Change the strategy and we must realign or check the alignment of everything down to individual reward systems. Otherwise, as in this next case, the strategy will not be carried through.

CASE STUDY

A change in the strategy badly communicated through the old reward system

A software company made a top-level strategy change to recognise a need to focus on the maintenance and active management of **costs**. The organisation could no longer afford to continue to develop feature-rich products without ensuring that the development costs were within agreed limits. Unfortunately, no one remembered to tell the people who designed the software. Experienced design engineers were proud of the fact that cost was not a consideration and that they could focus wholeheartedly on making the 'best' technically superior product possible.

The fact that the customer would no longer pay the price for the development work was vitally important to the long-term success of the organisation, but appeared to be irrelevant to the people performing the tasks and consuming resources.

Balancing reward structures

Balancing reward structures ensures that there are positive rewards for doing a good job and negative 'rewards' for doing a bad job. Many people find it uncomfortable to create negative rewards and poor performance tends to go unmarked. It is essential that poor performance is recognised from the point of view of changing behaviour and from the point of view of people who are performing to the necessary quality.

In terms of organisational sensitivity, meetings are an interesting example of a lack of negative rewards allowing unsatisfactory behaviour to continue. Many, many organisations openly recognise that their meetings are typically managed badly, with people frequently arriving late. In one of the UK's largest companies it is more or less guaranteed that every meeting, with the possible exception of key customer contacts, will start late. As the day progresses so the degree of lateness increases from the knock-on effect. This situation will not change until people are told how destructive their behaviour is on the performance of the group overall and meetings which are key to the worst offenders are summarily cancelled. It is also simple for a chairperson to thank the group for their prompt arrival. Unprofessional meetings cost organisations a lot in terms of lost time, poor decisions, lack of consensus and goodwill.

Unprofessional meetings cost organisations a lot in terms of lost time, poor decisions, lack of consensus and goodwill.

When using the word 'reward', people tend to think about pay and bonuses. However, most effective rewards relate simply to the words of feedback used by the manager or simple tokens of appreciation – they cost nothing! Here is a good example of this.

CASE STUDY

Using bacon sandwiches to build team commitment

One enlightened and committed manager in charge of a customer support team wanted to encourage the new way he wanted his team to operate. The 'what's in it for me' culture had set in after initial training, and so when he suggested that they meet as a team before work once a week he was met with anything but enthusiasm. However, with a simple gesture – the provision of free bacon sandwiches – these meetings became popular events and the team spirit and team performance quickly grew.

Providing feedback should be based on a simple premise that firstly people would rather do a good job than a bad job, and secondly that people are very effective 'self-correcting' mechanisms. This sounds reasonable enough but most organisations build their feedback mechanisms around a very different premise by which people only receive feedback about how effectively they are performing a task at their six-monthly or annual review. It is much more effective to give people feedback on performance as and when it happens, and let them respond to what it is telling them.

Many managers find providing feedback to their team difficult and are uncomfortable about doing it. The simple rule can be remembered using the pneumonic RATS. Feedback should be Relevant, Accurate, Timely and Specific.

Remembering that people are unique!

Rewards must be viewed from the perspective of the individual, since everyone responds differently to stimuli. For example, some people working on a project would love the prospect of making a presentation to senior managers about the work they have done, whilst others would hate it. Some are motivated by the challenge of the job, others by how comfortable they feel. This list could go on.

The implications for managers are that effective motivation of people requires a good understanding of them as the people they are. Many managers are uncomfortable about this and therefore avoid it. Without such knowledge, the only reward structures available to the manager are the organisational or 'formal' systems such as pay and remuneration. This will always be part of the solution but does not allow for the individuality of people.

Putting all the elements of the performance model into place (see Figure 9.2) may not guarantee success, but it will enable people and collectively the organisation to work to the best of its abilities.

What are the implications for structure design?

All of this brings us to the topic of designing a structure which is suitable for the sensitive organisation. There is, of course, no universally correct answer, but there are some concepts which will encourage the building of a sensitive rather than an insensitive organisation.

The starting point is clear. A clear strategy drives processes which will tend to dictate the structure. Having said that, the sensitive organisation will then use cross-functional planning teams to ensure that a sensible structure remains effective for a long time.

Defining design criteria

When faced with crises or a significant change in their marketplace, several organisations respond by changing their structure but little else. This approach of structural change to strategic concerns is almost bound to fail, and will typically result in further structural changes on an annual basis as though searching for some 'panacea'. These organisations typically operate in a form of chaos with nobody really understanding what they are supposed to do because the strategy has drifted and because the structure is uncertain.

Once the strategy and processes have been clearly articulated, then the selection of the 'best' structure should be based on a number of selection criteria. These criteria will relate to the degree to which the structure will help to achieve the strategy whilst at the same time take into consideration a number of other areas such as minimising disruption to operations, operating costs or the number of hand offs.

Developing the criteria for the design or selection of the structure should be done by a cross-functional cross-level management team in order to avoid the pitfalls created by previous structures based on personal power bases. A high level of involvement will also help to ensure commitment to the new structure so that 'making it happen' will be that much easier.

The same team will become the checking mechanism for the structure once agreed.

→ Is it suitable (does it fit with the strategy and processes)?

→ Is it feasible (can we make it happen with our limited resources)?

→ Is it acceptable (will people commit to making it happen)?

→ Is it enduring (how long will this structure be appropriate for and how easily can it be changed)?

This last point leads to an important conclusion. There is no doubt that changing a structure conjures up in most people's minds 'Where will I fit in?' The disruption to work during the period of uncertainty caused by a review of the structure can be catastrophic, to the extent where it is not certain that customers will be properly served. The conclusion must therefore be to decide on a strategy-driven structure and live with it.

Unfortunately the world will change and problems will be created by an out-of-date structure. The answer is to retain flexibility by using fluid structures based on cross-functional teams.

Creating fluid structures

Responsiveness and flexibility in the sensitive organisation is built around the planning teams which come together on a permanent or a temporary basis. They are merely an extension of the concept of a process team introduced earlier. Process teams were created with regard to a cross-functional process diagram which identified who was involved and what was their role in the process.

Fluid structures simply take this thinking one step forward by getting managers to think in terms of **process or project teams**. These teams are made up of the people you would naturally turn to on a particular topic. Using this concept, managers at all levels can look at a problem or a required change in process and decide on the need for a new process or project team. This team then comes together and goes through the process already discussed. Starting from a statement of the purpose of the team, deciding on its objectives and putting targets for achievement in place. This is done without changing the structure.

Europower has a problem with a separation of the responsibility for a major customer and the authority to deliver total satisfaction. The answer was not to change the structure, but to create a new planning team.

CASE STUDY

Europower: handling its biggest customer with a natural planning team

The biggest single customer of Europower electricity is the power procurer who works for the Grid Company. Europower also regards the end-user as its customer, but it is there primarily to satisfy the demands of the Grid.

On the distribution side this involves the allocation of resources, particularly maintenance resources, to places where Grid managers see priorities. The service is then provided by the geographic regions which have their own priorities for their finite resources.

Recognising this, senior management put a manager at Head Office in charge of the National Grid account. He had no direct control over the maintenance managers in the regions. The result was frustration for the Head Office manager who claimed the job was impossible without a change in reporting structures which gave him more power to allocate resources.

Instead of this, Europower decided that there was a need for a planning team consisting of the regional maintenance managers, the Head Office manager and one or two other people. This team came together in an atmosphere which, if not actually hostile, was very suspicious.

The planning process did its job. Helped by a facilitator, a purpose was agreed, the environment examined and a series of objectives and activities agreed. The problem had been solved without changing the reporting structures with all the political problems that go with such action.

The concept of process and project teams is the mechanism by which the internal barriers to organisational sensitivity are broken down. It is a simple concept which gives it the added attribute of being feasible.

Having broken down the internal barriers it is only a small step to work on the external ones and bring the customer into direct contact with the planning team.

CASE STUDY

Europower: involving the customer in the planning process

The planning team created to look after the power procurer in the National Grid started its environmental analysis quite rightly from the customer's point of view. It made a reasonable stab at what the Grid's management believed to be its purpose and then used SWOT analysis to try to understand the Grid's starting point.

It quickly became clear that the team lacked some knowledge and in any case it wanted to check some of its key assumptions. The customer was invited to join the team for one of its meetings. The team presented the Grid SWOT. The Grid representatives were first of all very impressed with the work that was being done, not bad for customer relations. They then became progressively more open about their own strengths and weaknesses, which added to the team's understanding of the situation enormously.

At the end of the meeting the next action seemed so obvious that it was hardly discussed before it was implemented. The customer agreed to join this 'natural' planning team on a regular basis, and the relationship and its effectiveness in delivering benefits to agreed cost and time parameters flourished.

One last point about process and project teams. Since they are the mechanism for ensuring that the organisation is sensitive to changing circumstances both internal and external, they must in turn be flexible to changes in the environment. A project team and even a process team may very well complete its task and when it has it should be congratulated, bought a drink and disbanded.

Moving from titles to roles

Getting people to focus on what they do rather than what they are called is a useful step in removing some of the 'politics' from the organisation. In many organisations people are being encouraged to adopt more of a 'portfolio' approach to their jobs and careers. What this means is that they may commit part of their time to one role and part to another. It gives the organisation a much greater flexibility and responsiveness to situations, whilst giving the person much greater diversity of work and fulfilment. This represents a change from 'division of labour' to 'portfolio workers' and is built on by the adoption of the concept of process and project teams.

In summary, process teams not only replace structures but work in different combinations. The traditional functional structures may continue to exist in order to manage the administration elements of managing people, but that is all.

Process teams are a form of permanent teams which are naturally right to execute the process. Short-term or one-off groupings are project teams.

Modifying the performance environment and creating fluid structures

KEY POINTS

Take a few minutes to reflect on each of these.

➡ No matter how effectively the strategy has been formulated or the processes designed, if people have neither the ability nor willingness to perform tasks expected of them, then the organisation will fail.

➡ Individual performance is affected by elements of the 'performance environment': requirements, capabilities, resources and rewards.

➡ When jobs are specified, everything should be done to ensure that people will succeed – the performance environment must be used as an enabler not an enforcer.

➡ People would rather do a good job than a bad job.

➡ Strategy should drive the design of the processes which in turn should drive the choice of structure.

SELF-ASSESSMENT

Rate your organisation or unit on a scale of 1 to 5.

1   Are job requirements jointly set by managers and those performing the tasks? ☐

2   Are they focused on the desired outputs and not on activities? ☐

3   Are requirements clearly articulated, communicated to and understood by those performing the tasks? ☐

4   Are the right people selected for the right jobs? ☐

5   Is there an effective career and succession plan? ☐

6   Are the skills needs for each job specified in terms of 'content', 'process', and 'people' skills? ☐

7   Are people given the skills and capabilities they require? ☐

8   Is there an organisation training plan? ☐

9   Do personal development plans exist? ☐

10 Are the necessary resources made available as and when required – people, information, equipment, facilities and materials. ☐

11 Are they of the right quality and quantity? ☐

12 Are budgets allocated in the most appropriate way – balancing the cost of resources with their application? ☐

13 Are people rewarded in a way that benefits the organisation's overall objectives? ☐

14 Are there positive consequences for doing a good job? ☐

15 Are there negative consequences for doing a bad job? ☐

16 Are people recognised as being individuals and unique? ☐

17 Is there flexibility in the system to allow each individual to contribute to their full potential? ☐

18 Are structures designed to support the efficient operation of the current processes and the performance environment, rather than being based on historical thinking? ☐

ACTION PLAN

Where you scored badly in your self-assessment, identify what
actions you will take to improve your performance.

What?	Who?	When?
1		
2		
3		
4		
5		

'But far more numerous was the herd of such
Who thinks too little and talks too much.'

John Dryden

CHAPTER

10

THE NEED FOR CRITICAL THINKING

Managing complex concerns and making good decisions.

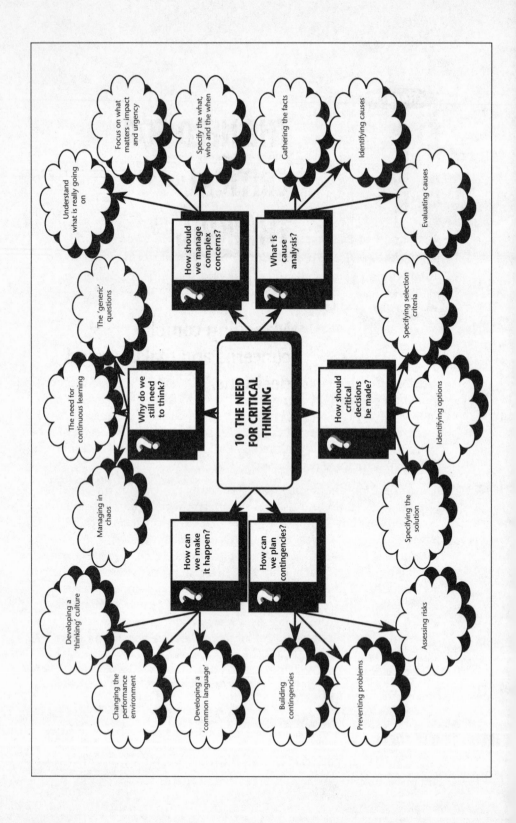

O rganisational sensitivity depends firstly on a plan and then on the ability of all concerned to react correctly when things change or go wrong. The culture has to encourage everyone to think critically about what could be done better.

At the end of this chapter, readers will be able to define and use a standard approach to analysing concerns and decide what to do about them having considered risk and contingency planning.

Why do we still need to think?

At the end of Chapter 5, the topic of continuous analysis was raised. We suggested that customer-focused analysis was a continuous process remaining sensitive to changes and trends in the marketplace. In this chapter we explore another never-ending element of organisational sensitivity, the need for all the people involved in the processes of satisfying customers, both internal and external, to think critically about what they are doing.

Standardisation on an approach to thinking critically in the areas of problems, decisions and risk has significant benefit if it is accepted by everybody as the 'common language'. This is particularly powerful when working with cross-functional teams, and is almost a prerequisite for their success. Short-term teams, such as project teams, or long-term teams, such as 'cross-functional process teams', by their very nature, combine people with different backgrounds, experience, expertise and approach. Bringing such a team together without an agreed way of debating concerns is a recipe for 'destructive conflict' – the team will never agree on the outcome because they don't even agree on the principles.

Critical thinking is the final management skill required in creating organisational sensitivity.

Managing in chaos

One way to manage in chaos is to think ahead and plan. We have discussed how to develop an organisation that is sensitive to its

> *One way to manage in chaos is to think ahead and plan.*

environment through the creation of its strategy, processes and analysis mechanisms. But on a day-to-day basis, even with the best strategy in the world, the organisation will still not manage itself.

As they carry out the 1001 activities which occur on a daily basis people have to think. We cannot plan for every eventuality or situation, and therefore, people still need to be able to resolve issues and concerns 'real-time', as and when they occur.

The need for continuous learning

A common set of 'thinking tools' can help to improve both individual performance and the performance of the team. This is the topic for this chapter, but it should be remembered from the discussion of the performance environment that giving people skills will improve their ability to resolve issues, but it will not affect their willingness to do so.

This takes longer and involves changes to all elements of the performance environment. The essential change is from an organisation where problems are solved for 'workers' by maintenance or management to an organisation where people are responsible for solving their own problems. The cultural element of this will be discussed in Chapter 14.

For the moment, it is interesting to note that the way people view their jobs needs to change. People must no longer turn up to do the job they did yesterday, they need to turn up to perform yesterday's task and to **improve** the way it will be done tomorrow. Ownership of driving positive change is being accepted by those who can influence it most, the ones doing the work. Here is a good example.

CASE STUDY

Improvement is part of carrying out the function

One of the staff of a car manufacturing line made a recommendation to change one of the processes involved in vehicle manufacture. The change was implemented and it saved the company several hundred thousand pounds. For his efforts, he was awarded a plaque and a bottle of champagne. When the press got hold of this story it was represented as miserly, a poor return for a massive benefit. However, when interviewed, the 'hero of the hour' made it quite clear that he viewed the identification and making of such improvements as part of his everyday job!

The 'generic' questions

Back in the late fifties, Ben Tregoe and Charles Kepner conducted some research into individual and organisational effectiveness which subsequently enabled them to construct an international organisation, transferring critical thinking skills to people of all cultures, languages and trades (*The New Rational Manager*, Princeton Research Press, 1981).

Their unique proposition was to identify the 'fundamental' principles for resolving issues. The concepts, which combined rational and creative thinking, were thus considered not to be a management 'fad' but to be simply applied common sense. They explained that critical thinking skills can be broken into four distinct but interconnecting principles, based around four generic questions.

➡ **What is happening?**

➡ **What caused this to happen?**

➡ **What can we do about it?**

➡ **What might happen?**

We will explore each of these areas in more detail under the headings of: Concerns, Causes, Choices and Contingencies. The logic behind the generic questions is that whenever we are faced with a new or complex situation, the first question has to be one that tells us what is going on. Unless we really understand the situation, the specific concerns we might have and their relative priority, we run the risk of taking action which may be inappropriate. The first question is therefore to understand what is really happening.

Once we understand the situation, we need to resolve it in the best way. Frequently, before we can 'fix' something, we need to understand what caused it to happen. For example, we cannot fix a 10 per cent fall off in sales until we know whether it is due to competitor activity, poor sales performance or changing customer expectations. The quality of the resolution is therefore linked to why the situation occurred. The second question seeks to find out what caused this situation to happen.

A clear understanding of what is going on and what caused it to happen is often enough to pinpoint what we need to do to fix it. Sometimes this is made more difficult by the complexity of the situation (possibly involving several functions), the novelty of the situation or the high degree of investment required. In either case, once the cause is known, we need to fix it, so the third question is 'What can we do about it?'

Finally, too often we put our 'fix' in place and run to the next task. However, many of the tasks we perform are correcting things that didn't go right in the first place. So before leaving the current situation, it probably makes sense to spend a few minutes, whilst the information is fresh in our minds, to speculate about 'What might happen?'

When we plot these questions against a timeline as in Figure 10.1, it becomes apparent why these are the four generic questions. If we understand what is going on, and then analyse the past, present and the future, then there is nowhere else to look.

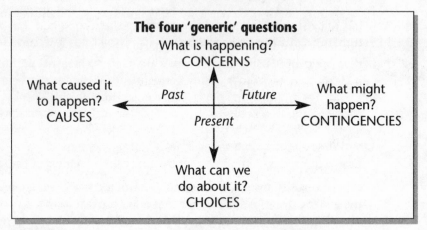

The four 'generic' questions

FIGURE 10.1

How should we manage complex concerns?

We need now to look at the detail and practical implications of the four generic questions.

Understand what is really going on

The tendency in many organisations is to act first and then think once things have gone wrong. In addition the stimulus for many actions is often based on very limited information. A customer phones up and complains that their computer system is 'down'. The operations manager says that a production machine is 'broken'. Sales say that the machine design is 'no good'. If these concerns are to be resolved, more information is required.

This is not to suggest that perfect information is needed to resolve each situation (an approach named 'analysis paralysis'), but a balance needs to be drawn between the need to move quickly and the need to get it right. All too often this balance is missed, and the pressure of needing to be seen to be doing something results in a bias to action within an information vacuum. By asking the right questions it is possible to move from a brief high-level understanding of the concerns to a point at which an 'action plan' can be created which pinpoints what needs to be done, by whom and when.

Concerns normally break into three areas: problems, process and people. Take a simple example of someone using a pick-axe when it breaks. The **problem** is that the pick-axe is broken – we need to do something about that. But if we reflect further, we might question whether there is a concern with our **processes** that allowed us to provide a bad pick-axe in the first place. Finally, we should not forget that the **people** using the pick-axes are likely to be upset and frustrated if this is a problem that occurs frequently, or if the lost production will impact their take-home pay. So we can see how in this simple example, the easy solution is to replace the pick-axe, but it may miss an opportunity to improve a process and therefore fix a problem once and for all. It may be that even if we did replace the pick-axe, productivity may fall off further because of the feelings of the people.

The first step is therefore to really understand all the dimensions of what is going on, and to list all of the concerns that exist.

Focus on what matters – impact and urgency

Looking for concerns can have the unfortunate outcome of finding them. Once found, they need to be fixed, but there is simply not enough time or resources to fix everything.

People tend to make decisions on what to do based on tasks that are enjoyable or whether they like the person that needs the help, or who shouts the loudest. It is vital to focus attention and resources on those concerns of greatest priority.

It is vital to focus attention and resources on those concerns of greatest priority.

To help with concern prioritisation, both the impact of the concern, and the urgency with which it needs to be fixed, should be considered. Impact will vary enormously from situation to situation, from project to project, but frequently four types of impact can be considered:

➡ impact on short-term 'profit' (or equivalent)

➡ impact on long-term 'profit' (or equivalent)

→ impact on customer satisfaction

→ impact on employee satisfaction.

For complex situations it is helpful to plot each concern against a two-dimensional matrix (see Figure 10.2) and ask 'Are we really resolving the concerns in the top right-hand corner?' It is often frightening to discover what is actually happening.

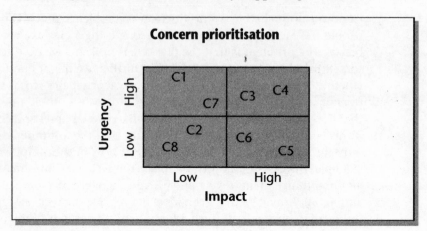

FIGURE 10.2

Some people would argue that the concerns of greatest 'strategic' importance should be those in the bottom right-hand corner. If concerns really are that important strategically, they should be managed 'proactively' and should therefore not fall into the 'urgent' category. Whilst this may appear idealistic, it does make us think about the concerns in a critical way with the realisation that all concerns are not equally important, and that some will have an immediate impact, whilst others are longer term.

Specify the what, who and the when

Having identified which should receive attention in the short versus long term, an action plan can be drawn up, specifying the what, who and when.

→ What is to be done to resolve each individual concern?

→ Who should be involved for success and who should take responsibility – complex concerns will typically require cross-functional involvement?

→ When should the concern be resolved by?

234

So, having discovered which concern we are gong to work on first, the time has come to move to the second generic question.

What is cause analysis?

Finding causes of problems is not always straightforward, and can be tackled using a logical process. First you need to make sure you have the information to hand.

Gathering the facts

Some problems take a lot of effort to resolve, and others seem to hang around for a long time. One reason why problems remain unresolved is a dearth of information or knowledge. Gathering data is time-consuming, and again a balance must be drawn between spending time building up a profile of the 'evidence', and 'getting on with it'.

The guiding principle is to ensure that every activity yields as much as possible in progressing the search for causes. This is particularly true when a problemsolver has tracked someone down and asked some questions, only to find that they have to repeat the exercise later on because they forgot something. Finding people in order to talk to them is not easy so it is important to make the most of it.

The conclusion of many hours observing people 'troubleshoot' problems is that most of the required information can be gained simply by asking more of the right questions at meetings and telephone calls that are happening in any case.

In seeking causes the first question is 'Why?' Whilst we may be involved in situations at the request of others, they will always have an opinion about causes. Certainly if we don't ask, there is no guarantee that they will offer their thoughts for a whole variety of reasons.

Then the Sherlock Holmes approach needs to be used as we look for clues. Clues can be found almost anywhere so a systematic structure is often helpful. When asking questions to gather facts use open questions: why, what, who, which, where, when, how much or many?

Good questioning technique is a matter of phrasing questions in a format that makes sense for each particular situation. This takes practise but, as with Sherlock Holmes, after a while becomes intuitive.

The other side of active questioning is active listening. Poor troubleshooters have an idea of a cause in their mind, and will selectively screen information that supports or opposes their idea. If they are right then great, but if they are not, they have to go back to the start. 'I must go and talk to Peter **again** ....'

Finally, once we have asked questions and listened to answers, the information must be recorded in a format that aids analysis at a later date or by others. This means that it should not appear in text format as a long 'essay'. The answers may be there but they will be no easier to find! Using the questions as headings, and adding facts in bullet point format into the appropriate section as and when they are gathered is probably the easiest way.

The saving in overall time in solving problems can be substantial if the thinking process is completed in a structured way.

CASE STUDY

A problem well described is a problem half solved

Whilst training Japanese and European staff in a common approach to problem solving and decision making, an analytic approach for describing the problem was introduced. This in-depth analysis was initially resisted by the Europeans who started from the point that they did not have time to sit down and think, they needed to *do something*.

On reflection, they realised that many of the actions that they took to resolve problems had no impact on their resolution. They also found that the reason that they didn't stop to think was essentially a cultural one – the managers had created an 'action-oriented' culture. This in itself was not bad, but it was starting to inhibit quality thinking. On the other hand their Japanese colleagues were very comfortable gathering data and analysing data before 'jumping to a solution'. There is an old Japanese proverb saying that 'a problem well described is a problem half solved' and when this organisation took it to heart, things improved.

Identifying causes

So, we have identified a problem, agreed that it is urgent and has high impact and we have gathered specific information from the people involved. Now we need to find out what caused it, or something like it, to occur before. If we have involved the right people in gathering information, we will already know something about the problem and its likely cause. Complex high-value situations such as production lines, health and nuclear power, will typically maintain logs of previous problems and their causes.

If a situation occurs frequently, experts can build software programmes which ask the right questions in the right order and produce the answer. It would be nice if it was always that simple.

The reality is that for many long-term difficult problems, causes could originate in many places. Reflecting on the facts that have been gathered often provides some clues. 'What could cause the problem to occur here and not in other areas – **what is different**?' What could cause the problem to occur at this time and not before – **what has changed**?'

Additional causes can be found through the use of a simple 'cause and effect' diagram as in Figure 10.3. This is a form of structured brainstorming, where possible causes are identified using the four Ms and the environment as headings.

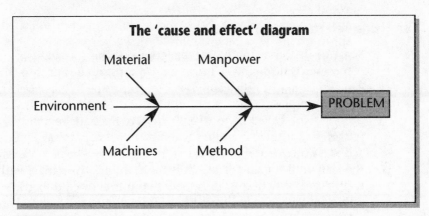

FIGURE 10.3

The brainstorm would thus take the shape of a series of questions. 'Could the cause of this concern be something to do with materials?' 'Could the cause of this concern be something to do with manpower?' And so on.

Evaluating causes

One difficulty with creative problem-solving techniques such as using cause and effect diagrams is that a long list of possible causes is often the outcome. There is rarely the time or resources to put a fix in place against each and every one, and we should not want to. We only want to put a fix in place against the true cause.

Each of the possible causes should be evaluated against the evidence gathered at the start, and those that don't make sense eliminated. The stronger and more complete the evidence is, the more likely it is that the list will be whittled down to a manageable number quickly. This is, of course, another strong argument for spending more time initially gathering facts in the case of complex problems. The remaining possible causes will each need to be evaluated, focusing on those that seem to conform best with the facts. Eventually, and before putting a fix in place, the true cause needs to be confirmed by checking facts or experimenting.

How should critical decisions be made?

We now need to make a decision on what we are going to do. To get to this point we have used good critical-thinking techniques, we can continue with this into the decision-making phase.

Specifying selection criteria

Some causes, once found, can be ignored if the probability of recurrence is negligible. Unfortunately, most do not fit into this category, and once the cause has been confirmed, it is necessary to put a fix in place. Fixes can be either short-term, often called interim, or long-term, called corrective. Corrective fixes are obviously preferred, but there are times when it is necessary to take interim action. A production line leaking oil may have a bucket placed under the leak until the end of the shift for example. The danger with taking interim action is, of course, that it is allowed to become permanent as people get used to a slight discomfort.

In either case, the most appropriate interim or corrective fix needs to be selected. Asking the question 'What did we do last time?' will often result in finding a workable solution, but simply defaulting to the last fix may miss a 'better' fix which may have been uncovered with a little thought.

But how are decisions made, and what do we mean by better? All too often decisions are made by comparing actual options against each other. This will tend to limit the potential fixes by what is already recognised and available. A better way would be to first think about what we want to achieve, and then evaluate each option against these 'selection criteria'. Brainstorming such criteria is best done with the involvement of all those people who will be impacted by the decision, probably a cross-functional team.

For most situations, the criteria will not all be of the same type nor will they be equally important. Take, for example, the case of the leaking machine on the production line. In choosing the best way to fix it, criteria to be considered may include the time taken to make the fix, the cost of the fix, the impact on production, the impact on the maintenance schedule, consistency with health and safety standards and the expected durability of the fix.

Some of these criteria may be mandatory, such as consistency with health and safety standards. Others will be entirely subjective. Furthermore, for the subjective criteria, some will be more important than others. For example, the production supervisor may consider the impact on production to be more important than the impact on the maintenance schedule. Where there is a difference in the relative importance of the subjective criteria, and there usually is, a simple weighting system can be used to reflect the thinking of the group, using, say a ten-point scale.

The resulting list of selection criteria provides a robust foundation against which to compare alternative options. What is meant by the 'best' is now clear, it will be the option that best satisfies the selection criteria.

Identifying options

Whilst it sounds obvious that we should think about what we want from a decision before selecting the answer, it is often not done. Two pitfalls get in the way. Firstly the 'status quo' or 'what was done last time' is an easy option accepted by default, and secondly, people tend to have a strong preferred option beforehand which inhibits further analysis. Sometimes such preferred solutions are also the best, in which case the selection criteria can be used to validate them.

If not, a range of options should be created using both rational and creative thinking. This process is often helped by the involvement of people who know nothing about the situation, but are willing to ask the 'stupid questions', again cross-functional involvement. A group consisting of only technical or marketing people will tend to come up with technical or marketing solutions, whereas the ideal may be some creative combination of the two.

The sound foundation created by a robust set of selection criteria allows people to be creative knowing that anything they come up with will still be evaluated in terms of those criteria.

Specifying the solution

Once the selection criteria have been agreed, and the options created, the hard work is done.

By evaluating each option in turn against each of the criteria, some will be rejected because they don't satisfy the mandatory criteria. The best performer will be the one that 'best' satisfies the subjective criteria. Again, a ten-point scale can be used to create a weighted score for each option. Where numbers are used, they should only be used to reflect the thinking of the team, and should not be used to create a science out of the art of critical thinking and decision making.

How can we plan contingencies?

So far we have looked at critical thinking in terms of finding causes of problems and choosing suitable actions to solve them. But stopping the problems occurring in the first place may well be a more profitable piece of critical thinking.

Assessing risks

Many organisations have a 'fire-fighting' mentality. Many even proudly claim 'it's what we're good at'. This 'cultural' difficulty is often compounded by the realisation that formal and informal reward systems actively reward fire-fighters. Reflect on who gets the glory – people who work hard for 24 hours to resolve crises once they have occurred, or those that work tirelessly to prevent crises that never actually happen?

It would be wrong to lose the capability to fight fires once they occur, but the potential gains from preventing fires in the first place is often enormous. There are two ways that future problems, 'risks', can therefore be managed. Preventing them in the first place or responding to them once they have occurred. The risk management 'dynamic' is shown in Figure 10.4.

Managers need to focus on those risks which represent the greatest threat. The size of the threat can be determined by reflecting on both the probability that each will occur, and the impact if it does. Clearly, focus for managing future risks should be on those that are both highly probable and likely to have a high impact.

Managers need to focus on those risks which represent the greatest threat.

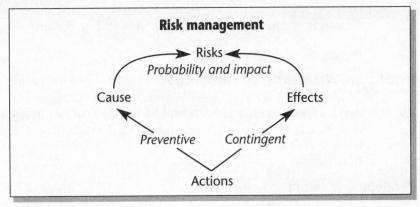

FIGURE 10.4

Preventing problems

When attempting to prevent problems, all actions are targeted at reducing the probability that they will occur. We have suggested that identifying causes is often a necessary step in fixing problems. In the same way, in order to identify actions that will prevent risks, it is useful to specify what is likely to cause each risk.

For example, the risk of a fire in a hotel has at least two likely causes – 'smoking' or 'electrical faults'. Eliminating this risk is therefore achieved by taking action to prevent the smoking and electrical faults causing a fire.

Identifying actions which will avoid risks does not mean that they will be taken. Taking any kind of action costs time and consumes resources. 'Is it worth it?' To answer this question, the cost of each preventive action should be compared against the benefits gained by reducing the risk.

Sometimes the cost of taking action to eliminate risk will be prohibitive. For example, a risk for field service engineers is that they may not be able to communicate with base because their mobile phones may malfunction. It is unlikely that a second machine would be issued to prevent this. In this case, contingencies would be put in place.

Building contingencies

Contingencies exist to reduce the impact of the risk should it occur. The impact is assessed through a detailed understanding of the effects that the risk is likely to have. The question to ask is simple 'What will we do if this risk does occur?'

However, cost–benefit analysis must again be considered and each contingency must cost less than the 'do nothing' option.

How can we make it happen?

Application of the concepts introduced in this chapter invariably leads to improved individual performance through the more effective resolution of problems.

Developing a 'common language'

We have said that a common approach to problems, decisions and risk is a major contributor to the smooth working of cross-functional teams. The likelihood of destructive conflict is high if managers cannot agree on the principles of debate, let alone on the best action plan.

This is one of the major difficulties faced by Boards of Directors. By definition they are a team of functional specialists who have very different, although probably complimentary, skills. Without an agreed way of debating issues, it is no wonder that debate in the boardroom often degenerates into 'corner fighting' or consensus through averaging as in 'democratic' voting.

The benefits of having a common approach through which unique skills can be combined are clear:

➡ faster decision making

➡ greater commitment to the solution

➡ a more robust 'fix' that satisfies cross-functional groups

➡ a greater understanding of what really drives organisational and functional performance – organisational sensitivity.

Through visibility of thinking and decisions, knowledge and understanding are automatically transferred to others.

If a common approach is to be achieved, it is also important that thinking is made visible. Through visibility of thinking and decisions, knowledge and understanding are automatically transferred to others. This visibility also improves managers' ability to gain the commitment of others.

Changing the performance environment

For individuals and the organisation to adopt and use 'critical thinking skills' intuitively, it will require people to change the way they behave in certain situations. As with all desired behavioural change, all change will need to be supported by changes to each and every element of the performance environment.

The **requirements** of key tasks will need to be respecified. For example, many organisations insist that a robust set of selection criteria are developed and agreed by managers from several functions before any managerial new hire is selected.

Changing the way a task is performed is difficult enough, but the real benefit comes when people start to think differently. Improving people's **capability** will take time, formal education and reinforcement of the ideas through regular review sessions. During these sessions, real concerns are evaluated using the concepts of critical thinking. Some additional **resources** may also be required. For example it is likely that information systems will need to be changed to provide people with the knowledge they require as and when they require it.

Finally, there must be positive **rewards** for people who achieve real performance improvements through use of the ideas. Unfortunately, experience also shows that there will be people who will try to resist the new 'way of working' whatever it happens to be. Therefore, there must also be negative consequences for people who decide to act as individuals against the interests and wishes of the team.

A common methodology for critical thinking helps to break down geographical and other natural barriers.

CASE STUDY

Crossing cultural and communication barriers

The language differences often experienced when working across functional boundaries are much more visible when divisions of an international organisation work across real language, cultural and geographical boundaries. A major Japanese car manufacturer trained engineers in Japan, UK and the US in a 'common approach' to problem solving and decision making based on 'best practice'.

One well-publicised application of the techniques involved selection of a new component for a new car. Senior managers at the plant were surprised at the outcome which effectively overturned the initial recommendation. They were even more surprised when they subsequently learned that the net saving to the company would certainly exceed £500,000, and that dialogue between the centres had significantly improved.

Developing a 'thinking' culture

The success or failure an organisation has in changing the way things are done is directly related to the level of leadership shown by the chief executive and the top team. No matter what people think of new concepts, if their boss doesn't use the ideas then sooner or later they won't either.

> *The success or failure an organisation has in changing the way things are done is directly related to the level of leadership shown by the chief executive and the top team.*

Furthermore, the use of critical thinking is so fundamental to an organisation's ability to implement the strategic and operational plans it has developed, that it should not be seen as just another training or HR initiative, but as part of the culture – 'first think, then act'.

The need for critical thinking

KEY POINTS

Take a few minutes to reflect on each of these.

➡ Performance can be improved through making people more effective individually, and through team improvement by developing a common approach for resolving concerns.

➡ When resolving concerns, four 'generic' questions reappear.

  – What's going on?
  – What caused it to happen?
  – What can we do about it?
  – What might happen?

➡ A simple four-step model can be used focusing on the '4 Cs': concerns, causes, choices and contingencies.

➡ Concerns should be identified, clarified and priorities set using an assessment of impact and urgency. An action plan can then be developed that specifies 'who does what and when' to resolve each concern.

➡ Causes should be evaluated against a systematically collected set of facts.

➡ Choices should be evaluated against specified selection criteria representing organisation priorities and all the stakeholders involved.

➡ Contingencies should be planned to allow the proactive management of future concerns.

➡ Critical thinking must combine rational and creative techniques.

SELF-ASSESSMENT

Rate your organisation or unit on a scale of 1 to 5.

1 Are concerns resolved proactively (before they occur) or reactively? ☐

2 Is a 'fire-fighting' culture supported? ☐

3 Could people resolve concerns more effectively either individually or as a team? ☐

4 Is there a common approach that allows functional specialists to work together as a team? ☐

5 Could teams work more effectively through use of a common language for resolving cross-functional concerns? ☐

6 Are concerns clarified and prioritised before action is taken? ☐

7 Do we 'act then think'? ☐

8 Is the impact and urgency of each concern understood before allocating time and money to fix them? ☐

9 Are the right people always involved and the right methods always used when resolving concerns? ☐

10 Are facts gathered in a logical and systematic way when finding causes? ☐

11 Is the true cause always confirmed? ☐

12 Are some fixes put in place that do not solve the problem? ☐

13 Are selection criteria specified before choosing between alternative options to fix the concern? ☐

14 Do the criteria reflect all stakeholders and are they prioritised? ☐

15 Are risks always assessed and proactively managed whenever making a change or putting a fix in place? ☐

16 Does the performance environment support a 'thinking' culture? ☐

ACTION PLAN

Where you scored badly in your self-assessment, identify what actions you will take to improve your performance.

What?	Who?	When?
1		
2		
3		
4		
5		

PART 4

CHANGES

What tools do managers need to create?

'In our company, all our successes are unplanned,
and all our plans are unsuccessful.'

Most salespeople at some point in their careers

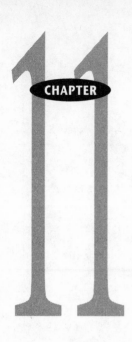

TAKING CONTROL

The plan-execute-reflect-
learn model (PERL).

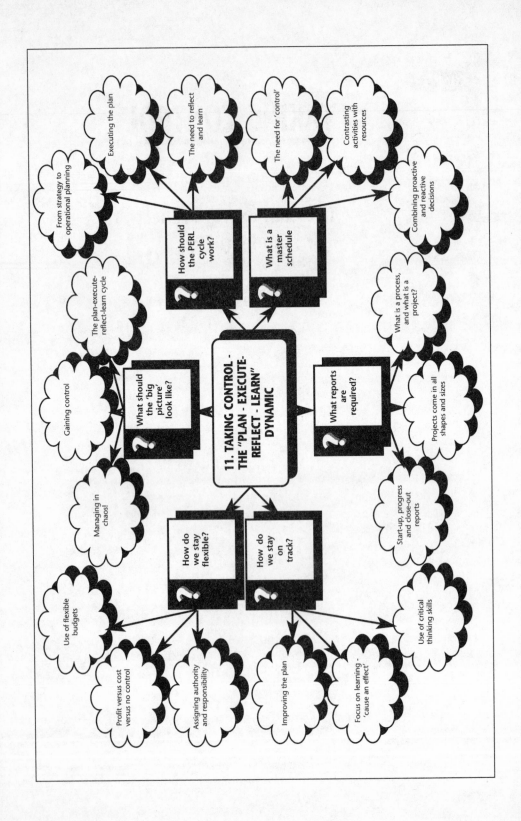

11. TAKING CONTROL - THE "PLAN - EXECUTE - REFLECT - LEARN" DYNAMIC

How should the PERL cycle work?
- Executing the plan
- The need to reflect and learn
- From strategy to operational planning

What is a master schedule
- The need for 'control'
- Contrasting activities with resources
- Combining proactive and reactive decisions

What should the 'big picture' look like?
- The plan-execute-reflect-learn cycle
- Gaining control
- Managing in chaos!

What reports are required?
- What is a process, and what is a project?
- Projects come in all shapes and sizes
- Start-up, progress and close-out reports

How do we stay flexible?
How do we stay on track?
- Use of flexible budgets
- Profit versus cost versus no control
- Assigning authority and responsibility
- Improving the plan
- Focus on learning - 'cause an effect'
- Use of critical thinking skills

How do managers link the strategic plan with the operating plans, cross-functional processes and major projects? And how do teams monitor and modify the implementation of the plan?

At the end of this chapter, readers will be able to use a method of reviewing progress and describe how a master schedule holds the key to control and budgeting.

What should the big picture look like?

The methods discussed so far, from customer-focused analysis to critical thinking will help to create an organisation which is sensitive to external and internal events and environmental changes. The problem then becomes one of continuing the processes and controlling them.

Managing in chaos

The degree to which an organisation manages in chaos is, to a certain extent, dependent on its ability to be proactive in managing changes in its external environment. For a few of the world's largest organisations, the 'chaos' that they work within is what they have chosen to allow. Microsoft's ability to dictate the development of the software markets is a good example of this. However, for most organisations this is a tactic they do not have the option to employ.

The result is that the planning of the sensitive organisation is always based on the best information currently available. Recognising this, there will always be a certain amount of chaos where flexible and rapid responses to crises may be the only way to survive.

This cannot mean, however, that management does not need to find processes for trying to lead and be in control.

Gaining control

Recognising that there will always be a balance between proactive and reactive management of the organisation does not imply that it is only the proactive side which requires effective management. Thus assume that the strategic plan has given priority to one or two key cross-functional processes, one or two key projects and that all of these are aimed at improving their potential for the future. Management still has to manage current processes and react to problems and changes as they occur.

Europower is facing this problem.

Europower: problems of linkage

A major review of processes at Europower Power Generating Division had been completed. As a result all functions and many cross-functional teams had a customer-oriented SWOT analysis, a series of new process teams and a number of newly reviewed maintenance and development projects.

What they then found was a problem in linking these to the normal operating plans and budgets. What was emerging were two levels of plan implementation, the new strategic plan with its change projects and the old work plans and output indicators. In the course of time this became a serious problem. Indeed managers were becoming relieved if a critical issue at the operating level cropped up as it gave them excuses for slipping the longer term exercises.

They needed a linking mechanism and stricter prioritisation. They needed a plan for resources, including their own time, to make real progress with longer term matters.

Organisations also need a process which ensures that the identification of the need for change can be linked with the ability and willingness to change.

As we will see, the master schedule will afford this linkage.

Organisations also need a process which ensures that the identification of the need for change can be linked with the ability and willingness to change. This, and the need to change by the right amount and in the right direction must not be left to chance.

The plan-execute-reflect-learn cycle

To help identify each of the elements in what might be called the 'control system' we can use the plan-execute-reflect-learn model shown in Figure 11.1.

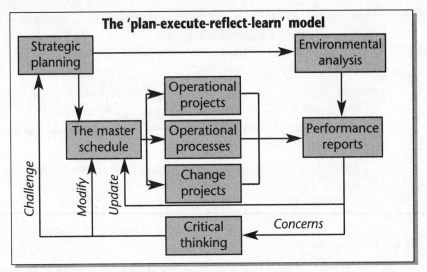

FIGURE 11.1

Some elements of the model will already appear familiar as we have covered them in earlier chapters. These include strategic planning, environmental analysis, operational (or cross-functional processes), performance reports and critical thinking. The master schedule is covered in this chapter, but essentially fills the gap between the strategic plan and the day-to-day activities completed within the organisation.

The model follows the logical progression from planning of organisational activities, execution of those activities, reporting of performance and concerns, and the continuous improvement of performance through challenging the strategy, and through the modification or updating of the master schedule. This gives us the linkage we require. This is how the cycle works.

How should the PERL cycle work?

There are two key linkages between the strategic plan and the day-to-day operating plans.

From strategy to operational planning

Two key outputs are produced from the strategic planning process which will drive the control system. They are firstly the **activity matrix** which contains details of what products and services will be provided to which customer or market groups, and what the forecast

255

volumes will be. Secondly, the strategic plan will identify **capabilities** required by the organisation which will be required for effective implementation of the strategy, but which do not currently exist.

Both of these outputs will be required as key inputs to the master schedule. This tool is a schedule of all activities to be completed by the organisation on a rolling 12-month basis in order to achieve targets set in the activity matrix, and in order to build capabilities through the execution of change projects.

The master schedule is a short-term planning tool. It takes the 'high-level' long-term view presented in the strategy, and identifies in very real terms what must be achieved in the short term.

Executing the plan

We have already discussed how the activities that are completed in order to produce the products and services from the organisation are linked together in the form of operational processes. For some organisations, they are not based around a continuous throughput style of operation, but around a series of independent and unique projects. These projects are predominantly cross-functional again, and it is often argued that they are still 'processes' with the special attributes of having a specified start and end point. By their nature, they are also typically more complex. If they were simple repeat projects, then essentially they become a process.

For example, in the case of Europower, a major refurbishment of a turbine would be a project, while the planning and execution of routine maintenance would be a process. Both are operational in as far as both represent how operational activities actually get completed.

The third category of activity performed inside the organisation has nothing to do with the meeting of specified customer orders. These are the 'change projects'. These activities are those that are necessary to complete the change projects identified in the strategy, and which are considered necessary for the organisation's ability to meet future orders. Such projects may include the design and installation of a new computer system, or the satisfactory conclusion of a major review of work practices and role changes. This last, as we have seen, may include the combining of jobs into more flexible job responsibilities.

The need to reflect and learn

We have already discussed the reason for and the importance of performance indicators. These are required to identify where elements of the master schedule are not being realised, and therefore where remedial action will need to be taken. This reflecting and learning process does not happen by itself, and regular reviews need to be conducted which integrate the effectiveness of all functions. The model also identifies how inputs from the ongoing external analysis will be needed to help identify causes for problems. For example, an internal indicator may identify that sales are low in a particular market, but without knowledge of competitor and customer trends in that market, it will not be possible to confirm what is the true cause.

If, on reflection, the plan is being achieved as and when specified, and all performance indicators are within target, then no further action will be required other than to update the master schedule on a monthly basis. However, if problems are identified then action will need to be taken. This analysis of the situation and determination of corrective action requires the use of 'critical thinking' skills. Some organisations call this the management of the 'churn'.

Two key objectives should be considered when reviewing concerns – what are we going to do about it, and how should we change our planning so that it does not happen again? The reality is that in most 'reactive' organisations, the first question is asked and answered, but somehow the organisation fails to learn for next time. This activity does not happen by itself and needs to be formally instigated, as well as supported through the organisation's culture. This will be covered in more detail in Chapter 14.

Once the concern is fixed, the 'learning' activity should confirm whether there is a need to review or challenge the current strategic thinking (can we really achieve our targets in our key markets?), or whether there is a need to modify the master schedule (was the plan overambitious in the first place?)

What is a master schedule?

Until managers have combined all the work implied by the strategy and operating plans, they will be unable to map resource requirements into the plans and set priorities where there are clashes of resource needs. This master schedule is the tool which brings all this together. Most organisations will require a master schedule at several levels.

The need for 'control'

All three activities (processes, projects and change projects) comprise the total activities performed by an organisation in pursuit of its short- and long-term commitments. As such, all three consume scarce resources. In order to ensure that the organisation has sufficient resources as and when required, the master schedule must identify requirements and availability, specifically for people and budget.

The plan will not be executed if there are insufficient resources when required, and the organisation will not survive into the long term if the organisation operates inefficiently with a surplus of resources. A balance is required and this must be specified within the master schedule.

Contrasting activities with resources

The master schedule contrasts the total commitments of the organisation, or parts of the organisation, against resource availability. It is divided into three independent and inter-dependent sections, operational processes and project commitments (depending on whether the organisation is process- or project-based), change project commitments and resources. See Figure 11.2.

Typically, it shows commitments against a rolling 12-month timeline, and allows managers to look out over the short term and identify how they will be able to meet their operational and change commitments. To do this, monthly production forecasts need to be produced for each product or service line, and project plans will be needed for each operational or change project. This should be standard practice in any case but unfortunately often is not. For many organisations, even though they know change activities will be required, they are rarely planned to the same degree as operational projects with people assuming that they will happen somehow.

Once it is known when projects will start and end, and what the total production forecasts will look like on a monthly basis, it is then possible to identify what resources, of what type will be required, again on a rolling monthly basis.

The resources section can be grouped by function or whatever is the standard organisational structure in use at the time (project team, divisional etc). In each of the monthly columns, for each of the functions, it should show the resource requirements in total for all project and process activities covered by the plan. Whilst the focus is often on the number and type of people required, full budgets will need to take into consideration all resource needs including facilities, materials and equipment.

This 'big picture' rarely exists inside most organisations, and yet the information itself exists but is spread across functional and project

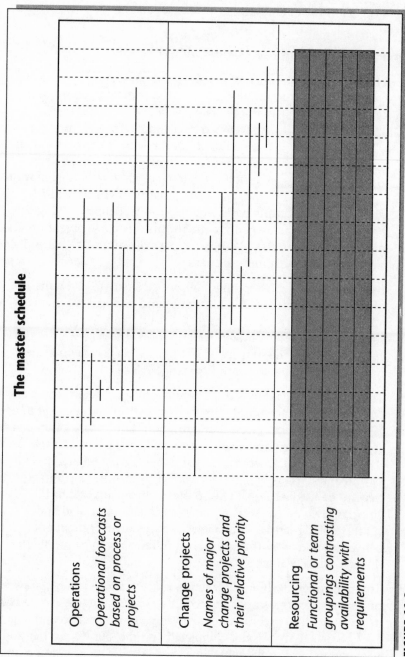

The master schedule

Operations

*Operational forecasts
based on process or
projects*

Change projects

*Names of major
change projects and
their relative priority*

Resourcing

*Functional or team
groupings contrasting
availability with
requirements*

FIGURE 11.2

managers. Information vacuums encourage functional thinking, because that is all managers can see. The master schedule presents people with the big picture, and everyone can see what is going on in all parts of the organisation.

Combining proactive and reactive decisions

The master schedule is a powerful tool if used correctly, and its creation is often far simpler than its degree of complexity would imply. Its degree of fine-tuning can be developed over time as the organisation becomes comfortable with the new way of planning and managing resources across functions. For example, several organisations now plot not only the resource requirements by function on a monthly basis, but also the availability, taking into consideration holiday periods etc. In this way these organisations can plan for the use of flexible or part-time staff, and plan their full-time staffing levels much more accurately.

The master schedule is a powerful tool if used correctly.

Its application has two primary purposes. Firstly to allow the organisation to plan its total activities and resource requirements in advance. It clearly answers the 'Is it feasible?' challenge to the strategy. It puts much more detail on 'how' and 'when' the targets specified within the strategy will be achieved and whether the necessary resources and cash flow will be available.

The second application is more reactive. The master schedule allows the organisation to consider how it can and should respond to events. Without this overall picture, organisations and groups often continue to accept more and more commitments in the belief that they will do it somehow. That, of course, is just not possible and one of a number of outcomes occurs: milestones will get pushed back; contractors will need to be used, the quality of projects or outputs will be compromised or, worst of all, people become exhausted and disillusioned. A crisis, when viewed in the larger context of all of the activities and commitments, takes a different perspective. 'Perhaps we don't need to deal with it today... .'

This control on dealing with the unexpected also assists with ownership of performance measures and accountability. Making regular decisions against the master schedule removes the 'fuzziness' of accountability. 'I know that activity was not completed on time, but we diverted to this pressing problem' stops being an excuse because the decision to divert is clear to the owners of the plan through the master schedule.

What reports are required?

The owners of plans need to have regular reports to check on progress. The owners of the plan must make sure that the bureaucracy of the planning process, that is reporting on milestones, does not become a substitute for making real progress. A key issue in this is the differentiation between projects with a defined life and processes which continue for ever.

What is a process and what is a project?

We have already discussed process performance reports in Chapter 8. However, projects do differ in as far as they have, as well as definable 'milestones' (event-driven review points), a start point, and an end point. In this regard, there are three additional reports we should briefly discuss. These are start-up, progress and close-out reports.

Projects come in all shapes and sizes

One of the biggest changes in project management thinking in recent years, is that 'project management' is not just the domain of the project manager. Project management used to be viewed as a technical or specialist skill, whereas nowadays it is viewed as a basic management skill for all levels and functions. The reason for this becomes obvious from the master schedule. Probably every manager involved in implementing the plan will have responsibility for activities contained in a project.

Projects come in all shapes and sizes. We have already identified two types, the operational project and the change project. But the size of the project is not material as to whether or not it is a project. Installing a new printer is as much a project as hiring a new member of staff, or fixing a customer machine, or building the channel tunnel. An example of a project in the finance field could be the determination of the starting or datum point for new performance indicators.

All projects consume resources, some at a greater rate. But if we add up all of the small projects they become significant, and must be accounted for in our planning. If we ignore the small projects because they are small, we will always find that we run out of time or go over budget at the end of the year.

Start-up, progress and close-out reports

Projects will have the same need for clearly defined performance objectives, indicators and targets. The clearer the picture of success, the more likely it is that it will be achieved. As an aid to this, projects have three additional reports, the start-up, progress and close-out reports. Start-up and close-out reports happen once at the start and end of the project, but progress reports will occur on a regular time- or event-driven basis, and will depend on the duration of the project.

Because projects, by their nature, are somewhat more complex than process (repeat activities), additional check boxes will appear in project reports. Many groups, often cross-functional, will participate in projects. For these 'teams' this is often the first time they have worked together, and some of the routine ground rules that will have been long established within existing processes will have to be agreed.

The start-up report will ensure that all success criteria are in place at the start of the project, and will ensure that the team is committed and knows what is required of it. Progress reports are essentially the same as process performance reports, but will also identify the key achievements in the most recent and the next reporting period, together with details of outstanding concerns.

The close-out report will ensure that the objectives set in the start-up report were achieved. The close-out report should also be the primary means by which the team and organisation learns from the project, and what it would do differently next time. In this way, it will challenge strategy or result in a modification of the master schedule for future projects.

Examples of start-up, progress and close-out reports are available from the authors on request.

How do we stay on track?

There are many similarities between the sensitive organisation and the learning organisation. In most cases sensitive organisations are also good learning organisations. In both cases, management builds a culture of cross-functional thinking and reflection on what has gone in the past in order to improve what will happen in the future.

Use of critical thinking skills

Where concerns are identified, it is clearly beneficial to resolve them as efficiently and effectively as possible. The use of critical thinking skills will not only help to keep the organisation or team on track, but will help to ensure a thorough diagnosis of the situation, which in turn will aid learning.

This was covered in Chapter 10 against the '4 Cs' technique of concerns, causes, choices and contingencies.

Focus on learning – 'cause and effect'

The review and redesign of processes must have a focus on learning. Managers must be aware that this may not happen because people are too busy, or because it is simply not in their interests to do so. It is often somebody else who benefits when we try to fix things for the future, so organisational sensitivity demands that all processes review and transfer learning points.

Learning from a situation requires a sound cause and effect analysis.

Learning from a situation requires a sound cause and effect analysis. What we see in a situation is the effect, low market share, high number of complaints, or high staff turnover. But to learn from these situations, we must identify cause, and then take the action necessary to prevent recurrence.

The process of learning and willingness to learn is again related directly to the culture within the organisation, and will be reviewed in Chapter 14.

Improving the plan

Once the key lessons have been learned, we must act. Taking appropriate action may require changing the strategic plan, and master schedule, or changing the way activities are completed. If a change is required at the strategic level then this must take place first, since there is no point in changing a process if the process will not be required tomorrow.

How do we stay flexible?

A well-constructed plan at top level will fail if its cascading to the next levels of activity is not accompanied by appropriate budgeting and reward systems. In the sensitive organisation, cross-functional teams deal with this in a thought through but flexible way.

Assigning authority and responsibility

Ownership of the PERL model must rest with the chief executive and the top team, since it defines how the organisation is controlled.

However, it is likely that each element will be the responsibility of a variety of people from across all parts of the organisation.

Certainly, the master schedule should be repeated at team or functional level. This is how managers proactively plan for how resources will be committed against change and operational activities within their own function or team. Interestingly, such 'planning boards' normally do exist at this level. It is higher up that you find the vacuum. For the organisation, the 'ideal' is that the master schedule for the organisation will simply be a consolidation from each of the teams or functions.

However it is managed, the key is to ensure that every element has responsibility clearly identified.

Profit versus cost versus no control

The process of planning is made more difficult because it is often driven by artificially set targets or budgets. There is a major trend in recent years to transfer control over budgets to local teams and groupings. This has the impact of transferring ownership for performance to a local level and to the place where improvements can be identified and actioned, and generally makes a positive contribution to organisational sensitivity.

Planning for the allocation and use of resources will be directly impacted by the reporting system used. Again, there needs to be a balance between giving the local manager the tools and authority to do the job, and not overly complicating the system without any clear benefit.

There is no absolute rule for this, although some general principles apply. No accountability for budget spend tends to lead to an inefficient allocation of resources, and the clear presence of operational drift. This is seen as 'resource hogging' just in case they may be required, structures that are out of date for the current market requirements and facilities that used to be fully utilised currently operating at half capacity.

The establishment of cost centres often helps to make people focus on internal costs, but will often drive pessimistic forecasting at the beginning of the planning period. Profit centres can give the individual manager the greatest degree of autonomy and responsibility, but there can be difficulties with transfer pricing, and if they are established around the old functional structures, then they can reinforce functional power bases and hierarchical thinking.

You can, however, take the profit centre principle too far.

Financial pressure can become counterproductive

One company, because it had got itself into serious financial problems, recruited a new Managing Director whose background was finance.

He rightly diagnosed the root of the problem as being in sales management. The sales managers were used to working with high gross margins and had developed expensive habits of discounting and providing free support.

They were not 'spending the company's money as though it were their own' and the company had become vulnerable to any slow down of revenue which threatened to cause further cash problems.

By Herculean effort the company's accountants produced the information and systems to push real profit centre management down to first-line sales managers.

This lasted only for one year. The sales managers became totally introverted about their p and l's and balance sheets. If, for example, a salesperson wanted to offer a trade-in of an old product to support a campaign to sell a new one, sales managers would spend a huge effort to unload the second-hand product on someone else's territory. If they failed to do so, the product was charged to their profit and loss account.

They would disallow sales in favour of making money in some other way.

It cannot be said that the year-long experiment did not work. Once the situation was made more standard by lifting the level of profit centres, the first-line managers were much more conscious of selling profitably.

We need a method of connecting budgets, cost and profit centres to the cross-functional teams created to review, redesign and implement the processes by which inputs are turned into outputs.

Use of flexible budgets

Clearly, one reason why the budgeting process is often of great influence is that it is used as the basis for the formal reward system. If it is to work, consideration must also be given to how to ensure that reward systems have a significant cross-functional 'team' basis.

Ultimately, the use of 'flexible budgets' appears to be giving organisations the best of both worlds. When set up correctly it gives individual managers the control over their operations, but it also ensures that they must work closely with managers from other areas internal and external. Flexible budgets also ensure that the focus on satisfaction of customer needs is done at an acceptable price.

The flexible budgeting process can then be linked directly with the master schedule. This will ensure that if a change is required to the plan, it is possible to do so. Furthermore, it will also be in the interests of each manager to get the change made. Many organisations seem to spend too much time doing things to stay on plan, even when the plan is clearly no longer appropriate. The reason is simply that they are operating to a fixed budget.

Taking control

KEY POINTS

Take a few minutes to reflect on each of these.

➡ Formulating strategy and designing processes does not guarantee success – operational and change activities must be managed and modified constantly.

➡ No matter how good the planning is, the organisation must still remain flexible and responsive.

➡ Use of a 'control model' shows the links between planning and control – plan-execute-reflect-learn.

➡ 'Plan' includes the longer term strategic panning and the master schedule.

➡ 'Execute' includes all operational and change activities, whether performed in processes or projects.

➡ 'Reflect' necessitates the creation and review of performance reports from both internal and external sources.

➡ 'Learn' requires the use of critical thinking skills to change the plan or improve the way activities are performed next time.

SELF-ASSESSMENT

Rate your organisation or unit on a scale of 1 to 5.

1   How effectively is the strategic plan linked to operational plans and activities? ☐

2   Do the activity matrix and capability needs drive activities? ☐

3   Are total commitments, both operational and change, clearly specified and planned against a timeline? ☐

4   Is the operational plan SAFE? ☐

5   Does the activity part of the master schedule exist? ☐

6   Are resource requirements for all activities identified and made available as and when required? ☐

7   Does the resource element of the master schedule exist? ☐

8   Are activities completed as and when specified in the plan? ☐

9   Are milestones or budgets missed? ☐

10 Is there a balance between commitment to getting today's jobs done (operational projects and processes), and preparing for tomorrow (change projects)? ☐

11 Is the priority defined? ☐

12 Is the master schedule used when assessing the potential impact of change? ☐

13 Are changes accepted in the belief that 'it will happen somehow'? ☐

14 Are the necessary reports produced to allow effective reflection and learning to improve planning and performance next time? ☐

15 Do projects have start-up, progress and close-out reports? ☐

16 Are there regular process performance reports? ☐

17 Are there activities planned to ensure organisational and individual learning? ☐

18 Is time allocated to learning and improving? ☐

19 Is the strategy really challenged and changed if needed or will people simply 'muddle through'? ☐

20 Are short-term operational plans changed without thinking about the long term? ☐

21 Do the budgetary and information systems support the use of a reflective control cycle and allow for the constant re-evaluation as the situation changes? ☐

ACTION PLAN

Where you scored badly in your self-assessment, identify what actions you will take to improve your performance.

What?	Who?	When?
1		
2		
3		
4		
5		

'Good, the more communicated,
the more abundant grows.'

Milton

CREATING THE ORGANISATION-WIDE KNOWLEDGE CENTRE

Organisational sensitivity
depends on shared
knowledge.

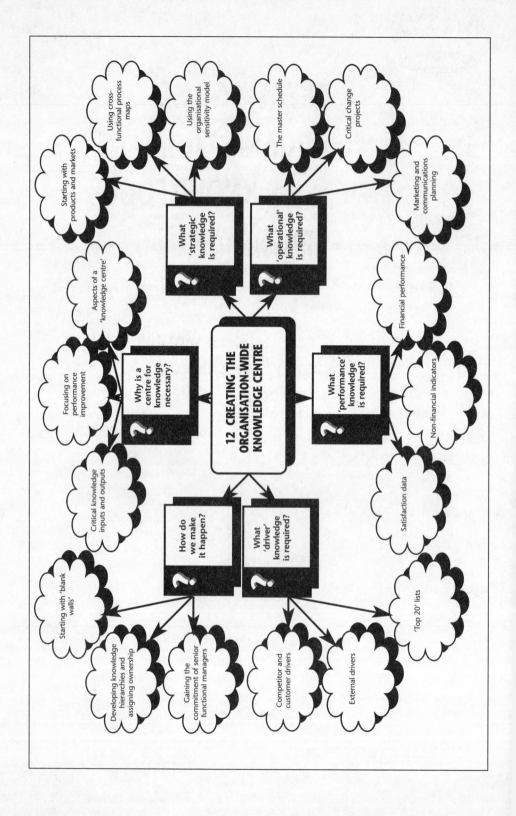

In order to implement a strategy and processes which are consistent and appropriate, and in order to be able to run the organisation, managers need to devise a framework of the knowledge which needs to be centrally available. The organisation-wide knowledge centre provides a tool that can help.

At the end of this chapter, readers will be able to identify what information, or knowledge, is necessary to run the organisation effectively, and to create a knowledge centre which would facilitate its collection and communication.

Why is a centre for knowledge required?

If you ask a man who runs a two-person building operation what his quick ratio is, he may very well say that he has no idea. If you then ask what is his bank balance, how much his customers owe him, how much he owes his major suppliers and when and how much is the next tax bill due he will, to an acceptable level of accuracy, be able to tell you.

Take this a step further. Ask the same builder why he does not go for some of the lucrative office renovations that are around, and he will say something like 'No, we do not want to work with that amount of sub-contracting, it's more trouble than its worth. We look for the domestic work which has gone wrong. When someone has made a pig's ear of something or gone bust or done a bunk or whatever. We are good at it, not many people are, and when we meet the clients they are desperate so it's profitable business too'. His strategy is clear and in his head. It is not difficult for him to articulate it.

Now ask him about his major projects, when they will be complete, what the major problems are and what resources he has available from within and without his organisation to complete them and once again there will be no problem in answering. His master schedule is in his head, as is the rest of his knowledge centre which is simply the knowledge that he needs to have and keep up to date in order to run his business. Such a man has been in the business for a while and has learned, possibly the hard way, exactly what he needs to know to stay in business and sleep at night.

Larger organisations could learn from him. Large organisations know that they have two assets in a builder's yard, a concrete mixer and some bags of cement, because their information systems tell them. The small builder knows that both these assets are useless because a labourer let the bags of cement harden in the concrete mixer. He has knowledge.

Organisational sensitivity is based on available and shared knowledge.

Organisational sensitivity is based on available and shared knowledge. In the end the sensitive company ensures that the internal left hand knows what the internal right hand is doing. This includes knowing what the other parts know if it is necessary to run the organisation.

Critical knowledge inputs and outputs

A knowledge centre is exactly as the title implies, a central location where all of the knowledge required to run the organisation is gathered and communicated. To be clear about the type of knowledge, it is not all the information needed to run the core and other processes of the organisation. Europower has a massive billing system, but only a small number of aggregated numbers from it are in the knowledge centre.

But if the knowledge centre is the answer, what is the problem? This question has already been answered earlier in the book. Let us reflect on some of the knowledge pitfalls identified in Chapter 3:

➡ trends are not being picked up from the external or competitive environments

➡ the wrong information is being picked up at the wrong times and transferred to the wrong people

➡ what information does exist is not analysed effectively

➡ some information exists but it is spread across functional units, or it is retained in people's heads

➡ knowledge of the customers, end-users and partners is limited

➡ internal communications are disjointed and ineffective

➡ no training or education in 'information management' is provided

➡ there is no central area for the gathering, organising or displaying of key information.

The physical creation of the knowledge centre requires that the organisation first of all identifies what information will be required by whom and in what format. This demands the creation of a communications matrix as described in Chapter 6 on the strategic framework. Answering these questions effectively requires a detailed understanding of how the organisation works and what is 'driving' it. The first benefit of committing to creating a knowledge centre is often a realisation that the knowledge that is really required simply doesn't exist.

Creating an effective organisational communications matrix started with identifying both internal and external stakeholders, all those people who have an interest in the success of the organisation. A detailed checklist was provided in Chapter 6. All stakeholders have communication needs, but this can be both in and out of the organisation. For each group ask 'What information do they need to know from us?' and 'What information do we need to know from them?'

Focusing on performance improvement

All information gathering and dissemination takes time and consumes resources. This is why all forms of communication should have the value they contribute to the performance of the organisation clearly understood. If it does not add value, then do not do it. The value will appear from the communications matrix.

The rule of thumb for timing of communication is 'The earlier the better'. You need to know from your customers when things are going slightly wrong even though performance is still tolerable. So do your suppliers, even if they are not aware of it.

Before confirming the communication matrix, an audit of current communication initiatives should be undertaken. In most organisations, reports are produced, meetings conducted, and information is gathered simply because 'That is how it has always been done'. The reason has somehow become lost in time, but the activity continues.

Typically an effective communication audit will eliminate as many unnecessary communication activities as it will create new ones. The difference will be between what information is currently available, and what is required, that is 'knowledge'.

Aspects of a knowledge centre

If the focus should always be on performance, however the organisation chooses to specify performance, then the knowledge centre should consist of all elements that relate to performance. The two key questions are:

➡ what information do we need to communicate to whom?

➡ what information do we need for inputs into our strategic and operational decision making?

These can then be structured under four major headings: strategy, operations, performance, and drivers. The more effective an organisation is at working through the elements of the organisational sensitivity model, the easier it will be to identify the elements that they need to focus on and hold in the knowledge centre. Every organisation is unique, and what it needs to focus on will be unique. An example of the constituent parts of a knowledge centre for Europower is contained at the end of this chapter.

Whilst every organisation is unique, some general principles will apply. For each section the focus will be on both communicating the 'big picture' and consolidating knowledge for decision making. One further consideration to bear in mind is that the exercise of creating a knowledge centre should not generate huge amounts of information, but should be highly selective and focused only on critical areas.

What strategic knowledge is required?

It is worth noting at this stage that this chapter tends to concentrate on the knowledge centre at the top of an organisation. It is, however, equally valid at all levels of groupings or teams. If a team has developed a strategic framework, it should think about what it needs in the team knowledge centre.

Starting with products and markets

All elements of the strategic plan impact performance. Whilst much of the detail should be retained in reports, the key points from the plan should be boldly displayed. They will include the values or guiding principles, the source of competitive advantage or purpose, the activity matrix showing the totality of products, services and customers as well as where the focus lies, the list of prioritisation criteria, and the list of high-priority capability needs.

No matter how well or badly the strategic plan has been created, sharing it with others in the organisation will help to gain commitment to it, to challenge it and therefore to improve it. By keeping it visible, it will be used to aid operational decision making rather than gathering dust in a drawer somewhere.

Using cross-functional process maps

The process maps of the organisation show how activities are linked together to deliver outputs, and therefore value, to customers. They show the cross-functional processes, and therefore show how functions are interdependent. This understanding and visibility of the high-level processes (sometimes called the core processes) is a vital part of breaking down the functional thinking and functional power bases.

The high-level process maps are often included under the 'strategy' element as they are the realisation of 'how' the strategy will be delivered. Where it is held in the knowledge centre is very much secondary to ensuring that at least the information is there. If a big idea is recorded, it will impact the activity plans no matter where it is recorded.

Having the processes clearly displayed will provoke debate and improvement.

CASE STUDY

The power of clear presentations

Following an examination of the full operation of a car manufacturer, a 'process map' was drawn up which contained all of the activities that took place within the organisation connected together in their natural sequence.

This map, prepared on large pieces of 'brown paper', filled one wall of their boardroom. Managers were then invited to review this 'picture of their organisation'. Whilst there were no new pieces of information on the map, and all managers knew in theory how their organisation operated, without exception they were amazed at how much they gained from it. Groups of managers started to debate aspects of their operations using the map as a focus of discussion.

Most organisations retain an element of a functional structure for convenience of administration if not operational management. If this is the case, then this should still remain visible. People like to see where they 'fit', and it may help to make clear to senior managers the total resource availability.

Using the organisational sensitivity model

Finally, in the area of strategy, the organisational sensitivity model is often displayed. This can be shown in its 'generic' format as shown earlier in the book, or tailored to highlight unique or vulnerable areas of the organisation.

One major advantage of many aspects of the knowledge centre is that it is highly educational in informing people how organisations work which is not done by our education system, or indeed by many MBA programmes.

What operational knowledge is required?

Operational knowledge is the knowledge needed to tell us if the 'how' is working. It is the control knowledge which tells us how the process activities, project activities and change activities are progressing.

The master schedule

A major source of operating knowledge is the master schedule as described in Chapter 11. It should appear in its totality as the primary operational planning and decision-making tool. It contains vital information relating to what activities are committed to, and what resources are available. It should therefore provide the basis for scenario or crisis planning, such as 'Can we take on another product line?' or 'How should we respond to this competitor move?'

Critical change projects

There will be a lot of change projects identified in the strategy and the master schedule, but a few will be critical to success. These should be treated somewhat differently as a greater degree of focus will be required. Often a single-page summary, perhaps the 'start-up report' will be displayed.

Here is Europower using the knowledge centre to monitor progress on a company-wide initiative with local variations.

CASE STUDY

Europower: industrial relations and the knowledge centre

To make a new start to poor industrial relations, a complete review of all the relationships of the organisation was undertaken. It included all the stakeholders, shareholders, suppliers and customers as well as the constituents of the primary relationship problem, unions, staff and management.

Chaired by an independent chairman, it came forward with some conclusions. These included setting up regular communication and consultation at all levels in the business. Such a significant initiative was then held separately in the knowledge centres of all the planning teams.

As a result of this, management were able to see and deal with problems and encourage some teams to use the experience of others in finding a new way forward.

Marketing and communications planning

Finally, in this section, key marketing and communication data is displayed. Marketing data often shows more detail of 'how' the priority areas in the strategic activity matrix will be achieved. This provides greater credibility and commitment, as well as helping to ensure that everyone in the organisation continues to focus on and give a consistent message to the customer.

What performance knowledge is required?

A key aspect of attaining the efficiencies connected with a sensitive organisation is making good decisions on performance indicators. There is no doubt that if senior managers set these without real consultation with the operating managers, they run a risk that the indicators will be inappropriate in some way. Either they will be achieved too easily, or they will cause the operating managers to take steps which move them towards the indicators, but which do not improve the quality or quantity of outputs.

On the other hand, most managers if allowed to set their own targets will make sure that they are achievable, perhaps to the extent of not being very stretching. They will be conservative with their estimates and consistently over-achieve. But there is no doubt either that the best people to know what are the vital ingredients of success in their part of the organisation are the actual practitioners. Consultation and discussion will reveal the right indicators and levels for each individual element of the organisation.

Financial performance

The type of performance information displayed in the knowledge centre will vary enormously depending on the budgeting system used, and whether the organisation is a commercial concern or a not-for-profit organisation. For most organisations budgets show the third level of detail, the activity matrix being the first, and the master schedule the second.

The use of ratios can reduce the total amount of information displayed, and if understood thoroughly, can give particularly useful insights into some of the detailed drivers of performance. These ratios will vary between industries and will be influenced by the selected strategy, but can be grouped into the following general headings:

➡ profitability ratios

➡ liquidity ratios

➡ gearing ratios

➡ asset utilisation ratios

➡ employee ratios

➡ production cycle ratios.

The key to the use of financial data and ratios is to keep them brief and focused. Just because the accounting software can produce a 20-page report does not mean to say that it is useful or even that people will read it. Keep it focused on what is actually important. Most managers can tell you, like the small builder, what are the key measures of their financial performance.

Management should not forget the indicators for projects. If a project has an estimated profit and loss account together with cash flow predictions, then the project should be measured against them. Many management teams believe that once a decision to invest in a project is taken, there is little point in monitoring its financial return on the grounds that you cannot unspend money. This ignores the learning element of project management.

The final point on financial indicators is to make certain that they keep pace with the strategy. If, as in the following example, a company has reached a point in its development which calls for consolidation of its current markets and an improvement in profitability, it is no use if the financial performance indicators are still chasing volume.

Leaving the indicators unchanged in a changing strategy

A worldwide telephone operator had been through a protracted period of massive growth in two markets where deregulation had allowed them in to compete. It had accompanied this growth with huge investment in infrastructure, ie the network.

As part of the thrust for growth the company had, with great razzmatazz, set up electronic scorecards for each district, region and country to display their progress against the very aggressive growth targets.

However, as the markets became more competitive, it became vital for the company to concentrate on what it already had, and squeeze much more out of the existing infrastructure. 'Our strategy is one of making best use of our fixed assets', trumpeted the annual report.

The main indicator the Board wanted to pursue was return on assets. Given that the whole culture and all the performance targets of the two operating companies concerned were focused on new business, it seems obvious that a major communications exercise was necessary to alter the focus. Obvious it may seem in hindsight, but it was not done. The growth display boards remained, the first-line sales managers hardly altered their behaviour of chasing new business and new markets. The communication of the new direction had failed and the company went through a very bad patch as a result.

Non-financial indicators

Financial indicators often paint a short-term snapshot of organisational performance, but this can sometimes be misleading. The strategic performance indicators identified in the strategy should be clearly displayed in the knowledge centre as the prime source of performance data, allowing managers to check for consistency.

Key indicators here should also include progress against the execution of change projects if this information is not included already in the master schedule.

281

Satisfaction data

Finally, in the performance areas, focus should also be on the longer term. Satisfaction data, if built in consultation with the customer, is often an indicator of tomorrow's performance rather than today's.

These should include an understanding of customer, end-user and employee satisfaction. Measuring staff turnover, for example, is already too late. It implies that we will wait for the crisis to happen and then react to it.

What driver knowledge is required?

Finally, the question of what is driving performance needs to be asked. Whilst the plan detailed in the strategy activity matrix states the intent of the organisation, the reality can often be very different. The indicators developed to monitor the strategy have to give early signals that reality is parting from intention. In the case above, for example, it was necessary for the Board to have early warning signals that no real improvement in return on assets was being achieved.

'Top 20' lists

The Pareto principles discussed earlier apply here. Not all customers or projects or products or services are equally important. So it is important to know which right now are the greatest contributors. We have called this the 'top 20 list', but the number will vary depending on the type of organisation. As a general rule, the customers, projects, products and services that contribute the top 50 per cent by revenue or budget is a useful cut-off. It is surprising how few will be on the list.

External drivers

The trends in the external environment identified in Chapter 5 on customer-focused analysis will constantly change as will the greatest opportunities and threats faced by the organisation. Understanding these and making them visible helps to keep people throughout the organisation thinking strategically, maintaining the short- and long-term balance in their thinking, and thinking about the solutions.

Competitor and customer drivers

Exactly the same applies for customer, competitor and partner trends. All of these things are important as they will influence how jobs will need to evolve to continue to counter competitor threats, and changing customer or end-user expectations. The summary held in the knowledge centre ensures that this knowledge is quickly available throughout the organisation.

How do we make it happen?

As usual the contributors and users of the knowledge centre hold the key to its successful implementation.

Gaining the commitment of senior functional managers

We have discussed the variety of information that is shared within a knowledge centre and the reasons why it might be useful. But the sharing of information of this nature is often perceived as very threatening to senior managers. It involves making their thinking visible. It also involves a different way of managing and a perceived loss of power through information retention. This resistance can be very destructive and results in some of the pitfalls identified in Chapter 3.

The benefits, however, can be enormous if the top team all commit to it. The selling point is to ensure that only information of real value is contained in the knowledge centre, there should be no 'timewasting' data or gratuitous padding. Secondly, for each of the stakeholders, and the functional managers will each be key stakeholders, the question 'What's in it for me?' should be answered. There should be clear benefits for all managers from such information sharing.

With this in mind, the justification for starting such an exercise is to ask what concerns managers currently have with the way information is transferred around the organisation, and the resultant list provides not only the justification for the creation of the knowledge centre, but it also provides the guidelines as to what it should contain. If a good environmental analysis has been produced by each of the key teams, then it is quite possible that this information is already available. It is then an administrative job to produce this list and check it with managers.

Developing knowledge hierarchies and assigning ownership

Within the knowledge centre is information with different attributes. Some of it, such as the guiding principles, will remain reasonably static throughout the year, whereas other items of information will require monthly updates. Whatever the information is, there should be clearly identified responsibilities for what to update, who should do it and when.

Ultimately, the ownership of the organisation-wide knowledge centre is the domain of the chief executive. He or she may not have responsibility for updating any particular piece of information, but they must use it. Its prime objectives of communication and the provision of the inputs required for strategic and operational decision making will not be achieved if it does not get used.

Board meetings must be conducted in the knowledge centre so that Board decisions are made in the context of what is driving performance for the organisation. Otherwise it is too easy to lose focus, deliberately or accidentally.

Teams conducting cross-functional meetings should be encouraged to use the room as much as possible, cascading knowledge throughout the organisation, and encouraging cross-functional 'organisational' thinking. This implies that the knowledge centre should be a physical room with enough space to conduct meetings. This certainly works best, and whilst some organisations are experimenting with the use of a virtual centre using computers, a physical knowledge centre encourages team spirit.

A key consideration with use of a physical location is going to be the question of confidentiality. Whilst it is true that a limited amount of information will be too sensitive, generally, information is far less sensitive than people imagine. Start with the premise that all information should be made available to all internal stakeholders and then insist on selective justification where this should not be the case. This situation can be managed by having one 'lockable' display board, with the remaining knowledge on permanent display.

Starting with 'blank walls'

There are a number of ways of starting. If the knowledge centre is seen as a new initiative, then the chief executive should call a meeting of all cross-functional managers and influential stakeholders and conduct a structured brainstorming session based around the four headings: strategy, operations, performance, and drivers. If the chief executive can, he or she should allocate a blank wall for each.

This exercise asks managers to think hard about what information they really require to run the organisation effectively. It is often a frightening exercise, however, as it highlights just how little of the

The Europower 'knowledge center'

STRATEGY	OPERATIONS	PERFORMANCE	DRIVERS
Product/market matrix Statement of competitive advantage Product/market matrix High emphasis areas Key capability requirements	**Master schedule** Activity forecasts (short-term and historical) Major internal change projects Resource availability schedule Current year time-scale major events	**Financial plan** Budgets and financial forecasts Revenue performance Profit performance Key financial ratios	**Top 20 lists** Year-to-date list of customers by £ Year to date list of products by £ Year to date list of projects by £
Process maps Top level 'core' process map Reflection of source of advantage Organisation chart End-to-end process map Critical risk areas identified	**Project plan** Definition phase and Gantt chart (Major internal change projects) Resource requirements matrix	**Non-financial indicators** Key indicators of strategic success Key indicators of operational success Key indicators of change project success	**External drivers** Changing shareholder expectations External environmental trends Substitute product trends Supplier trends
Organisational competency model Elements expanded	**Marketing plan** Definition phase and Gantt chart Resource requirements matrix	**Satisfaction data** Customer satisfaction data 'Clientshare' data Employee satisfaction data (management, operations and support staff)	**Customer drivers** Changing customer expectations Competitor performance and trends New competitors and substitute products

FIGURE 12.1

right information is available, and how poorly the current strategic plan actually helps to guide decision making. Whilst frightening, it is of course particularly powerful as highlighting deficiencies in this way allows the team an opportunity to correct them before it is too late. The alternative is to allow them to be highlighted through poor and possibly disastrous performance in the marketplace.

You have to look at the best way for your particular situation. Either look on the creation of the knowledge centre as a new initiative, remembering BOHICA of course, or you can to build on work that is already done and processes already put in place. A good example of building on existing processes is to take a consolidation of the SWOT analysis developed earlier, and include it in the knowledge centre, changing it as progress is made.

Cross-functional exercises such as these help to build understanding of the organisation and commitment to the outputs. When conducted effectively with trained facilitation, they are also the most effective form of team building at senior management level.

The concept of the knowledge centre is by no means applicable only to the organisation as a whole. Again the starting premise that all concepts contained in this book apply equally well to organisational, team and individual levels applies. Product line, service line and functional knowledge centres are powerful management and communication tools at a local level.

Figure 12.1 is an example of the contents of a Knowledge Centre.

Creating the organisation-wide knowledge centre

KEY POINTS

Take a few minutes to reflect on each of these.

➡ The right information must be provided to the right people in the right format at the right time – a 'centre for knowledge' can help!

➡ Two key questions need to be addressed in the knowledge centre: 'What information do we need to communicate to whom?', and 'What information do we need for inputs into our strategic and operational decision making?'

➡ Knowledge can be grouped into four categories: strategic, operational, performance, and drivers.

➡ Knowledge should not be used as a source of individual power but as a potential source of advantage for the organisation – everyone has potentially useful knowledge, and everyone has a need for specific knowledge in order to maximise performance.

➡ Knowledge is useless unless it is used – use of knowledge is significantly increased through visibility.

SELF-ASSESSMENT

Rate your organisation or unit on a scale of 1 to 5.

1 How effectively is knowledge shared within the organisation? ☐

2 Is the right information transferred to the right people
   at the right time? ☐

3 Are strategic and operational decisions often made in an
   information vacuum – a sophisticated wide-angled guess? ☐

4 Is the information unavailable or too difficult to find? ☐

5 How effectively is the strategy communicated and
   understood at all levels and in all functions? ☐

6 Does everyone know what their role in strategy
   formulation is? ☐

7 Does everyone know how the organisation 'works' – the
   way inputs are processed as customer outputs are
   produced and value is added? ☐

8 Does everyone know what factors impact performance? ☐

9 Are operations managed with all factors in mind? ☐

10 Is there an organisation master schedule? ☐

11 Is it accessible and visible? ☐

12 Is the master schedule used? ☐

13 Is it current? ☐

14 Is there a balance between financial and non-financial
   performance data? ☐

15 Is information on both customer and employee satisfaction
   complete, current and visible? ☐

16 Are the key drivers of current performance identified and visible? ☐

17 Do you know who the largest or most profitable customers of product lines are? ☐

18 Is knowledge about the external and competitive environments available, current and displayed? ☐

19 Is it used? ☐

20 Is the knowledge available when all major management meetings are conducted? ☐

21 Is the required information at people's fingertips when decisions are taken? ☐

ACTION PLAN

Where you scored badly in your self-assessment, identify what actions you will take to improve your performance.

What?	Who?	When?
1		
2		
3		
4		
5		

'Every reform was once a private opinion, and when it shall be a private opinion again it will solve the problem of the age.'

Ralph Waldo Emerson

CHAPTER

UTILISING
TECHNOLOGY

Making sure that new
technologies offer
opportunities rather
than threats.

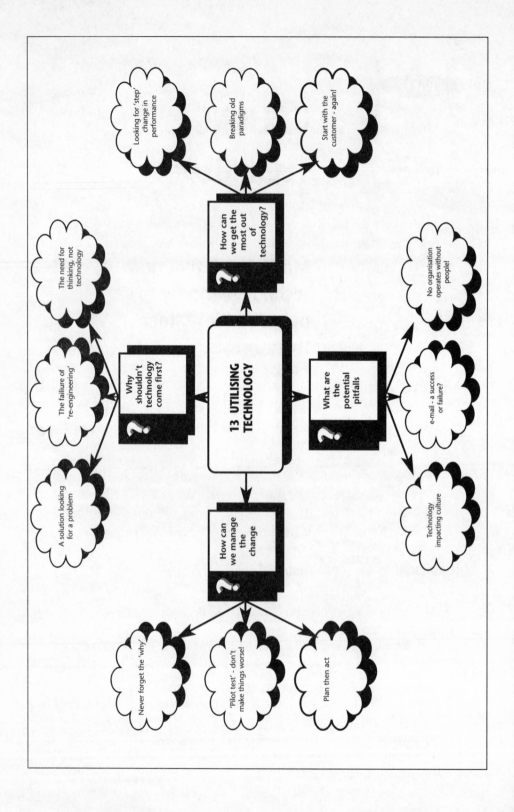

Technology has the potential to enhance significantly or to destroy organisational sensitivity. The emphasis must be on performance improvement and strategic fit.

At the end of this chapter, readers will be able to start the plan for how technology can assist and improve the strategy and processes they are reviewing.

Why technology should not come first

When computer technology was gathering pace in the early days, it was allowed, because of the potential benefits it offered, to dictate strategy. Getting the billing system on to the computer was the aim, not getting the money in faster.

We got wiser, and started to insist that the organisation goals and objectives should drive the technology. The control here was technical. The spends were large and generally handled at the centre. Then the technology changed and managers became able to deploy technology piecemeal using their own discretionary budgets. The danger is back that technology will be put on people's desks without proper thought on how it will benefit the outputs and support the strategy.

A solution looking for a problem

These rapid changes in the field of technology and information processing in particular present organisations with both significant opportunities and threats. The opportunities come from the potential 'step' changes possible in performance in certain processes through use of technology. The threats come from two sources.

If an organisation chooses to ignore the potential then it will rapidly find itself losing ground in the marketplace, because at least one of its competitors will be getting it right. Secondly, if the organisation attempts to use technology and gets it wrong, it has the potential to have enormous adverse consequences on performance over and above the cost of the technology itself.

The situation has been confused by the lack of understanding that the average manager has of computers and other forms of technology. And you cannot blame them if you focus on the technology itself. It is complex, technical and changing rapidly.

> *The situation has been confused by the lack of understanding that the average manager has of computers and other forms of technology.*

The result of this 'technological ignorance', both in respect of what it is and what it can do, has been to rely over-heavily on the technological specialists within the organisation. There is a well-known phrase that 'if you only have a hammer, then everything begins to look like a nail'. Placing control of change projects in the hands of technical specialist results in a technological bias to the end solution.

The failure of 're-engineering'

The resultant authority to change, combined with huge budgets has increased the profile of the information technology or information solutions departments enormously. This fact is seen by some managers as one of the main reasons why so many re-engineering projects have had poor results.

Some re-engineering projects are reported to have cost a lot of money and actually made performance worse. Whilst hindsight is always a marvellous thing, there are perhaps some general concerns frequently expressed. Firstly, that the solution was not focused enough on performance improvement. The objective once again has become the installation of the computer system in itself, or the redesign of the process rather than improved benefits to customers. Secondly solutions are too heavily focused on the technology, without enough thought being given to how the changes will affect real people doing real tasks. Thirdly, there is no clear understanding of where it fits within the strategy of the organisation as a whole, no holistic view. Finally, such changes often have a direct and fundamental impact on the underlying culture of the organisation, and this is not always considered to be a good or practical thing.

This brings us back to a principle theme in the creation of organisational sensitivity, critical thinking.

The need for thinking, not technology

This situation has to be resolved. Technology is here, and here to stay. We must adapt to its potential and to a new way of working, but we must do so in a way that is right for us and our organisation. The steps to achieving this are clear. First we formulate strategy, then redesign the process, and only then do we ask how technology can help us to do what we want to do in the way we want to do it. In fact, think first then act.

An example of using technology as a tool can be seen in the use of project management software inside project-based organisations. If people are given the software alone, without the conceptual understanding of how to manage both the technical and people elements of projects, then they become slaves to the software. However, those that gain an understanding of the concepts first are able to utilise the software as a 'tool' as and when it will add value. The ownership and control must rest with the person responsible, not with any technological system.

How can we get the most out of technology?

Looking for 'step' change in performance

There is typically a huge cost to the introduction of new technology. This includes the direct purchasing costs, the lower performance typically experienced during the teething phase, and the ongoing maintenance cost of both technical support and support for the people changing how they carry out their jobs. With such significant potential costs, which are almost always underestimated, the potential improvement must be significant. If it is not, then the investment will certainly be more trouble than it is worth.

To try to ensure that any changes do significantly impact performance, start by focusing on the high-value activities identified in an earlier exercise. There are, therefore, two ways in which technology offers improvement. It offers continuous improvement when we improve the way we use it and a step change in performance when a process is changed to use new technology.

Breaking old paradigms

The technology field is changing so rapidly, what is possible is often far more, far faster, and much cheaper than people imagine. Unfortunately, computers have created a bad impression with many due to lost data, unfriendliness, crashing, and lack of capability. Most managers have had some bad experience in the past. This means that

297

to evaluate new opportunities, it is first necessary to dispel old, but very real concerns.

Some of these are personal and lead to problems for individuals such as this Financial Director.

CASE STUDY

We may not need to understand the technology, but we must understand what it can do for us

The Financial Director of a manufacturing company was not at all computer literate. Whilst 20, or even 10 years ago this would have been acceptable, nowadays it places him at a significant disadvantage. Firstly, his staff were more or less able to write their own job specifications as they were all now working on computers. Secondly he was not aware of the potential insights he could offer other managers about individual product or customer profitability.

The opportunities afforded by recent trends in technology allow managers to rethink completely some problems which up until now have been insurmountable. The following list only picks up some of the issues we discussed earlier. Managers need to step back and think about how many of these opportunities are relevant to them.

➡ By careful study of how an expert goes about his or her function, you can build *expert systems* which allow lower skilled people to carry out the same task subsequently to the same quality.

➡ *Telecommunications* networks offer the opportunity of combining the benefits of a centralised and a decentralised approach to managing the organisation.

➡ Linked to this is the release of field staff from being tied into visiting an office on a regular basis to retrieve and input information. *Home working* can offer massive benefits in terms of productivity, staff satisfaction and customer service.

➡ *Interactive videodisk and video-conferencing* can revolutionise the supplier–customer relationship. The effectiveness of customer contact is truly measured in effectiveness, as opposed to assuming that personal contact is the best type of contact.

➡ *Shared databases* are a further step to achieving the chief executive's instruction 'Get the information in front of all the right people at the right time'. Suddenly information can be in more than one place at a time.

➡ Instead of the regular review of plans at set times with its attendant risk of being more reactive than proactive, *high-performance computing* allows the instantaneous and continuous updating of plans. The result offers an improvement in decision making.

➡ Decisions are also improved by the availability of decision support tools, such as *access to database information* and *modelling software* giving managers an infinite number of 'What if?' questions.

➡ We can even get computers to tell us where things are by using *identification and tracking technology*.

This list does show the level at which all managers need to understand what technology can do for them, so that they see potential applications which solve real business issues.

It is unsurprising that the starting point is the customer whether internal or external.

Start with the customer – again!

The selection criteria technique discussed in regard to critical thinking can be useful here. To answer the question 'How can we get the most out of technology?' a set of customer-focused selection criteria can be developed. In this way, whilst it is sometimes difficult to tie down the exact benefit of investment in technology, performance against criteria provide an effective substitute for value or profit.

More specifically, we might ask 'How will this improve the benefits we are able to offer customers?', or 'How will this improve our 'time-to-market?', or 'How will this reduce our costs and make us more competitive?' Before confirming any selection or change, each suggestion should be validated against the same **SAFE** filter: suitability, acceptability, feasibility and endurance.

What are the potential pitfalls?

In seeking to achieve organisational sensitivity, an organisation or team should already have some significant aids to avoiding the pitfalls of applying technology. However, there are pitfalls which are usually more concerned with the people applying or using the technology rather than the technology itself.

No organisation operates without people!

The constant drive towards operational efficiency is encouraging organisations to seek to design the 'people-free' operation. In reality, this will not happen on any meaningful scale for a variety of reasons:

➡ the chaotic environment informs us that whilst we can predict and manage proactively many aspects of change, the picture is too complex to predict every likely scenario

➡ there will always be a human relationship aspect to almost all customer–supplier transactions, whether these relationships are internal or external

➡ the technology itself will always be designed, built, programmed, commissioned and maintained by people

➡ finally, the quality of the outputs achieved is only as good as the quality of the inputs that people provide. The old adage still applies – garbage in, garbage out.

The imperfections, uniqueness and unpredictability of people must be taken into consideration when utilising technology to fulfil part of any operational process. And of course the positive side of people involvement is their ability to make suggestions leading to performance improvement.

Taking one well-tested technology, e-mail, we find evidence for its doing harm as well as good.

E-mail – a success or failure?

There is a huge increase in the use of e-mail as a means of communicating within and between organisations. The authors of this book benefited from this technology by e-mailing each other draft versions of chapters between the UK and Spain. Such communication of large volumes of text just would not have been possible without the technology. The benefit of this was a marked improvement in time to market.

However, many organisations are suffering from the adverse impact e-mail systems appear to be having on teamworking and quality. The fault lies not in the technology, but in the over-reliance people have come to place on it.

Used solely for the transfer of information e-mail has few limitations. But if it is a particular 'message' that you are trying to put across then the body language which accounts for 85 per cent of the communication of a 'message' is lost in e-mail. At the moment that is.

It will be interesting to see if video telephony as an adjunct to e-mail will prove beneficial in this area.

The problem does not rest in the technology, but when and how it is used.

The problem does not rest in the technology, but when and how it is used. The 'fix' to this particular pitfall is straightforward. Managers must design the processes first, then ask how and when can technology help. In answering this question they should also recognise that all technology has the potential to create or destroy value.

Technology impacting culture

Above and beyond any impact on key performance indicators, it must also be recognised that any change to technology will potentially have an impact on the organisation's culture. This can be very significant.

It is all too easy to put in place a fantastic technological solution to a real operational problem, only to find that the people within the organisation refuse to use it. The reason being that it is against their culture, as simple as that. The change clearly hadn't passed the 'acceptability' filter.

The use of mobile phones in the health service was rejected by many people for this reason, and took many years for managers to accept that the gains outweighed the discomfort many felt with the technology.

Often there is a timing problem with this, in that the people are introduced to the new concept too late in the process. There is a temptation to leave the people whose jobs are going to be changed until the detail of the application is decided upon and it is possible to start with training. This is too late. The people whose jobs are going to change must be involved at the outset when the objectives of the exercise are being agreed. If processes are being owned by cross-functional process teams, then, of course, the chances of a successful implementation are greatly enhanced.

How can we manage the change?

The management of technological change follows the rules of change we have already discussed with a few specific additions.

Plan then act

Once the potential for improvement has been identified, and the recommended changes have passed all four of the filters, an effective implementation plan is required. Implementation requires the use of professional project management techniques, where the project manager is often someone from the operational side of the organisation, not the IS/IT department. It is completely logical that if an application is in banking, the implementation project should be managed by a banker.

Because technology projects frequently cut across several processes and functions, certain activities must be completed as part of any successful project, echoing, incidentally, the steps gone through in the change process in Chapter 7:

➡ an assessment of the project stakeholders – who needs to be consulted or involved

➡ familiarisation sessions with all the stakeholders

➡ clearly defined performance objectives for the project with specific targets which identify what 'success will look like', and ensure that the project delivers more value than it costs

➡ a comprehensive list of activities which will be undertaken in order to ensure success, each with quantified resources and allocated responsibilities

➡ review milestones to ensure the project stays on track, and a planned formal 'start-up' and 'close-out'

➡ an assessment of the principle risks, and a statement of how each will be addressed.

Scoping and planning projects effectively does not take long, but is often done very badly. Technology is exciting, and the opportunities great. This tends to make people just want to get on with it. Unfortunately, as we have already identified, mistakes can be monumental. Time spent in planning is never wasted.

At Europower the symptom that people were not implementing the available technology eventually revealed the real problem.

CASE STUDY

Europower: you may have to go a long way back in the process to find why technology seems not to be effective

The managers of the Power Generating Division were concerned about how many centrally produced computer systems were being poorly implemented or used in the power stations. The potential benefits of the system were being lost because of lack of commitment or even interest.

They gave a manager the task of reselling the systems and encouraging the people in the stations to come on side. After a while the real problem emerged. The systems were being rejected because the managers in the power stations did not see them as strategic to what they were trying to do, and saw them as being irrelevant to the main performance indicators they were pursuing. Going back one step further it became clear that the power stations did not really have a strategy, or that it was not understood or bought into by most of the people.

What was needed was to go back to customer-focused analysis, build a cross-functional team and agree a strategic framework. From that would emerge the processes which needed review and redesign, and from that would emerge the real relevance or irrelevance of the existing computer systems.

'Pilot test' – don't make things worse!

No matter how well the implementation of the new technology is planned, it is unlikely to go right the first time. Major changes to how processes are conducted should always have a form of 'pilot' test. This is an initial phase where the technology and approach is evaluated in a small, controlled environment to make sure it will work. Make sure this is conducted in a way that involves all of the major stakeholders identified during the scoping and planning phase.

One of the major keys to successful implementation is that the project manager is prepared for some hard-hitting feedback and willing to change the final installation on the basis of the lessons learned. This is not as easy as it sounds, since people are quick to warm to a particular solution and defensive of their own ideas.

With many operational projects, such as building a machine for a customer, there is often a second chance to put things right, assuming that the problems are picked up without the customer being overly inconvenienced. The great difficulty with change projects is that there is often only one chance. Introduce total quality management inside an organisation and get it wrong, the second time you try to introduce it there will be so much resistance to it that people will, knowingly or otherwise, make sure that it fails; the BOHICA effect again.

There are legions of examples of changes introduced badly, which will never appear again on the agenda of the organisation. Perhaps the UK government's attempted introduction of a 'poll tax' was a good example of this. Whether you believe it was right or wrong was essentially irrelevant because the way it was introduced had such a dramatic and negative response.

Never forget the 'why'

Whilst we have covered this point already, it is so vital that it is worth reiterating. Major technology projects take so long that the justification for them can change throughout their lifetimes. This can happen because of changing customer expectations and competitor performance. For example, banking customers wanting queries handled differently at their local branch. If, six months into the project, a new firm introduces telephone banking, however unlikely this may appear, the original project may well become redundant, the reason 'why' will have changed or disappeared.

Focusing on the 'why' throughout the project will help to ensure that the desired benefits will be achieved.

Focusing on the 'why' throughout the project will help to ensure that the desired benefits will be achieved.

Utilising technology

KEY POINTS

Take a few minutes to reflect on each of these.

➡ Technology should be used as a 'tool' to improve effectiveness and efficiency once the processes have been specified. In this way it should never be the starting point of organisational change.

➡ The emphasis should always be on 'thinking.' In this way successful technology projects are managed by line managers and driven by customers.

➡ Utilising new technology is often required for survival. But accepting such change often requires a change to existing paradigms.

➡ It is not necessary to understand the technology itself, but simply what it can do for us.

➡ As with all major changes, the SAFE hurdles can prove invaluable if the project is not to become another BOHICA initiative!

SELF-ASSESSMENT

Rate your organisation or unit on a scale of 1 to 5.

1   How effectively have technology projects worked in your organisation? ☐

2   Did performance improve significantly? ☐

3   Did it ever make things worse? ☐

4   How open or receptive is your organisation to change? ☐

5   Will people accept new technology if it results in a change to the way the job will be performed? ☐

6   How familiar are managers with current technology – not what it is but what it can do for them? ☐

7   Has new technology been introduced within a clear strategic remit – 'How will this improve our ability to perform in the future?' ☐

8   Has new technology been introduced with clear performance improvement targets? ☐

9   How effectively were the needs and expectations of people taken into consideration when planning new technology introductions? ☐

10 How effectively was each element of the performance environment changed to support the introduction of new technology – job requirements, capabilities, resources and rewards? ☐

11 Are pilot tests conducted? ☐

12 Are the right people involved at all stages? ☐

13 Are problems resolved before the 'go live' date? ☐

14 How much are operations adversely impacted short term? ☐

15 How effectively is the project evaluated once completed? ☐

16 Were performance targets met? ☐

17 What were the difficulties? ☐

18 How easy was implementation? ☐

19 Is there really a belief that technology is a requirement for long-term survival? ☐

20 Do we know why and how? ☐

21 Do we know what customers and competitors are doing? ☐

ACTION PLAN

Where you scored badly in your self-assessment, identify what actions you will take to improve your performance.

What?	Who?	When?
1		
2		
3		
4		
5		

'Whenever I hear the word culture, I release the safety catch of my revolver.'

Hanns Johst, Nazi writer

CHAPTER

14

A CULTURAL TRANSFORMATION – CREATING THE SENSITIVE ORGANISATION

All the analyses and process designs in the world will fail if the culture of the organisation is at odds with their implementation.

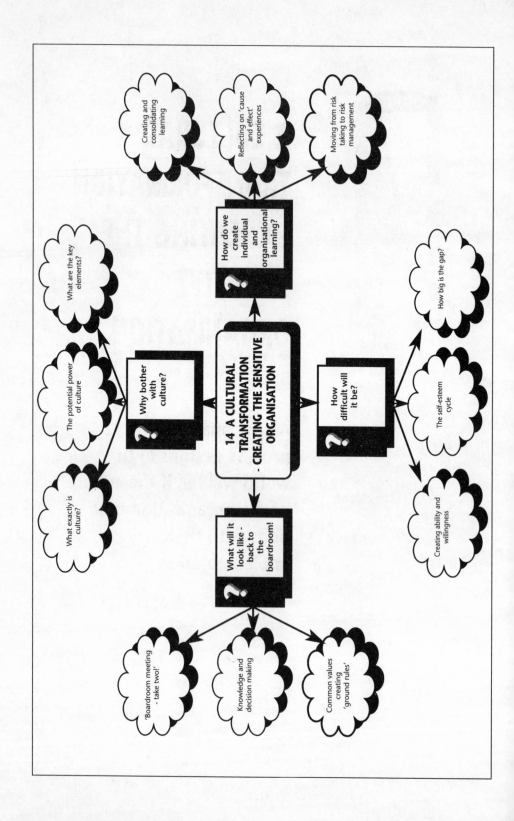

14 A CULTURAL TRANSFORMATION - CREATING THE SENSITIVE ORGANISATION

Why bother with culture?
- What are the key elements?
- The potential power of culture
- What exactly is culture?

How do we create individual and organisational learning?
- Creating and consolidating learning
- Reflecting on 'cause and effect' experiences
- Moving from risk taking to risk management

How difficult will it be?
- How big is the gap?
- The self-esteem cycle
- Creating ability and willingness

What will it look like - back to the boardroom!
- 'Boardroom meeting - take two!'
- Knowledge and decision making
- Common values creating 'ground rules'

O rganisational sensitivity requires that there are some common and widely accepted beliefs which guide the behaviour of the people in the organisation.

At the end of this chapter, readers will be able to create a plan to change the culture of their organisations, groups or teams by using a number of checklists for change.

Why bother with the culture?

So far in this book, we have developed a systematic approach to the design and creation of organisational sensitivity. We have talked about basic concepts of what drives organisational performance, gone through the inter-related elements of strategy, processes, knowledge and people, and ended with the 'tools' that help to keep the organisation sensitive once it has been achieved.

We have also discussed how vital it is for the culture of the organisation to be supportive of the new way of working.

What exactly is culture?

Culture is a difficult word to define. It is often said that you normally know if you have got the culture of the organisation right or wrong without being able to define exactly what makes it right or wrong. The term is used with regard to change projects where a supportive culture is said to be a critical success factor, but that does not entirely help us to understand what it means. Perhaps the best definition is by an example we have already mentioned.

CASE STUDY

The HP way

Dave Packard the co-founder of Hewlett-Packard is credited with describing the attitude and behaviour of HP people as 'the HP way'. In this case it is a definite series of beliefs and values, although even they have some misty edges. HP managers are very confident of the power of the HP way.

> The Chief Executive of HP was showing a senior businessman around a large HP facility. The visitor was very impressed by the openness with which he was treated. He expressed this surprise by stating that there seemed to be no fear that competitors could learn and gain from such openness. 'Not so,' replied the Chief Executive, 'because they could not implement the ideas without importing the HP way as a new culture.' HP managers simply do not believe that it can be done.

Perhaps, then, the nearest we can get to a definition is that the culture of an organisation is a common and accepted set of beliefs which the organisation holds and can communicate, and which makes it possible for the organisation to meet its objectives and carry out its strategy.

In this regard, the culture of the organisation has been defined to a large extent within the guiding principles laid down in the strategic framework.

The potential power of culture

A culture that works against what the change is trying to achieve will stop the initiative dead. What is worse, culture is often extremely difficult to change, perhaps more difficult than any other element of the organisational sensitivity model. Some organisations would rather die than change their culture. Some people would rather let their jobs become untenable rather than change how they work and interact with their colleagues.

Sometimes, however, failure to build an appropriate culture is not caused by a stubborn refusal to change by an antiquated workforce, but by a lack of a clear vision and guidance in how to change. It is like telling someone who is unhappy to 'cheer up'. Changing culture, like changing our emotions, is not easy, and the organisation and the people in it must be willing and able to make the change.

Examples of where a cultural change was required but not achievable can be seen in the computer industry. Some of the world's best-known companies developed a 'quality is everything' culture. When it became apparent that, because of changes in the competitive environment, organisations would have to compete on price, orders were sent out from head office. Unfortunately, a cost-cutting culture involves a way of thinking that is fundamentally different from building in maximum quality; it permeates through every activity the organisation performs. The changes took many years and a significant loss of market share occurred before performance under new market conditions was stabilised. Many people chose to leave voluntarily along the way. Others were asked to leave.

It has been interesting to note the progress of one top-quality car manufacturer, as it was forced to change its culture from one of absolute build quality to customer-defined quality. A period of poor financial performance provided it with a significant incentive, but the change was dramatic and not without pain.

What are the key energising elements?

An analysis of culture can be structured in many ways, but will ultimately affect every part of the organisation. Definition of the stated culture will appear explicitly in both the statement of guiding principles in the strategic framework and in each element of the performance system, requirements, resources, and rewards.

It is plain that the culture that permeates the organisation must actively support the way of working defined in the strategy, processes, knowledge sharing and the management of all people associated with the organisation.

Some aspects of the culture consistently have a dramatic effect on performance, and we have tried to consolidate these in the list below. As you read through the list, you might find it useful to reflect on your own organisation or team, and decide whether your culture provides the vital energy required to fulfil its strategy, or whether it actively works against it.

 'Strategic' energising elements

➡ *Values – practised not ignored*

Once the values that the organisation and individuals hold are understood and defined, they must either be practised or changed. If one set of values is stated, and another set practised, this will undermine efforts in all of the following elements.

➡ *Management of the future – proactive not reactive*

No matter how dynamic the external and competitive environments are, people who take responsibility for outcomes and manage issues before they become crises always perform more effectively. In general, people often have more control of their destiny than they imagine. However, they tend not to seek that control unless they are helped and encouraged.

➡ *Changes – externally (customer) not internally driven*

All changes to any of the four elements of the sensitivity model must be driven by customers and changes in the external environment. If we do not understand the link to the customer, then we are likely to perform tasks in the wrong order of priority and to the wrong set of performance indicators. This also holds true for organisations which are affected to a significant extent by a regulator.

➡ *Planning – realistic, not optimistic or pessimistic*

Many organisations have almost a standard practice that sales forecasts are always understated so that they will be exceeded, and budgets always overstated so that they are always achieved. When this becomes common knowledge, their value as a motivator or control tool is lost. Organisations which are new to cross-functional planning frequently overestimate what they can get done when they see the need for changes to processes. Only when planning becomes more mature do their plans become more realistic.

Many of the following operational issues have already been raised in previous chapters as part of the process of creating organisational sensitivity, or as one of the tools which help managers to implement it.

 ## 'Operational' energising elements

➡ *Thinking – rational* and *creative, not rational* or *creative*

The most effective teams and individuals use processes when thinking through issues, such as those described under 'critical thinking skills'. However, these must not be purely rational, which can hinder the development of a truly creative solution, or purely creative, which risks coming up with a solution which just would not work. Both rational and creative thinking should be used in combination.

➡ *Issue management – first thinking not acting*

If there is a crisis and you are found sitting down thinking, then you risk being asked why you are not doing anything. But, of course, thinking should always be the first activity when faced with concerns that require a solution that is not obvious. Whilst 'analysis paralysis' should be avoided, people should never be discouraged to think when faced with a concern.

➡ *Problem management – solution not blame*

Finding true causes should be done from the perspective of ensuring that the best solution is put in place to fix the problem and prevent its recurrence. If blame is always sought, it will dramatically suppress the free flow of willing information and helpers for future problems.

➡ *Decision making – knowledge-based not guessed*

It is easy to say that we do not have the time or budget to get the necessary information, and use this as an excuse to have a guess. Perfect information is never available, but a little information can often be all that is needed. For each decision it is a question of understanding what information really is required, our definition of knowledge, and ensuring that, at the very least, it is obtained.

➡ *Risk management – prudent acceptance not avoidance*

Organisations, teams and individuals will not improve and develop unless quantified and effectively managed risks are taken. To avoid taking risks prevents development; to prevent development encourages long-term decline. It is a truism, but nevertheless a truth, that we cannot stand still.

➡ *Resource utilisation – justified not hoarded*

No organisation has enough resources for all the activities it wishes to do for both operation and change. The 'hoarding' of resources on a 'just in case' basis results in compromise in other parts of the organisation.

➡ *Knowledge management – sharing not hoarding*

Knowledge in one area of an organisation will often be of use in several other areas. For example, understanding a change in customer requirements will be of value at least to sales, R&D, and manufacturing functions. If it is not shared because people are protecting personal power bases, then the organisation as a whole will perform below its optimum.

The interaction of people in the organisation is the next issue in setting up an appropriate culture. These are the tests which reveal how well your organisation is harnessing the vital energies of interaction.

 'Relationship' energising elements

➡ *Leadership – by example not dictate*

There is no substitute for leading by example. We can design every element of the sensitive organisation to perfection, but if the Chief Executive does not 'live' the model, then it will soon fall into disuse. People who do not lead by example lose credibility and this results in the loss of both 'mechanistic' and 'personal' management tools.

➡ *Working with others – willingly not through compliance*

Formal hierarchies exist, but if these are used exclusively for the management of people, then lack of mutual respect and 'teamworking' results in an informal 'work to rule'. Many organisations recognise that much of their work is produced outside the formal working hours through the willing contribution of staff at all levels. Some organisations can achieve this during a crisis, a major storm for example, but not during everyday working life.

➡ *Relationships – open not hidden agendas*

Honesty when dealing with others is always the best policy. Despite all there are no exceptions to this rule. Hidden agendas become unhidden at some stage in the future. Relationships are rarely 'single transactions', and hidden agendas may win the battle but will not win the war.

➡ *Managing people – acceptance not denial of others' individuality*

People are what they are. We cannot change them easily even if that were a good idea. It is best to accept their individuality, and instead of looking for how they can be cloned, recognise where they can be given 'best practice' techniques and put to use their individual strengths.

➡ *Contracting – win-win not win-lose or lose-win*

When conflict arises, look for a creative solution that gives both sides what they need. This does not have to be a compromise, and even where it does, the strengthened long-term relationship should outweigh any short-term loss.

➡ *Loyalty – organisational not functional*

Functions should be used for administrative management of people, not the management of the job. Loyalty to any team whose operations are often at conflict with the overall purpose of the organisation is risky. Loyalty should exist to any process or project team, and steps must be taken to build this, but overall, respect and loyalty to the organisation must be built. This will have to be earned.

➡ *Progression – learning not assumed right*

Time in a job should not guarantee any automatic right to progression. Growth for individuals will come from the development of them as people, and as such personal development planning should help towards this objective.

➡ *Individual development – roles not titles*

The person is what they are and what they do, not what badge they wear. No matter what job title people have, the part that they contribute to the organisation's performance depends not on knowing what they are called, but knowing where they fit into the processes.

Finally there are two elements of individual contributions to an appropriate culture which determine by how much the attributes described above will enable the organisation to achieve sensitivity.

'Individual' energising elements

➡ *Energy levels – active not passive*

Performance on nearly all jobs is improved when the people performing the tasks have high energy levels. This is obvious in physical jobs, but in many other tasks, such as making sales presentations, high energy levels result in greater enthusiasm and commitment. Energy levels will be impacted both by people's physical conditions and lifestyles, and their level of motivation.

➡ *Attitude – positive not negative*

It is said that there are two types of people in this world – those who say that a glass is half full and those who say it is half empty.

The facts are the same, but different people interpret facts in very different ways. Both are dependent on the same element – attitude. There is no doubt that people with positive attitudes are more effective, apart from making the work environment a much happier place. Whilst personality can have a role to play here, behavioural techniques can be employed which will significantly change the way people choose to view the 'world' they live in. These are beyond the scope of this book.

Organisational learning and attitude to risk are two fundamental areas which encapsulate many of the above energising elements, and so we will look at them in more detail.

How do we create individual and organisational learning?

Creating and consolidating learning

If old habits die hard, then we need to 'unlearn' before we can learn. If we reflect on the four-stage model for individual learning it becomes clear that if something is already programmed into our unconscious memory, a form of 'reprogramming' will be required.

The four stages start from '**unconscious incompetence**' where we are not even aware that a competency exists. A backwoodsman who has never seen a car is unaware that he cannot drive. The second stage is '**conscious incompetence**' where we become aware that a capability exists and that we do not have it. Sit the backwoodsman in Piccadilly Circus for a while and he will become aware that he cannot drive. Training gives rise to '**conscious competence**' where we have the competency but need to think about the ideas as we use them in a concentrated way. 'Into third, check the mirror, signal, check the mirror, change lanes', etc. Finally we reach '**unconscious competence**' where we freely use the competency hardly aware that we are doing so. At this stage our backwoodsman is driving, listening to the radio and smoking a cigarette. The fourth phase of unconscious competence is in effect intuitive. The example of driving reminds us also that without some periodic reminder of the basics of the competence, we can easily return to the first phase of unconscious incompetence.

If people are to move from organisational confusion to organisational sensitivity, then they must make sure they understand how things happen at the moment. This is more easily said than done. When we reflect on something as simple as decision making, it is often not clear what 'process' we are using. Changing the way decisions are made is much easier if we first understand how we do it now. This will allow internal frameworks to be built upon or replaced as appropriate.

Having a stated objective of applying new ideas, or learning from a new experience is half the battle. Such opportunities do not just happen, they need to be made to happen. Sometimes this is simply a matter of changing the way routine tasks are done (for example every tenth time it is done a formal learning exercise is conducted), but at other times it is necessary to create special learning opportunities. Benchmarking, bringing in new hires, reading journals which publish 'best practice' articles are just some of the ways in which people can challenge the current mind-set and way of working, assuming that they are sufficiently motivated to do so.

Reflecting on 'cause and effect' experiences

The cause and effect experiences discussed earlier in the book are a prime example of how individuals and teams learn. 'This action was taken, and it resulted in this outcome.' Organisational learning will only result if the knowledge gained by individuals and teams is somehow consolidated, so that if other people require the knowledge in the future, the same 'cause and effect' experience does not have to be repeated.

This does not happen in most organisations. Once a problem has been resolved or a project completed, operational pressures make it easy simply to move on. Systematically spending a few minutes recording key learning points, and recording them in a centrally accessible location will transform organisational learning. In some organisations, this learning activity is formally built into their processes and into both operational and change projects. This takes place through the completion of such things as close-out reports. Short and simple they may be, but if the person who had the experience leaves, the knowledge that they have acquired does not.

Adoption of the PERL model, where learning is defined as a distinct activity, can also have a significant impact. Avoiding the blame culture remains vital, since learning must never happen in order to apportion blame. Where this simple rule is violated a new model can be recognised. Called the PERLWF model it stands for plan, execute, reflect, learn, witch-hunt, fire! It's a model for continuous destruction rather than continuous improvement.

Moving from risk taking to risk management

Risk management techniques were covered in Chapter 10 on critical thinking skills, but here we will discuss the cultural implications which accompany a move from risk taking to risk management. We know that risks are necessary if an organisation is to survive, but we also know that taking risks is very difficult for some people to do. Taking identified risks openly involves moving into changing environments and into the unknown.

However, if the wrong risks are taken at the wrong time disaster can result. Risk taking has to be encouraged at the right time, but must also be managed. A culture of risk taking must not result in a cavalier attitude towards responsibility for performance. No risk should be taken without thinking through: the likelihood of occurrence and size of the risk; actions that will lower the likelihood and actions to minimise the size.

How difficult will it be?

It is worth restating that culture is the most difficult element of an organisation to change. Simply, if it requires change, it will not be easy.

How big is the gap?

An audit of the current culture, and a subsequent comparison will give an idea of the size of the gap, or what we might call 'cultural drift' since it was probably the most appropriate culture at one time. Use of a checklist such as the one above on energising elements is helpful. Changes are likely in many areas, and just as with any change project, it will need to be planned out as a project involving the representation of all the stakeholders.

As well as getting an objective idea of the size of the gap in specific areas, sometimes 'mind-sets' or ingrained prejudices need to be challenged. Sometimes a new broom will help, but as this example shows the old brooms need to be receptive.

CASE STUDY

The need to challenge old habits

An ageing Board at an old, established and traditional manufacturing company appointed a young and able female Human Resources Director on the retirement of the previous incumbent. Over the next 12 months, every effort that she made to change the way the Board and company operated was met with polite smiles but total inactivity.

The fact was that she kept challenging the existing way of doing things. What was worse she was young (so what would she know?), and she was female (so what would she know?) Unfortunately for the company her ideas were actually necessary for survival and growth but they never listened to her. At the end of 12 months, she felt obliged to resign her position. The company started an accelerating decline. Old paradigms and mind-sets are difficult to change and it does often take new blood to act as the catalyst for change – unfortunately, people need to be prepared to listen first!

The acceptance cycle

People resist change, and no change more strongly than cultural change. Their suspicions that the change will be in favour of stakeholders apart from themselves is most people's starting point, and this is true whichever stakeholder they represent.

> *People resist change, and no change more strongly than cultural change.*

The most common mistake in pushing through change, is to try to make people go straight from this deep suspicion all the way to complete acceptance of the change. In fact there are stages in the process which everyone goes through. They can be summarised as follows.

The acceptance cycle

1	*Ignorance*	No awareness
2	*Indifference*	Awareness (but it will never happen – BOHICA)
3	*Resistance*	Awareness (and it's going to happen)
4	*Discomfort*	Competence – (the conscious competent)
5	*Acceptance*	Recognition that it is here to stay
6	*Internally supportive*	Recognition that it is right
7	*Externally supportive*	Recognition that others will benefit

A project manager of a change project needs to plan how to take people through each stage in an orderly manner. It is a mistake to attempt to take people straight from stage 1 to 7 without recognising that they need to visit 2 through 6 on the way. It is also a mistake to address people at different stages in the same way. If you make a presentation to two people one of whom is at 'discomfort' and the other at 'resistance', you are as likely to take the 'discomfort' person back to 'resistance' as you are to make progress with the one at 'resistance'.

As well as ensuring that the transition from 'ignorance' to 'externally supportive' is as swift and smooth as possible, the adverse impact on performance will need to be minimised. During the change process there is a perceptible decrease in performance or delivery summed up by the graphical representation of the stages in Figure 14.1.

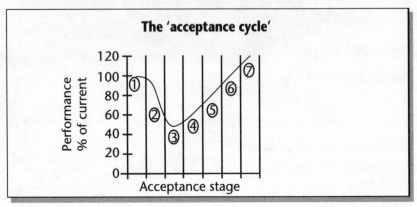

FIGURE 14.1

Creating ability and willingness

Once the new culture has been defined, the size of the gap or cultural drift determined and the likely negative impact on performance estimated, each element of the performance environment, (requirements, capabilities, resources and rewards) should be reviewed. As with all change, modifications to the performance environment will be required to support the new way of working, and to create both the ability to work within the new culture, and the willingness to do so.

What will it look like – back to the boardroom?

A strong and agreed culture is the starting point for removing potential conflict within a team at Board level or elsewhere. It is not surprising, therefore, that project teams start by defining the 'ground rules' they will follow when working together. These ground rules will determine the culture of the team. The stronger the values, the stronger will be the team. Agreed values and ground rules will, of course, be useless unless the whole team agrees to live by them.

Knowledge and decision making

One of the greatest cultural transformations required of senior managers and the Board in particular is the need to make decisions based on knowledge. This ties back with the ideas of organisational learning, critical thinking, performance reporting and the use of a knowledge centre. Senior managers often find this difficult because many of the decisions they make relate to the future, and in that regard are based on assumptions and uncertainty. What we have tried to demonstrate, however, is that if time is spent on designing and managing the organisation using the principles of organisational sensitivity, senior managers can make decisions and make better decisions because the right information should be available at the right time in the right format.

Decision making in a knowledge vacuum is not tolerated at other levels of the organisation. A salesperson is expected to know who the competition is; a production operator is expected to complete information for statistical control systems; maintenance operators are expected to prevent future failures through 'predictive maintenance'; telephone operators are expected to log each call; and so on. A knowledge vacuum should not be tolerated at management levels simply because fixing it is more difficult.

The same applies to all forms of management development. This can be a highly sensitive and political area, and a great deal of diplomacy is required. If changes are required, however, managers must make them happen. It starts from the top. Senior managers need to recognise their own development areas and their own cultural drift. They have their vanity though, and sometimes the choice of words to describe their development can be important.

CASE STUDY

What's in a name? A ruse by any other name would do the trick

Once the strategy had been set for a manufacturer, it was necessary to plan the actions for implementation. To do this a two-day session had been organised where basic project management concepts were to be discussed and then applied to the critical issues faced by the company. Unfortunately, when the Board heard someone referring to this session as a training day, there was immediately a revolt. 'We don't need training!'

The session eventually went ahead, but only under the heading of a 'workshop'. This team desperately needed some basic management tools, but over the years of managing through charisma and confusion it had become impossible for them, as directors, to admit that they might in some way benefit from 'training'.

This is not untypical of many senior staff, and the way in which things are packaged is as much a factor in their eventual acceptance as the quality of the outputs.

'Boardroom meeting – take two'

We have now completed the rational and creative development of the principles of organisational sensitivity. Before concluding, let us now revisit the boardroom of Europower as they meet to address the same major concern as was discussed in Chapter 3. This time we will assume that they have gone through many of the processes involved in creating organisational sensitivity. How different would things have been?

To recap the concern

To describe what has happened at the oil-fired power station, known as the Mulger Station, as a concern is an understatement. It is a disaster. As part of the long-term growth in electricity generation capacity, Europower had purchased a new turbine for Mulger. The project to install took six months and was completed on time and pretty much within budget. In fact it was shortly after the bonuses for completing on time were handed out at a celebration party which senior managers attended mob-handed that the 'incident' occurred.

A bolt worked loose from its seating, dropped into the turbine, broke into millions of shards and wrecked much of the machine.

The following afternoon the Power Generating Division (PGD) Board met.

Amongst those present were:

Joop van Daylaan	–	Managing Director
Claus Raes	–	Director of Human Resources
Michelle Surtain	–	Director of Coal-powered Stations
Panos Goumez	–	Director of Oil-fired Stations
Paco Diaz	–	Director of Marketing
Ian MacDonald	–	Director of Finance.

A company which has achieved a measure of organisational sensitivity meets a crisis

The location is the PGD knowledge centre in the Head Office building. Those present are sitting round a boardroom-style table while on the walls are charts with all the information mentioned in the Europower knowledge centre document at the end of Chapter 8.

Joop Well, ladies and gentlemen, we will try to cover some of the items on the normal agenda later, but plainly we need to start by reviewing events at Mulger. In brief, our worst scenario actually occurred. The installation team had calculated the risk that such a traumatic incident would take place as very low indeed. So despite the fact that we knew that if the risk did occur it would be both high-impact and high-urgency, we decided to complete the powering up of the new unit. Panos will give you the details.

Panos The first powering up during the pilot test was supervised by the supplier and had gone perfectly. We had signed the acceptance documentation since the installation had achieved all of the milestones and technical criteria set at the beginning of the project. However, when our people powered the unit up they got a printout from an instrument which had detected very, very slight vibration inside the turbine. The installation team suspended the operation and called back the supplier for a meeting of the normal cross-functional project team. The team drew information from some of the supplier's other installations. In the end four possible causes were listed, one of which, by a long way the most unlikely, was that something was loose in the unit. For that cause there were two possible fixes. The first was to do nothing but monitor the printout closely as the unit continued to power up. The second, I'm afraid, was to re-start the installation by stripping down the turbine. The cost of doing that was some £150,000 plus a delay of 3 months. The cost of doing nothing was virtually zero. There was, of course, the high-impact risk of damage to the turbine which is currently estimated at £250,000 and a delay of some 6 months. That was the risk we took. There **was** something loose in the unit and it parted company with its seating and caused the damage. It leaves us with three problems. First of all, how do we make up for the loss of capacity without causing problems for our customers, for which we have a pretty well worked out contingency plan already started? Secondly, we need to reconstitute a project team to dismantle the unit and get the necessary parts back to the supplier. The problem here is that all the resources were committed in the master schedule to other projects starting in two weeks' time. Thirdly, we have a major personnel problem. The Station Manager and his people are devastated. They have gone from feeling like the top team in the company to feeling that when they walk into a roomful of their colleagues, things are going to go quiet whilst their colleagues whisper 'Those are the Mulger people'.

Joop Yeah, well you know it's tough at the top, but as you say we will have to get to that. Let's talk in the first place about the contingency plan.

Panos We have delayed the commissioning of the new unit at Preyent, as planned. The people are unhappy about it naturally. We pointed out that they had already agreed to this as part of the contingency plan and they are working at rearranging their schedules and shifts.

Claus We must beware of the difference between the plan and the reality. All these people agreed to being part of the contingency plan, but the reality is quite a lot of disruption to their working and home lives, some are even cancelling holidays. And they are, as agreed, not getting much extra money. I think a note from you, Joop, and a visit as soon as you can, will help them to come to terms with the situation.

Joop I'm not certain, but I think it's already in my diary. Good point. OK, let's just make sure we're SAFE on this. The suitability of the plan to maintain uninterrupted supply is plainly in tune with the strategy. Would you also, Claus, say that it fits with how we're trying to develop our people?

Claus Certainly. It fits in with our multi-skilling projects and our gradual but perceptible movement towards much more flexibility. In fact at Preyent, we might even be able to speed up the implementation of the technician grade, which is a key part of the multi-skilling strategy.

Joop Good. We've discussed acceptability with regard to our people, and although Claus has made us aware we mustn't take their co-operation for granted, it looks as though they will see us through. With regard to the Mulger people, couldn't we help their morale by getting them heavily involved in the learning part of this incident?

Michelle As you know, I've been invited in to chair the team on the review of the incident. I'm sure the team will be happy to get the Mulger people busy, without, of course, risking the objectivity of the study. Incidentally, we've got the people at Arachaig, the only other station we've got with that particular turbine, to re-examine their past records to check there's no risk there, and report on how this particular part of the installation programme went down there. The

Manager has promised to have a short preliminary report in to the knowledge centre by the end of the week.

Joop   OK. The other part of acceptability is the customer angle. There is a risk, albeit a remote one, that if something nasty happens to the temperature and we get an unusual peak, that there will be some interruption to supply. How are we handling it, Paco?

Paco   Well, the contingency plan with the Big 6 went well with five and like a lead balloon with the sixth. The account managers of all 6 spoke to them within 24 hours as they are required to do by the process concerning possible interruption to supply. Five of them agreed immediately to reduce usage significantly at four hours' warning, but made it clear that this temporary fix was not suitable for anything longer than the very short term. The sixth went ballistic and threatened us with dire consequences if we interrupted supply. They are in the middle of a long manufacturing process so I think we will have to make them priority number one. But nevertheless the Account Manager has got to persuade them away from their present position, which is to seek urgent guarantees of supply. Actually, by giving them priority the risk is minimal.

Ian   Now where have I heard that before?

Paco   Yes, well, ignoring that, I'll move on to the bulk of our customers. The Chairs of all the national and regional user groups have been informed and are being extraordinarily supportive. Actually, of course, the whole nation is aware that we have a problem because of the short press conference last night. My people are working on a low-key advertising campaign where we very gently ask people to economise a little with their use of power. That was very effective after the big storm of 18 months ago, but we can't be sure how well such an appeal will go with this one, since a number of people, including our competitors and enemies, are calling this a self-inflicted wound.

Joop   OK. Let's look at feasibility.

Michelle   Joop, give us a chance. We don't have full enough information to check out how the master schedule will have to change. It's coming in, but I think it will be at least a week before we thoroughly understand all the implications. We should wait that long because it doesn't actually interfere with the short-term contingency plan.

Joop   Right, but keep the pressure up. You know how people get used to an interim fix. We must see as soon as possible the long-term impact on resources. Which brings me to the 'E' of SAFE – enduring.

Frankly, what we are doing at the moment fails this test. We cannot have our ability to supply as fragile as this in the future. The current investment plans will fix it eventually but we need to make the case to the Minister for speeding up that programme. The trouble is that those at the Department of Energy have got it into their heads that competition from outside will solve this problem, not the best solution from our point of view. However, rather than present it as a crisis, I think we need to make it the first agenda item for the next departmental liaison team meeting.

If you look at the competitor's timescale on the external trends sheet, you will see that our best estimate of their supplying some of our customers is 18 months away, even if they get the political OK. It's going to be tough. Let's finish this first part of the Mulger agenda on the people. We have made it clear to the world that this incident took place against a background of calculated risk. We need to ensure that internally our own people do not believe that to be mere public relations. There was a properly assessed management decision on a risk in which a number of teams and process owners took part. On the other hand, let's not get romantic about it either. If there are development areas among the Mulger people's capabilities, we need to know about them and address them. What do you suggest Claus? ...

Europower summary

It is difficult to think of a worse incident than the one above, but it has happened. As a result the company suffered, particularly financially, as did the other stakeholders, the people and the customers. But it does illustrate the effect of a successful implementation of many of the issues concerned in creating organisational sensitivity.

A cultural transformation – creating the sensitive organisation

KEY POINTS

Take a few minutes to reflect on each of these.

➡ Culture is the common set of beliefs which the organisation holds and can communicate, and which makes it possible for the organisation to meet its objectives and carry out its strategy.

➡ No matter how effectively the strategy, processes, knowledge and people have been planned, without a supportive culture the organisation will fail.

➡ Culture has a dramatic (positive and negative) impact on energy levels. These can be categorised into: strategic, operational, relationship and individual energising elements.

➡ Key elements of culture which are necessary for success include: how effectively the organisation learns, its approach to the management of risk, and the use of knowledge in decision making.

➡ The acceptance cycle is a useful tool for assessing the impact of change on individuals and culture – moving people thorough each stage of the cycle takes time and needs to be planned.

SELF-ASSESSMENT

Rate your organisation or unit on a scale of 1 to 5.

1 Is there a common and communicated set of beliefs? □

2 Do these beliefs guide strategic and operational decision making? □

3 Do they guide day-to-day activities? □

4 Does the culture support or oppose the organisation in what it is trying to do (its strategy) or how it is trying to do it (its processes)? □

5 How supportive are your strategic energising elements? □

6 How supportive are your operational energising elements? □

7 How supportive are your relationship energising elements? □

8 How supportive are your individual energising elements? □

9 How effective is your organisation at learning from the past, present and future activities? □

10 Are mistakes repeated? □

11 Is individual learning consolidated into organisational learning? □

12 Are risks taken and proactively managed? □

13 Is the organisation too risk averse or too carefree? □

14 Are the principles of cultural change and the 'acceptance cycle' understood and applied? □

15 Is knowledge – however limited – seen as a necessary requirement for effective decision making? □

ACTION PLAN

Where you scored badly in your self-assessment, identify what
actions you will take to improve your performance.

What?	Who?	When?
1		
2		
3		
4		
5		

THE CHOICE IS YOURS

Thank you for reading our ideas and for challenging some traditional perspectives on organisational design and management.

You can choose between:

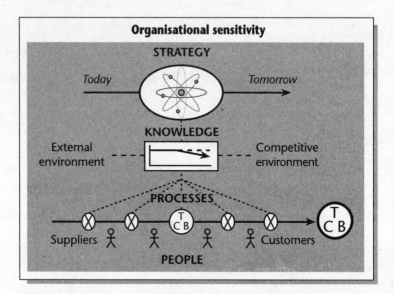

or:

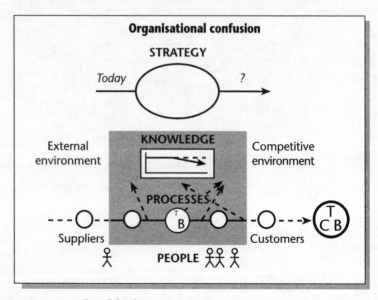

The choice is yours. Good luck.

INDEX

and culture 301
electronic mail 88, 300–1
implementing changes in 301–4
and information 121
and people 300
pitfalls 299–301
trends 108
telecommunications 298
thinking culture 244
time-to-market focus 90
timeframes 137
Timex 37–8

training 211, 213
Tregoe, Ben 231
trends 104, 107, 108

value added 166–7, 191–2, 214
value analysis 113–15
value chain 161
value statements 138
vertical compression of jobs 164
video-conferencing 298

Waterman, R.H. 141